Contents

3 Editorial: Warnings and the Embrace of Grace

7 *Chris Armitage*, Jesus and Elijah Redivivus: The Messianic Apocalypse, Matthew 11.4–5/Luke 7.22 and Jesus Memory Theory

25 *David Lertis Matson*, 'Put Your Sword Back into Its Place' (Matt 26:52):
The Rationale Behind Jesus's Sword Directive (and It Isn't Pacifism)

47 *Craig S. Keener*, Casting Out Mountains—Mark 11:23

66 *John A. Davies*, Luke–Acts as Prophetic Proclamation

82 *Craig L. Blomberg*, The Fourth Gospel and a Fourth Quest of the Historical Jesus

108 *Arco den Heijer*, The Two Ways of the Lord in Luke and Acts: Distinguishing Two Metaphorical Uses of One Term

123 *Nickolas A. Fox*, Decentralization in Luke-Acts

Thesis Reports

143 *Denise Powell*, Who Are the Righteous?: The Narrative Function of the Δίκαιοι in the Gospel of Luke

146 *Andrew Stewart*, The Three Accounts of Paul's Conversion in Acts 9, 22 and 26: A Study of Consistency and Creativity in Narrative Retelling

Book Reviews

148 *David M. Jacobson*, Agrippa II The Last of the Herods. Routledge Ancient Biographies (London and New York: Routledge, 2019)

151 *Constance M. Furey, Brian Matz, Steven L. McKenzie, Thomas Römer, Jens Schröter, Barry Dov Walfish and Eric Ziolkowski (eds.)*, Encyclopedia of the Bible and Its Reception 18: Mass – Midnight (Berlin, Boston: De Gruyter, 2020)

154 *Craig L. Blomberg*, The Historical Reliability of the New Testament: Countering the Challenges to Evangelical Christian Beliefs (Nashville: B&H Academic, 2016)

157 *Bruce Harold Henning*, Matthew's Non-Messianic Mapping of Messianic Texts: Evidences of a Broadly Eschatological Hermeneutic (Leiden and Boston: Brill, 2021)

159 *Hans M. Moscicke*, The New Day of Atonement: A Matthean Typology (WUNT 2.517. Tübingen: Mohr Siebeck, 2020)

161 *Holly Beers*, The Followers of Jesus as the 'Servant': Luke's Model from Isaiah for the Disciples in Luke-Acts (LNTS 535. London and New York, Bloomsbury T & T Clark, 2015)

164 *Benjamin E. Reynolds & Gabriele Boccaccini (eds),* Reading the Gospel of John's Christology as Jewish Messianism: Royal, Prophetic and Divine Messiahs, Mark, Luke and John (Leiden, Brill, 2018)

167 *Eve-Marie Becker, Helen K. Bond, and Catrin H. Williams (eds),* John's Transformation of Mark (London: Bloomsbury, 2021)

169 *Joshua Noble,* Common Property, the Golden Age, and Empire in Acts 2:42–47 and 4:32–35 (LNTS. London: T&T Clark, 2020)

171 *Eric Clouston,* How Ancient Narratives Persuade: Acts in its Literary Context (London: Rowman & Littlefield, 2020)

Warnings and the Embrace of Grace

At that time, some people came and reported to him about the Galileans whose blood Pilate had mixed with their sacrifices. [2] And he responded to them, 'Do you think that these Galileans were more sinful than all the other Galileans because they suffered these things? [3] No, I tell you; but unless you repent, you will all perish as well. [4] Or those eighteen that the tower in Siloam fell on and killed—do you think they were more sinful than all the other people who live in Jerusalem? [5] No, I tell you; but unless you repent, you will all perish as well.' (Luke 13:1–5)

What was Jesus thinking? To urge people to repent is often considered rather rude and inappropriate at the best of times, let alone in the context of disasters and human tragedy. Haven't people got enough to worry about as they cope with their own mortality, shown to be so fragile in the face of other human beings losing their lives, whether at the hands of malevolent politicians or equally malevolent natural forces? Even if we grant that Jesus was one of the most empathetic persons known to human history, surely he lacked a sense of timing on this particular occasion?

Last September, the COVID 19 pandemic was already well advanced. This September it seems entrenched. Humans being what they are, rather than pulling together against a common enemy the ideologues are still seeking to score points against one another—although in some quarters both right and left join forces against governments deemed to be too heavy-handed in removing freedom in the pursuit of safety. If the pandemic wasn't enough, the legitimate government in Afghanistan has collapsed to the Taliban following the removal of troops from war-weary western nations. As the shock-woes disturb an already anxious world, the horrendous prospects for Afghani women are only eclipsed by thoughts of future global terrorism backed by anti-western superpowers.

Perhaps the current megaphone is larger and louder, but the warnings of the Nazareth teacher already pointed the world to the lessons inherent in its own suffering. The context of human history has, is, and always will be, the same:

EDITORIAL: GRACE IN PANDEMIC PROPORTIONS

> When you hear of wars and rumors of wars, don't be alarmed; these things must take place, but it is not yet the end. For nation will rise up against nation, and kingdom against kingdom. There will be earthquakes in various places, and famines. These are the beginning of birth pains. (Mark 13:7–8)

With that context in view, his lesson was simple: 'Watch yourselves!' (Mark 13:9). As the world continues to be divided against itself, and struggles to survive the disruptions of both politics and nature, there may well be special difficulties thrown against those who live under the name of the Christ (Mark 13:9–11). But Christ's mission to the nations is still to be the first priority (v.10). Within that 'apocalyptic' context, urging survivors to take advantage of the time remaining is a warning that comes from the God of grace. As the warning is heeded, mortal human beings find a gracious Saviour with his warm embrace.

As never before—and as always before—if we recognise the nature of the times in which we live, then now is a time for the proclamation of God's grace in Christ to continue to the nations.

In this issue of *JGAR*, now five years old, Chris Armitage explores the expectation of a coming Messiah who would raise the dead, as reflected in a text from the Dead Sea Scrolls, 4Q521. The life-changing effects on those who heard Jesus' teaching about his own role in the light of such an expectation made an impression which left a trace in our Gospels (Matt 11:4–5//Luke 7:22). Well-aware of the violence inherent in a world of 'wars and rumours of wars', Jesus was himself confronted by its violence as he was arrested in Gethsemane. But, as David Matson shows, it was not the moment to answer violence with violence, for in service of God's gracious purposes, the Prince of Peace had come to die. Turning to Mark 11, Craig Keener argues that Jesus spoke of the mountain-moving power of faith made available to his disciples through prayer. Even before the resurrection day with its ultimate solutions, in prayer mortal human beings have access to God's resources. Examining 'the word' as a prophetic message proclaimed in and through Luke-Acts, John Davies shows how Luke's narrative calls upon its hearers to repent and live in accordance with God's purposes. Reporting on the renewed interest in the Gospel of John as a source for historical Jesus studies, Craig Blomberg notes the significance of Jesus' concerns for purity, as a bridge between the Jewish and Gentile worlds of his day. Rather than today's churches defensively concerned about being corrupted by the world around them, perhaps grasping the vision of a contagious holiness might help to regain some greater influence instead. In his discussion of Luke-Acts' use of the expression 'the way', Arco den Heijer reveals how both Jewish and Gentile disciples are connected to God's instruction from ancient times concerning the way of life. As the same narrative tracks the movement of the gospel from Jerusalem to the nations, Nickolas Fox traces the 'personal decentralization' that goes along with it, as people from all nations are changed by the Spirit of God and take their place in the advancement of the gospel of the risen Christ.

As the foundational documents which both arose from, and were in support of, the proclamation of this gospel, research into the Gospels and Acts remains both a relevant and an urgent task for today's troubled world. May the contributions of the present volume assist the better understanding of the Christian message and its mission, so that many might hear behind the present warnings, and embrace God's grace anew.

Peter G. Bolt
Executive Editor

Jesus and Elijah *Redivivus*
The Messianic Apocalypse, Matthew 11:4–5// Luke 7:22 and Jesus Memory Theory[1]

CHRIS ARMITAGE

Abstract

The Q saying in Matt 11:4–5//Luke 7:22 attributed to Jesus may or may not be genuinely dominical. Mal 3:23–24 [ET 4:5–6], in light of the reconstruction of 4Q521, 'The Messianic Apocalypse', by Puech may be seen to suggest that the notion of Elijah reappearing as a forerunner of the Messiah, and of the raising of the dead by the forthcoming Messiah, was known in Jewish circles before the Common Era. However Faierstein may have successfully broken the consensus that Mal 3:23–24 [ET 4:5–6] is to be read this way. If so, since it cites Mal 3:23–24 [ET 4:5–6], perhaps 4Q521 ought not be read this way either. So we may need to turn to Jesus Memory Theory to try to establish whether the Q saying in Matt 11:4–5//Luke 7:22 is probably dominical, asking whether it has its basis in the impression Jesus made on those recalling his sayings, having regard to its life-changing effect on them. Using these methods, we can say that this Q saying probably goes back to the historical Jesus and is dominical.

Introduction

Of the possibility that Matt 11:4–5//Luke 7:22 is probably a dominical saying, Flint writes:

> The discovery of 4Q521 [The Messianic Apocalypse] calls for a re-evaluation of Luke 7:20–23 (=Matt 11:2–6). Unlike the Lukan and Matthean passages, the term *messiah* (line 1: למשיחו, 'to his messiah') is explicitly used in 4Q521. Moreover, the Gospel passages contain seven distinctive features, three of which are prophesied at Isa 35:5–6, and one more at Isa 61:1–2; four of these are featured in 4Q521 [....] Finally, the act of raising or reviving the dead is not found in Isaiah, but is included in 4Q521 (line 12: ומתים יחיה, 'and he will make the dead live'). This feature in 4Q521 constitutes an important correspondence with Luke 7:22 (=Matt 11:4–5). This remarkable singularity between 4Q521 and Luke 7:21–22 (=Matt 11:4–5) supports the view that a list of activities associated with the Messiah similar to the one in Q was familiar to at least some Jews before the Common Era. *This makes it feasible that the words recorded*

---

[1] My unstinted thanks are due to Prof Emerita Alanna Nobbs and Assoc Prof Paul McKechnie of Macquarie University's Department of Ancient History and to my anonymous peer reviewers for their many valuable suggestions and corrections, largely adopted in the final draft of this article. The views expressed and any errors or omissions in it are mine alone.

in Luke 7:22 go back to the historical Jesus, and that he saw himself as, and claimed to be, Israel's Messiah.[2] [emphasis added]

The aim of this short paper is simply to investigate whether or not it is probable that the words recorded in Luke 7:22 'go back to the historical Jesus'.

Tabor and Wise, in an article written not long before the reconstruction of 4Q521 by Emile Puech,[3] make the critical point that the phrase ומתים יחיה, 'and he will make the dead live',[4] in 4Q521 frag. 2. 2.12 does not occur in the Hebrew Bible at all.[5] They suggest that because, of the six signs of the Messiah in Luke 7:22 (Matt 11:4–5), the two remaining phrases 'lepers and cleansed' and 'the dead are raised' have no basis in Isa 35:5 and 61:1 or related passages in the Hebrew Bible, this Q saying[6] 'probably reflects an understanding of John and Jesus as fulfilling the mission of Elijah/Elisha figures', which was 'based on the cycle of stories in 1 and 2 Kings together with the prophecy of Mal 4:5–6, the prophecy that such a figure would arise in the last days'. They note that both Elijah and Elisha raise the dead, and Elisha heals Naaman the leper (1 Kgs 17:17–24; 2 Kgs 4:18–37; 2 Kgs 5:1–14).[7] They postulate that 'although it is unlikely that Luke knew the Qumran text directly, it seems that he shares with its author a common set of messianic expectations'.[8]

Collins agrees that 4Q521 frag. 2, 3.1–2, 'And I will free them with [...] it is su[re:] the fathers will return towards the sons [...]',[9] is a clear reference to the return of Elijah because, as Puech rightly recognises,[10] in the last line there appears a citation of Mal 3:24 [ET 4:6], which predicts that God will send Elijah before the day of the Lord and 'he will turn the hearts of fathers towards their children and the hearts of children to their fathers'. Collins notes that the same phrase appears in the Hebrew version of Sir 48:10, which commences with a statement that Elijah is 'prepared for the time', נכון לעת, using the same word, נכון [... as] in 4Q521'.[11] But Collins points out that the expectation of Elijah as the forerunner of the Messiah is not attested in Jewish texts before the rise of Christianity. He refers here to Mal 3:23 [ET 4:5], with 'Elijah [...] cast as an eschatological prophet, not a royal Messiah'.[12]

Here Collins agrees with Faierstein, who seeks to rebut the arguments of Wink,[13] Jeremias,[14] Klausner[15] and Mowinkel,[16] that the idea of Elijah as forerunner of the Messiah was current in Jewish thought before the rise of Christianity, by pointing to their reliance on Jewish and Christian texts of the second century CE and later. Consequently, Faierstein suggests, almost no

---

2   Flint, 'The Qumran Scrolls and the Historical Jesus', 279.
3   See Puech, 'Une Apocalypse Messianique (4Q521)'.
4   García Martínez and Tigchelaar, *The Dead Sea Scrolls Study Edition*, 1044-1045 (editors' translation).
5   Tabor and Michael O Wise, '4Q521', 157; see also Wise and Tabor, 'The Messiah at Qumran', 63, for a similar but more briefly expressed view.
6   In this an all subsequent references to 'Q', this paper does not assert the existence of the much-disputed written Q source: it merely uses 'Q' to refer to synoptic material shared by Matthew and Luke, and not by Mark. For a brief but fair summary of the scholarship for and against the existence of an actual, written Q source underlying Matthew and Luke, see Turner, *Matthew*, 13; and see also France, *Matthew*, 21–22; Bock, *Luke*, 1.9.
7   Tabor and Wise, 'On Resurrection and the Synoptic Gospel Tradition', 160.
8   Tabor and Wise, 'On Resurrection and the Synoptic Gospel Tradition', 161.
9   Martínez and Tigchelaar, *The Dead Sea Scrolls Study Edition* Vol 2, 1044-1045 (editors' translation)..
10 Puech, 'Une Apocalypse Messianique', 509.
11 Collins, 'The Works of the Messiah', 102–03.
12 Collins, 'The Works of the Messiah', 103–104.
13 Wink, *John the Baptist*, 28, 31.
14 Jeremias, ''Ηλ(ε)ίας', 928–941.
15 Klausner, *The Messianic Idea in Israel*, 451-57.
16 Mowinkel, *He that Cometh*, 278.

contemporary evidence survives showing that the concept of Elijah as forerunner of the Messiah was widely known or accepted in the first century CE, so that 'the further possibility, that the concept of Elijah as forerunner is a *novum* in the NT, must also be seriously considered'.[17]

This possibility may mean that Flint's suggestion, that in Luke 7:22//Matt 11:4–5 the Q statement that 'lepers are cleansed' and 'the dead are raised' reflects an understanding of John and Jesus as fulfilling the mission of Elijah/Elisha figures, needs questioning. This, in turn, may raise a problem for Flint's statement that:

> a list of activities associated with the Messiah similar to the one in Q was familiar to at least some Jews before the Common Era. This makes it feasible that the words recorded in Luke 7:22 go back to the historical Jesus, and that he saw himself as, and claimed to be, Israel's Messiah.[18]

This article examines the cogency of Collins' and Faierstein's arguments, and then asks whether, even if they are right, Jesus Memory Theory provides another route for seeing Luke 7:22/Matt 11:4–5 as genuinely dominical.

Elijah as Forerunner in the OT

Elijah in the OT is portrayed as possessing powers of healing and raising of the dead (1 Kgs 17:8–24). For quite a time, the received wisdom was that in the OT, Elijah was seen as the forerunner of the Messiah. Strugnell, for example, considered that the Mosaic eschatological prophet was, in the thought of Qumran, and possibly of Mal 3:23 [ET 4:5], identical with Elijah *redivivus*.[19]

This hypothesis has come under question in more recent years. Fitzmyer maintains that the Elijah forerunner concept is not a logical deduction from Mal 3:23–24 [ET 4:5–6] because no Second Temple writings relate the coming of the Messiah on a day of the Lord.[20] Further, he argues that 'form-critical studies on the Baptist accounts in the Synoptics have shown that John the Baptist expected Jesus to be Elijah and that it was Jesus himself who corrected this notion, teaching that John was Elijah *redivivus* (Matt 11:3–14)'.[21] Nolland too sees John as Elijah in this sense,[22] as does Witherington.[23]

This identification may not be quite correct because, as Hagner writes, 'what has been implied in the quotation of Mal 3:1 in [Matt 11] v.10 now comes to exact expression', when in v.14 Jesus says of John, αὐτός ἐστιν Ἠλίας ὁ μέλλων ἔρχεσθαι, 'he is Elijah, the one who is to come',[24] but adds εἰ θέλετε δέξασθαι, 'if you are prepared to accept it'. What this may mean 'is not that John is actually Elijah *redivivus* [...] but that he functions in the role that was ascribed to Elijah just before the end time'.[25]

What is that role? Mal 3:1, speaking of 'my messenger who will prepare the way', ופנה־דרך לפני מלאכי, is immediately followed by Mal 3:2–3 which, in an echo of Isa 1:25, reads 'But who can survive the day of his arrival, and who can be the one standing when he appears? He will be like the fire of a refiner or the soap of launderers. And he shall sit as one refining (מצרף) and one purifying and

---

17   Faierstein, 'Why Do the Scribes Say that Elijah Must Come First?', 86.
18   Flint, 'The Qumran Scrolls and the Historical Jesus', 279.
19   Strugnell, 'Moses Pseudepigrapha at Qumran', 234.
20   Fitzmyer, 'More about Elijah Coming First', 295–96.
21   Fitzmyer, *Essays on the Semitic Background*, 137.
22   Nolland, *Matthew*, 459.
23   Witherington, *Matthew*, 234.
24   This writer's translation appears in this and all subsequent OT and NT citations unless the contrary is indicated.
25   Hagner, *Matthew 1–13*, 308.

refining (מְצָרֵף) silver'. The same verb, צרף, 'refine',[26] occurs in Isa 1:25b, 'and I will purge (וְאֶצְרֹף) your dross', and in Mal 3:2–3. Isa 1:25 is eschatological, speaking of the actions of the Lord himself in the end-time. So too is Mal 3:2–3, speaking of the day when the events presaged in Mal 2:2–3 will occur. And Mal 3:23 [ET 4:5] reads 'Behold, I am sending you Elijah the prophet before the terrible day of the great Yahweh'.

Read together, Mal 3:2–3 and 3:23–24 [ET 4:5–6] may imply that Elijah is in fact the Lord's messenger who will prepare the way in Mal 3:1 before the end-time. The same may apply to Luke 7:22. But this does not prove that in Matthew 11, John the Baptist *is* Elijah *redivivus* where in v.14 Jesus says of John, αὐτός ἐστιν Ἠλίας ὁ μέλλων ἔρχεσθαι, 'he is Elijah, the one who is to come', but adds εἰ θέλετε δέξασθαι, 'if you are willing to accept it'. What it shows is simply that John 'functions in the role that was ascribed to Elijah just before the end time',[27] a fine but real distinction.

In fact, exegetically, there is much in Faierstein's argument that when Mal 3:23–24 [ET 4:5–6] is read 'without *a priori* assumptions', the idea of Elijah as forerunner of the Messiah is *not* found there, because 'Elijah stands in relation to "the great and terrible day of the Lord", a phrase which implies a particular time and not a person', and because 'there is no reference in these verses to the Messiah or to any other non-divine being who may be identified with the Messiah'.[28] There is a strong argument that Faierstein is right in his contention that exegetically, Mal 3:23–24 [ET 4:5–6] does not support the notion of Elijah as forerunner of the Messiah in the OT.

Once one reaches that conclusion, Faierstein's attempted refutation of the array of references to extra-biblical works in the arguments of Wink, Jeremias, Klausner, Mowinkel, and others becomes strictly unnecessary, because if Mal 3:23–24 [ET 4:5–6] do not support the notion of Elijah as forerunner of the Messiah in the OT in the first place, the echo of Mal 4:5 in Matt 11:14 cannot control the exegesis of that verse—or for that matter Luke 7:22—even if many extra-biblical Jewish works before the rise of Christianity do speak of Elijah as forerunner of the Messiah.

Klausner finds evidence in 1 Macc 4:46 and 14:41 of the concept of Elijah as forerunner of the Messiah, finding in 4:46, 'until a prophet comes to tell them what to do with them' (speaking of the altar stones), conceptual similarity to the rabbinic phrase, 'it must be left until Elijah comes'. He contends that the role of the unnamed prophet in 1 Macc 14:41, to end the Hasmonean reign and begin a new Davidic dynasty, will be fulfilled by Elijah.[29]

However, Ferguson appears to be correct in considering these attempted identifications inconclusive, firstly because these texts might just as well refer to a prophet other than Elijah, and secondly because the rabbinic literature relied on by Klausner postdates Maccabees by centuries.[30] Ferguson does however also concede that Mal 3:23–24 provides *circumstantial* evidence of the concept of Elijah in pre-Christian Jewish thought as forerunner of the Messiah, viewing this text alongside other passages referring to the Messiah's arrival on a future day of the Lord. He refers here also, inter alia, to 4QpIsa (4Q161) 7.10, 3.22 interpreting Isaiah 11 as referring to an eschatological '[shoot] of David who arises in the la[st] days'.[31]

The problem about the whole concept of circumstantial evidence, however, is that unless it, alongside other evidence, supports at least a probable inference of a historical fact, its probative value falls away. Inferentially, 4QpIsa (and Isaiah 11) may just as will be seen as referring to the

---

26 BDB, 6884, 'smelt' or 'refine'.
27 Hagner, *Matthew 1–13*, 308.
28 Faierstein, 'Why do the Scribes say that Elijah Must Come First?', 77.
29 Klausner, *The Messianic Idea in Israel*, 260.
30 Ferguson, 'The Elijah Forerunner Concept as an Authentic Jewish Expectation', 131.
31 Ferguson, 'The Elijah Forerunner Concept as an Authentic Jewish Expectation', 133.

coming of a Messiah whose arrival is quite unconnected with Elijah's as forerunner. Little is added to the meaning of Mal 3:23–24 [ET 4:5–6]. The same applies to Ferguson's citation of 4QM (4Q285) 7.2–4, developing the imagery of Isa 10:34–11:1 by predicting the appearance of the branch (of Jesse) in the context of an eschatological war. This too adds comparatively little to the meaning of Mal 3:23–24 [ET 4:5–6].

Elijah as Forerunner in the Messianic Apocalypse

The case for seeing the Messianic Apocalypse, 4Q521 as evidence of the idea of Elijah as forerunner of the Messiah in pre-Christian Jewish thought is somewhat stronger. We have seen that Collins argues that 4Q521 frag. 2, 3.1–2, 'And I will free them with [...] it is su[re:] the fathers will return towards the sons [...]',[32] is a clear reference to the return of Elijah because 'there is in the last line a citation of Mal 3:24 [ET 4:6] which says that God will send Elijah before the day of the Lord and 'he will turn the hearts of fathers towards their children and the hearts of children to their fathers',[33] and because Sir 48:10 [Hebrew] 'begins with a statement that Elijah is "prepared for the time", נכון לעת, using the same word, נכון [... as] in 4Q521'.[34] Becker cavils with Collins' view that a *specifically* Messianic reference occurs in 4Q521 fr. 2, 2.1 and following.[35] However, this criticism may give insufficient weight to the citation of Mal 3:24 in the last line.

To be fair, Faierstein's 1981 study preceded Puech's 1992 article on the Messianic Apocalypse, so that Faierstein did not have the opportunity of considering the possibility that 4Q521 provides evidence of the concept of Elijah as forerunner of the Messiah in pre-Christian Jewish thought. However, an argument is still available that this is so, in that quite specifically, 4Q521 frag. 2, 3.1–2 in its last line cites Mal 3:24–25, providing some evidence of the concept of Elijah as forerunner of the Messiah in pre-Christian Jewish thought at Qumran.

Although there are features of a messianic figure presented in Isa 61:1–2, and in Matt 11:5, who gives the blind their sight and cares for the poor. Despite the Damascus Document quoting Ps 146:7–9 concerning God caring for the oppressed, prisoners, the blind, the bowed down, strangers, widows and orphans, Qumran harboured a marked distaste for the lame, blind, deaf or dumb (1QSa 2.4–8) or the insane (CD 15.5), all of whom were banned from membership of the community.[36] It may then be that 4Q521 does not have Isa 61:1–2 specifically in view.

And certainly Faierstein's argument that when Mal 3:24–25 are read without *a priori* presumptions, the idea of Elijah as forerunner of the Messiah is not found there, deserves exegetical weight. This is because, as he says, 'Elijah stands in relation to "the great and terrible day of the Lord", a phrase which implies a particular time and not a person', and 'there is no reference in these verses to the Messiah or to any other non-divine being who may be identified with the Messiah'.[37] It then becomes difficult to argue in turn that the citation of Mal 3:24 in the last line of 4Q521 is a clear indication of the concept of Elijah as forerunner of the Messiah in pre-Christian Jewish thinking.

If so, then to further interrogate Faierstein's suggestion that the idea of Elijah as forerunner of

---

32 Garcia Martínez and Tigchelaar, *The Dead Sea Scrolls Study Edition* Vol 2, 1044–1045.
33 Puech, 'Une Apocalypse Messianique', 509.
34 Collins, 'The Works of the Messiah', 102–03; see also Bailey, *Jesus through Middle Eastern Eyes*, 149.
35 Becker, '4Q521', 79–80.
36 Scheffler, 'Putting Qumran, Jesus and his Movement into Relief', 6.
37 Faierstein, 'Why Do the Scribes Say that Elijah Must Come First?', 77.

the Messiah—and indeed, by implication, the messianic claims of Jesus himself in Matt 11:4–5//Luke 7:22—may be a *novum* in the NT, and may not 'go back to the historical Jesus',[38] we may need to resort to Jesus Memory Theory, in the sense developed by James Dunn, allied to social memory theory as developed by Jan Assmann and supplemented by other more recent scholarship, in order to shed some light on this issue.

Maurice Halbwachs, Jan Assmann, Alan Kirk, Tom Thatcher, Barry Schwarz, Social Memory Theory and Matt 11:4–5//Luke 7:22

Form criticism sees the oral Jesus tradition as shaped by the needs of current social realities, and as not necessarily representing the actual words of Jesus in any form. Speaking of form criticism, Bultmann himself puts it simply: 'certainly there is no guarantee that all the sayings in the Gospels in which Jesus cites words of Scripture were really spoken by him; many were surely put in his mouth by the church, in order to justify its own position'.[39] He says the aim of form criticism is therefore 'to rediscover the origins and the history of the particular units and thereby to throw some light on the history of the tradition before it took literary form'.[40]

Bornkamm differs from Bultmann, maintaining that in John's relations with Jesus, John stood for the time of preparation, and Jesus for the time of fulfilment: between their missions, a decisive 'shift in the aeons' took place.[41] But Bornkamm never broke decisively with the form-critical approach of asserting the impossibility of isolating the genuine oral 'Jesus tradition' in scripture, as against insertions by later redactors.

The French sociologist **Maurice Halbwachs** held that it is 'in society that [people …] normally acquire, recognise and localise their memories', so that 'there is no point […] in seeking where [memories] are preserved in my brain or in some other nook of my mind to which I alone have access'.[42] Halbwachs explains the process whereby emerging Christianity appropriated the past:

> Society is aware that the new religion is not an absolute beginning. The society wishes to adopt these larger and deeper beliefs without entirely rupturing the framework of notions in which it has matured up to this point.[43]

Hence, Halbwachs says, 'if Christianity had not been presented as a continuation in a sense of Hebraic religion, it remains open to doubt whether it could have established itself as a religion', referring in this regard to Jesus' appropriation of the Levitical command to love the neighbour as yourself (Lev 19.18) in Matt 22:37–39.[44]

In reality Halbwachs takes his argument well beyond form criticism. As the biblical scholar and social memory theorist Chris Keith remarks:

---

38 Flint, 'The Qumran Scrolls and the Historical Jesus', 279.
39 Bultmann, *Jesus and the Word*, 51.
40 Bultmann, *History of the Synoptic Tradition*, 4.
41 Bornkamm, *Jesus of Nazareth*, 50–51; Dunn, *Jesus Remembered*, 452.
42 Halbwachs, *Collective Memory*, 38; Ollick and Robbins, 'Social Memory Studies from "Collective Memory" to the Historical Sociology of Mnemonic Practices', 109; and see Duling, 'Memory, Collective Memory, Orality and the Gospels', 6, for a good summary of Halbwachs's central ideas.
43 Halbwachs, *Collective Memory*, 86.
44 Halbwachs, *Collective Memory*, 87.

> From the continuity perspective of social memory, the failure to consider seriously the ways in which the past could have contributed to early Christians' presents is a severe oversight; for the early Christian communities were not theologising castles in the sky detached entirely from pasts that led to their presents. [...] Previous typologies provided categories for the present, and thus structure or restrain the interpretative freedom to an extent as groups assimilate the *novum* to the known.[45]

But if we see Matt 11:4–5//Luke 7:22 as a *novum* assimilated by early Christians to the known past, with its predictions in Isa 61:1–3, social memory theory as developed by Halbwachs does nothing *per se* to refute this, and to establish the actual historicity of Jesus' sayings there. That is because Halbwachs views the religious past as mainly, if not wholly, a social construction conditioned by the present: of Christianity as a historical event, he says of Jerusalem 'it is above all there that the essentials of the Christian myth were transposed into a tale of events—perhaps a century after the fact'.[46]

Halbwachs illustrates his view that 'the entire substance of Christianity, since Christ has not reappeared on earth, consists in the remembrance of his life and teachings' by turning to Durkheim's analysis of Buddhism, where he says that 'Buddhism has religious elements (without which it would perhaps be no religion at all) in addition to a morality, but the religious element is entirely reducible to remembrances'.[47] This conception of the transmission of religious ideas in no way depends on their *truth*: to Durkheim, they were wholly the product of society.

To **Kirk and Thatcher**, 'as Maurice Halbwachs argued, in the interplay between the past and the present, current social realities provide the frameworks for the appropriation of the past', so 'the dynamics of this reception are the dynamics of social memory, and the history of the Gospel tradition is in fact the history of the reception of Jesus' image in various contexts'.[48] But this statement needs to be read alongside their previous dictum that 'the form critics sharply (if unreflectively) distinguished between "memory", understood as personal recall, and "tradition", a term that comprehended both the "forms" these recollections took in oral preaching and teaching and all the processes by which the Gospel writers patched these pieces together'.[49] This hardly sounds like wholesale endorsement of the form-critical assumption that one *cannot* disentangle historical fact from the *kerygma* produced by a community's historical situation. Elsewhere, Kirk puts it this way: 'the form critics—and Bultmann in particular—understood that the history of the tradition is inseparable from the historical situatedness of the tradent communities—in other words, that present realities affect appropriations of the past'.[50] Of course—but Kirk is not here denying that historical fact may be discoverable beneath a community's *kerygma*. This is a subtle but important difference between Kirk and Thatcher and the form critics, Bultmann in particular.

Barry Schwartz criticises Halbwachs, writing that his 'greatest failure is his inability to see commemoration as anything more than an elaborate delusion', because:

> Halbwachs advances a pejorative conception of collective memory, one that distrusts and works to undermine established beliefs. He assumes that memory, as opposed to history, is inauthentic, manipulative, shady, something to be overcome rather than accepted in its own right. He cannot grasp what sacred sites accomplish, how they transmute reality to mobilise

---

45 Keith, 'Social Memory Theory and Gospels Research', 520.
46 Halbwachs, *Collective Memory*, 215.
47 Durkheim, *Les formes élémentaires*, 44; Halbwachs, *Collective Memory*, 88, 89.
48 Kirk and Thatcher, 'Jesus Tradition and Social Memory', 33.
49 Kirk and Thatcher, 'Jesus Tradition and Social Memory', 29.
50 Kirk, 'The Memory-Tradition Nexus', 134.

and sustain religious sentiment and, above all, elevate Jesus and sustain faith in what he did and represented.[51]

This is potentially a potent criticism, but whether it is a fair one is debatable. It is fairer to say that Halbwachs does not view collective memory pejoratively, but is simply conscious of its limitations, viewing it as establishing only the *existence* of collective beliefs, not the *truth* of those beliefs. Schwartz is on firmer ground when he criticises the assumption that because memory can be assembled from parts of a story, its constructed products are not what they seem, precisely *because* they are constructed. As Schwartz says, such reasoning is obviously circular and invalid.[52] He is also right to see a common failure by Halbwachs and Bultmann in 'their refusal even to *ask* how pericopae, texts and physical sites reflected what ordinary people of the first century believed'.[53]

But an important distinction was drawn by the German sociologist **Jan Assmann** in a significant further development of Halbwachs' ideas. Asmann mirrors Durkheim's view that 'the collective ideal which religion expresses is far from being due to a vague innate power of the individual, but it is rather at the school of collective life that the individual has learned to idealise', because 'society has constructed this new world in constructing itself, since it is society itself which this expresses'.[54]

However, Assmann distinguishes 'communicative memory', *kommunikative Gedächtnis*, from 'cultural memory', in that communicative memory 'can be used of communities still close to their origins, a period characterised by face-to-face circulation of foundational memories' which are 'biographically vested in those who experience originating events: it is the time of eyewitnesses and living memory (*Augenzeugenschaft und lebendigen Erinnerung*)'.[55] Assmann traces the concept of cultural memory to Thomas Mann, but associates it particularly with the work of Aby Warburg and Maurice Halbwachs in Zurich in the twenties.[56]

Assmann holds that the farthest time-limit of 'communicative memory' is the deaths of those who were in contact with the original generation, that is, three or four generations or eighty or a hundred years.[57] Therefore, communicative memory is not able to sustain group memories beyond this period.[58] At about the forty year threshold, at which the generation of living carriers of memory start dying, the community has to turn to more enduring cultural memory (*kulturelle Gedächtnis*).[59] In oral societies, such foundational stories appear in genres suitable for oral transmission, and continually integrate the society's present with its past.[60]

As Assmann remarks, *es handelt sich, um die Transformation von Vergangenheit in fundierende Geschichte*,[61] 'it concerns the transformation of the past into well-grounded history'.[62] He postulates that cultural memory is founded in the communicative, historical memories of original memory-carriers. In this, Assmann is to be distinguished from the form critics, who held that in the process of transmission of oral tradition to the written text, genuine, historically accurate

---

51 Schwartz, 'Christian Origins', 49.
52 Schwartz, 'Christian Origins', 43–44.
53 Schwartz, 'Christian Origins', 49 [emphasis added].
54 Durkheim, *The Elementary Forms of the Religious Life*, 423; Esler, *The First Christians in their Social World*, 5.
55 Assmann, *Das kulturelle Gedächtnis*, 1–25, 88; Dunn, 'Social Memory and the Oral Jesus Tradition', 184.
56 Assmann, 'Thomas Mann', 149.
57 Assmann, *Das kulturelle Gedächtnis*, 56; Dunn, 'Social Memory and the Oral Jesus Tradition', 184–85.
58 Assmann, *Das kulturelle Gedächtnis*, 50.
59 Assmann, *Das kulturelle Gedächtnis*, 218–21.
60 Assmann, *Das kulturelle Gedächtnis*, 49–50.
61 Assmann, *Das kulturelle Gedächtnis*, 92; Kirk, 'Memory', 168.
62 My translation.

tradition became entangled with non-genuine insertions by redactors, which then needed to be disentangled, to produce a smaller stratum of genuine tradition—a project unlikely to succeed. It is not without ironic significance that Assmann's wife Aleida, herself no mean critic, was Bornkamm's daughter.[63]

Kenneth Bailey, James Dunn, Dale Allison, Richard Bauckham and Matt 11:4–5//Luke 7:22

Kenneth Bailey argues that the concept of social memory, as the likely source of Jesus' sayings in the Gospels, is in line with Middle Eastern storytelling practice, both in the first century CE and at the present time. In a somewhat contested example, he relates his own experience of what he calls 'formal controlled oral tradition', when in the late fifties of last century he encountered a villager in Egypt who proudly recounted the preaching a hundred years beforehand of a Scottish evangelical minister, John Hogg, who said in Arabic, of dried cow manure set before him in response to his preaching on the Gospel injunction to eat what is put before one, 'this is food for a fire: give me food for people and I will eat it'. Bailey is fully confident that this is an exact record of Hogg's words a hundred years beforehand.[64] He contests the form-critical notion of 'informal uncontrolled oral tradition', whereby genuine memories of Jesus become so entangled with false memories and inventions that it is impossible to tell which is which.[65] On the basis of his experience, related in the above anecdote and others, he argues that Middle Eastern storytelling, in a 'formal controlled oral tradition', preserves what is believed and practised in its religion by 'a carefully nurtured methodology of great antiquity that is still practised and held in high regard by both Christians and Muslims'.[66] It is impossible to do justice to Bailey's subtle argument here, but it appears to stand or fall to some extent on the accuracy of his real-life examples, which are at times somewhat parlous. One prefers to put things as Dodd does, in a passage quoted by Bailey as a 'median position':

> When all allowance has been made for [...] limiting factors [...] the changes of oral tradition, the effect of translation, the interest of teachers in making the sayings "contemporary", it remains that the first three Gospels offer a body of sayings on the whole so consistent, so coherent, and withal so distinctive in manner, style and content that no reasonable critic should doubt, whatever reservations he may have about individual sayings, that we may find reflected here the thought of a single unique teacher.[67]

This is not really a 'median position': essentially it supports the historicity of the Gospels' accounts of Jesus' sayings, as opposed to the form critics' view that they are largely later reconstructions.

Weeden attacks Bailey's examples, pointing to internal inconsistencies in them and arguing that on the basis of these supposed inconsistencies, his whole theory does not hold water. He argues that in such Middle Eastern storytelling, the speaker moulds the story to meet the occasion on which it is told. Thus, he says, in the absence of rigorous social-science methodology and

---

63 Nordhofen, 'In der Spur-Gedächtnis als Ereignis', 726.
64 Bailey, 'Informal Controlled Oral Tradition and the Synoptic Gospels', 8.
65 Cf. Bultmann, *Jesus and the Word*, 51.
66 Bailey, 'Informal Controlled Oral Tradition and the Synoptic Gospels', 6.
67 Dodd, *The Founder of Christianity*, 22, quoted in Bailey, 'Informal Controlled Oral Tradition and the Synoptic Gospels', 5.

testing, Bailey's theory of 'formal controlled oral tradition' remains unproven.[68]

Weeden's criticisms, in turn, have their critics. Keener points to various respects in which non-crucial details are recorded differently by different speakers in Bailey's examples, while preserving the integrity of the central story, and arguing that social-science rigour cannot be expected in theorising in the humanities.[69] Potently, he argues that 'Most of those who use Bailey's information are not tradition-inerrantists', but 'Rather, their normal argument is simply that communities preserve the core of their key traditions'.[70] This is a sensible and moderate proposition. Elsewhere Keener notes with approval Assmann's suggestion that 'memory of individuals may continue orally from three to four generations to roughly eighty years, but a crisis often happens midway, at about forty years', which 'may help explain why authors began producing written accounts about Jesus within roughly this timeframe (cf. Luke 1:1)'. His view is that 'Mark, if it is the first finished story about Jesus, which we cannot know, stems from within about forty years'.[71] It is inappropriate to reach any conclusion about Mark's date here, but certainly, as most scholars now think it is the earliest of the Synoptic gospels, its date of composition is likely to be early, in relation to Jesus' death in circa 30 CE.

James Dunn too criticises Weeden, on the basis that Weeden considers he has demolished Bailey's theory merely by pointing to variations in the telling of his storytelling examples at different times.[72] Dunn suggests that Weeden falls into the trap of 'assuming that there can be only one, "original", "historically accurate" and "faithfully transmitted" version of any one story or episode', pointing to Matthew's and Luke's different purposes in telling the story of the centurion's servant (Matt 8:5–13; Luke 7:1–10), 'they simply tell the same story differently, to bring home somewhat different lessons for their readers/audiences—both lessons drawn quite fittingly from the same story'.[73] This has a commonsense appeal: *of course* it is unremarkable if in the telling, differences in detail occur in the same story told to different audiences for different purposes.

A good example of this phenomenon is the different wording of the sayings of Jesus recorded in Clement's First Letter to the Corinthians at 13:2 compared to Matt 5:7, 6:14, 7:12a, 7:1 and 7:2b and Luke 6:31, 6:38a, 6:37a and 6:38c, as noted by Strickland.[74] Weeden has not really 'caught out' Bailey by finding differences in the telling at various times of the stories in his examples. Dunn's position here is not far from Dodd's sensible one in the passage quoted earlier. Bultmann and his followers miss this essential point in finding the Gospel accounts of Jesus' teaching unreliable and inconsistent.

A short paper of this kind cannot do full justice to Dunn's expansive argument in his classic work, *Jesus Remembered*, but his central thesis is nicely brought together at the end of the book. Dunn offers these 'bare propositions':

(1) The only realistic objective for any "quest of the historical Jesus" is Jesus *remembered*. (2) The Jesus tradition of the Gospels confirms *that* there was a concern within earliest Christianity to remember Jesus. (3) The Jesus tradition shows us *how* Jesus was remembered; its character suggests again and again a tradition given its essential shape by regular use and reuse in oral mode. (4) This suggests in turn that that essential shape was given by the

---

68 Weeden, 'Kenneth Bailey's Theory of Oral Tradition'.
69 Keener, 'Weighing T.J. Weeden's Critique of Kenneth Bailey's Approach to Oral Tradition in the Gospels'.
70 Keener, 'Weighing T.J. Weeden's Critique of Kenneth Bailey's Approach to Oral Tradition in the Gospels', 73.
71 Keener, *Christobiography*, 482.
72 Dunn, 'Kenneth Bailey's Theory of Oral Tradition'.
73 Dunn, 'Kenneth Bailey's Theory of Oral Tradition', 52.
74 Strickland, 'The Integration of the Oral and Written Jesus Tradition in the Early Church', 134–35.

original *impact made by Jesus* as that was first put into words by and among those involved as eyewitnesses of what Jesus said and did.[75]

He explains that the initial formative impact in shaping the Jesus tradition was not 'Easter faith', although the characteristic motifs and emphases of the original tradition themselves demonstrate that they were established without, and possibly before, any Easter influence. We can look behind the impact to the one who made it, but we cannot expect to find 'a historical Jesus' other than, or different from, the Jesus who made that impact. That impact itself took the form of tradition. Those who had been influenced decisively by the life-changing impact of Jesus could not fail to have spoken of it to others who shared this new experience of God's kingship and its consequences in living in the here and now. So to Dunn, this impact expressed in verbal formation was itself the beginning of the Jesus tradition proper.[76]

Dunn rejects the form-critical approach: 'they neglected to enquire very far about the faith stimulus which *started* the traditioning process'.[77] To Dunn, the recognition that forms have a '*Sitz im Leben*', (life setting) diverted attention excessively from the process of transmission to the communities which shaped the forms. It succumbed to the 'assumption that there is a recoverable reality (an "original" form) behind the text untouched by faith'. But again, he says, we have to ask whether we have in the synoptic tradition *any* data which are untouched by faith from the outset.[78] Put another way, Dunn deplores the form critics' attempt at separation of the Jesus of history from the Christ of faith: he holds that *all we have* is the Jesus of history in the memories of those whose lives were changed by contact with him.

In his later volume, *The Oral Gospel Tradition*, Dunn criticises what he sees as Halbwach's failure to make a 'real attempt to discuss the dynamics of oral tradition or too engage with the idea that the earliest churches lived by and kept alive the initial memories of Jesus by regular repetition and celebration of their (oral) tradition'.[79] We have seen that Halbwachs says of Jerusalem 'it is above all there that the essentials of the Christian myth were transposed into a tale of events—perhaps a century after the fact'.[80] It is therefore not unfair to say that Halbwachs fails to engage with the possibility that 'the earliest churches lived by and kept alive the initial memories of Jesus by regular repetition and celebration of their (oral) tradition' because it was (and is) *true*.

Here Dunn notes that Assmann 'agrees with Halbwachs that memory is constituted by social frameworks of memory, and that the identity and continuity of a community depends upon its constant revitalisation of its constitutive memories', but moves on from Halbwachs in making 'a helpful distinction between 'communicative memory' and 'cultural memory'. Dunn notes that 'communicative memory', *kommunikative Gedächtnis*, 'can be used of communities still close to their origins, a period characterised by face-to-face circulation of foundational memories', which are 'vested in those who experienced originating events'; it is the time of 'eyewitnesses and living memory (*Augenzeugenschaft und lebendigen Erinnerung*)', the outer limit of which is 'the passing of those able to claim contact with the original generation'.[81] It has been important to quote Dunn directly here, because he raises the possibility that *alternatively* to the limitations of Halbwach's

---

75 Dunn, *Jesus Remembered*, 882.
76 Dunn, *Jesus Remembered*, 882–83; similarly Dunn, 'On History, Memory and Eyewitnesses: In Response to Bengt Holmberg and Samuel Byrskog', 478–79.
77 Dunn, *Jesus Remembered*, 127.
78 Dunn, *Jesus Remembered*, 128.
79 Dunn, *The Oral Gospel Tradition*, 235.
80 Halbwachs, *Collective Memory*, 215.
81 Halbwachs, *Collective Memory*, 236.

ideas, 'Assmann's distinction of "communicative memory" from "cultural memory" may be more relevant, given the limited time span in view in the period in which the Synoptic tradition was formed'.[82] Thus Dunn recognises the crucial divergence between Halbwachs and Assmann on social memory. He does not rely on Assmann in forming his own view of the formation of memories of Jesus here, but an essential part of his argument is the short time span between the events depicted in the Synoptic Gospels and their time of writing.

Dunn of course is not without his critics. In what are representative criticisms, Kirk argues that Dunn 'dismisses social and cultural memory analysis', which 'prevents him from recognising important ways that the tradition actually sustains vital connections to the past'.[83] As we have seen, however, Dunn does not deny the form critics' insight that 'tradition [...] sustains vital connections to the past': he simply asserts that 'they neglected to enquire very far about the faith stimulus which *started* the traditioning process',[84] which is a different thing altogether. Nor does Dunn 'dismiss' social and cultural memory analysis. Instead, he takes an impliedly positive view of Assmann's distinction between 'communicative memory' and 'cultural memory'—although he does not rely on it. Dunn merely dismisses the limitation Halbwachs placed on social memory, that 'it is above all there [at Jerusalem] that the essentials of the Christian myth were transposed into a tale of events—perhaps a century after the fact',[85] because Halbwachs fails to engage with the possibility that 'the essentials of the Christian myth' may be *true*.

With Dunn's explanations of his overall project in mind, we note that to him, the Sermon on the Mount/Plain stresses the importance of *hearing* and doing Jesus' words (Matt 7:24,26//Luke 6:47,49), recalling the *shema* with its overtones of heedful hearing.[86] Noting that Matthew, unlike Luke, appears to repeat without elaboration in Matt 11:5 what he found in the putative source Q, Dunn suggests that Matthew reminds his hearers that material poverty was not the most serious fate in which people could find themselves. This, he says, demonstrates that Jesus' attitude to poverty sets him wholly within the traditional law and spirituality of poverty,[87] predicated on the Deuteronomic assumption that the poor, as part of the covenant people, were entitled to a share in the nation's prosperity.[88] This cogent view tells against Matt 11:4–5 as a *novum* in the NT, as does Dunn's view that in Matt 11:4–5//Luke 7:22, John the Baptist's disciples are probably referred to Isa 61:1–3,[89] in pointing to Jesus' success in bringing about the healings Isaiah anticipated in the age to come.[90]

As **Dale Allison** notes, in Isa 61:1–3 in the LXX we find εὐαγγελίσασθαι πτωχοῖς,[91] 'to preach glad tidings to the poor', and τυφλοῖς ἀνάβλεψιν, 'the recovery of sight to the blind'. If that were a free fabrication, one would expect to find a record of the Baptist's positive response. There is none.[92] If, on the other hand, Allison writes, this passage exhibits a correct memory of the gist of

---

82 Halbwachs, *Collective Memory*, 237.
83 Kirk, 'The Memory-Tradition Nexus in the Synoptic Tradition', 144.
84 Dunn, *Jesus Remembered*, 127.
85 Halbwachs, *Collective Memory*, 215.
86 Dunn, *Jesus Remembered*, 491.
87 Dunn, *Jesus Remembered*, 525.
88 Dunn, *Jesus Remembered*, 526; see also Love, 'Jesus Heals the Haemorrhaging Woman' 92–93; Focant, 'La Christologie de Matthieu à la Croisée des Chemins', 82, 85.
89 Hagner, *Matthew 1–13*, 662; Allison, *Constructing Jesus: Memory, Imagination and History*, 275; Rodriguez, 'Textual Orientations', 205.
90 Hagner, *Matthew 1–13*, 771.
91 The verb εὐαγγελίζω is invariably used in the NT to connote bringing *good* news: BDAG, 317.
92 Allison, *Constructing Jesus*, 275.

an actual exchange between Jesus and the Baptist, this may permit an inference that the Baptist's apocalyptic warning about 'the one who is to come' (11:3) refers, not to God or an angel, but to a human agent, and that Jesus saw himself as that agent—as indeed Matthew identifies him in 11:2[93]—so that Jesus' self-conception incorporated the Baptist's eschatological expectation.[94] As Allison writes, the inference that Jesus' self-conception incorporated the Baptist's eschatological expectation is supported by these two sentences in Luke 12:49–50, 'I came to bring fire to the earth, and how I wish that it were already kindled! I have a baptism with which to be baptized, and what stress I am under until it is completed'. As he says, they are found *only* in Luke, and 'these two sentences, which should not be dissolved into two separate sayings with separate tradition histories, were not Luke's invention'.[95]

And there is nothing in Isaiah that might have inspired the inclusion in Matt 11:5//Luke 7:22 of the logion λεπροὶ καθαρίζονται, 'lepers are cleansed', so it may be present there only because it was generally believed—and by Jesus too—that he had indeed cleansed lepers.[96] During Jesus' earthly life and ministry his deeds showed who he was for the believer (11:2–6), but his true identity was realised only after the resurrection.[97] 'Talk of the works of the Messiah in 11:5 alludes to the prophetic promise of salvation in Christ'.[98] Dunn's approach is based on oral hermeneutics, but inevitably he 'foregrounds' the role of memory.

Richard Bauckham too rejects the form-critical notion that the Gospels combine authentic and inauthentic tradition: all history is 'an inextricable combination of fact and interpretation, the empirically observable and the intuited or constructed meaning'.[99] Bauckham criticises Theissen's view that Jesus himself gave his miracles of exorcism and healing an eschatological meaning, but that this meaning is found, not in the miracle stories themselves, but in the sayings tradition, referring, inter alia, to Matt 11:2–6, and that the miracle stories underwent a 'popular adaptation', whereby the distinctive character of the miracles was 'smoothed out'.[100] In refutation, Bauckham remarks that 'the disciples themselves are bound to have told these stories from the beginning, and it is not plausible that their accounts are wholly unrepresented among the miracle stories of the Gospels'.[101] This is an extremely plausible argument: why, one might ask, would the miracle stories in Matt 11:2–6 and elsewhere need to undergo, in the short time between the events depicted and the likely date of Matthew's and the other Synoptic Gospels, a 'smoothing out' of their distinctive character? The explanation of the differences in detail between Matthew's and Luke's accounts of what appear to be the same events is more likely to be accounted for, one might think, as Dunn puts it, by the fact that 'they simply tell the same story differently, to bring home somewhat different lessons for their readers/audiences—both lessons drawn quite fittingly from the same story'.[102]

---

93   Van de Sandt, 'Matthew 11:28–30', 318.
94   Allison, *Constructing Jesus*, 275–76.
95   Allison, *Constructing Jesus*, 276.
96   Hagner, *Matthew 1–13*, 450.
97   De Jong, 'Dominion', 442, 451 n.35.
98   Konradt, 'Die Rede von Glauben in Matthäusevangelium', 437 (my translation).
99   Bauckham, *Jesus and the Eyewitnesses*, 7–8; Keith, *Jesus' Literacy: Social Culture and the Teacher from Galilee*, 49.
100 Theissen, *The Miracle Stories of the Early Christian Tradition*, 276–86.
101 Bauckham, *Jesus and the Eyewitnesses*, 53.
102 Dunn, 'Kenneth Bailey's Theory of Oral Tradition', 52.

Conclusions

Considering the popular dating of Matthew's Gospel at a time pre-70 CE,[103] (and even if the most popular alternative dating shortly post-70 CE is preferred), the memories of Jesus' saying recorded in Matt 11:4–5//Luke 7:22 still lie within the timeframe of Assmann's *kommunikative Gedächtnis*, because they sit within the time of *Augenzeugenschaft und lebendigen Erinnerung*, and need not be explained in form-critical terms as a *novum* inserted by the writer/redactor of Matthew's and Luke's Gospels. Applying Assmann's distinction, which appears sensible, Matt 11:4–5//Luke 7:22 may not simply be a *novum* assimilated by early Christians to the known past, with its prediction in Isa 61:1–3, but may be, as Dunn and Allison theorise, a record of the memories of eyewitnesses who heard and saw Jesus make the statements recorded there, who had every reason to remember them, considering what was probably the life-changing effect of their encounter with Jesus.

We do not, for present purposes, need to decide finally whether Matthew or Luke was written before or after a time pre-70 CE, at a time prior to or after what has been called the 'parting of the ways' of church from synagogue,[104] because most scholars place both as written before the turn of the first century CE, at a time before the passing of the first generation who had person-to-person contact with Jesus, and therefore well within the time of Assmann's 'communicative memory'. While a scholarly consensus favours a post-70 CE but pre-100 CE date for Matthew,[105] those in favour of a pre-70 CE date for Matthew include Hagner,[106] Quarles,[107] France (cautiously),[108] and a number of others. Those favouring a pre-70 CE date for Luke include Bock,[109] and Jeffrey,[110] and a number of others. The many favouring a post-70 CE but pre-100 CE date for Luke include Fitzmyer, Bruce, Bovon, Kümmel, Danke, Tiede, Maddox, Esler, C.A. Evans, C.F. Evans, and Johnson.[111]

If Matthew was written pre-70 CE, however, it becomes even more understandable that, in the sense Halbwachs identified, Matthew 'was presented as a continuation in a sense of Hebraic religion'.[112] It may then be more likely that Jesus would himself present his messianic claims by appealing to OT predictions. More recently, Boyarin and others have questioned whether we can speak of a single split with one entity which we can label 'Judaism',[113] and Lieu adverts to this problem, pointing to ongoing Judeo–Christian interactions after the alleged 'parting of the ways'.[114] Still, Matthew's Gospel tends to display a more positive attitude to the Law compared to that portrayed in John's (cf. Matt 5:17–20; John 1:14; 9:29), although John is not unambiguous (cf. John 5:45).

Flint's observation, that the 'remarkable singularity between 4Q521 and Luke 7:21–22 (=Matt 11:4–5) may indicate that a list of activities associated with the Messiah similar to that in Q was familiar to at least some Jews before the Common Era', may be unsound.[115] However, using Jesus Memory Theory, within the limitations of recall inherent in laying down oral tradition in writing, and even allowing for significant changes of meaning, due to the pressures of the transmissional context,[116] we can say that it is still probable that Jesus' saying in Matt 11:4–5//Luke 7:22 is genuinely dominical.

---

103 Hagner, *Matthew 1–13*, lxxiv–lxxv.
104 Lieu, *Neither Jew nor Greek*, 11–30.
105 Turner, *Matthew*, 13.
106 Hagner, *Matthew 1–13*, lxxiv–lxxv.
107 Quarles, *Matthew*, 6.
108 France, *Matthew*, 21.
109 Bock, *Luke Volume I: 1–1–9.50*, 18.
110 Jeffrey, *Luke*, 6.
111 Bock, *Luke Volume I: 1–1–9.50*, 16 n.7.
112 Halbwachs, *Collective Memory*, 86.
113 Boyarin, *Border Lines*, 32.
114 Lieu, *Neither Jew nor Greek*, 26 –29.
115 Flint, 'The Qumran Scrolls and the Historical Jesus', 279.
116 Kloppenborg, 'Memory, Performance and the Sayings of Jesus', 117–18.

Bibliography

Assmann, Jan — *Das kulturelle Gedächtnis, Schrift, Erinnerung und politische frühen Hochkulturen* (München: CH Beck, 1992).

Assmann, Jan — 'Thomas Mann und die Phänomenolagie der Kulturellen Erinnerung' in *Thomas Mann Jahrbuch* (1993), Vol. 6, 133–58.

Bailey, Kenneth E. — 'Informal Controlled Oral Tradition and the Synoptic Gospels', *Them* 20.2 (1995), 4–11.

Bauckham, Richard — *Jesus and the Eyewitnesses: The Gospels as Eyewitness Testimony* (Grand Rapids: Eerdmans, 2006).

Becker, Michael — '4Q521 und die Gesalbten', *Rev Q* 18.1 (1999), 73–96.

Bock, Darrell L. — *Luke Volume I: 1–1–9.50* (Grand Rapids: Baker Academic, 1994).

Bornkamm, Gunther — *Jesus of Nazareth* (London: Hodder & Stoughton, 1960).

Boyarin, Daniel — *Border Lines* (Philadelphia: Philadelphia University Press, 2004).

Brown, Francis — *The Brown–Driver–Briggs Hebrew and English Lexicon* (Peabody, Ma.: Hendrickson, 8th printing, 2004; original ed. 1908). (=BDB)

Bultmann, Rudolf — *The History of the Synoptic Tradition* (Oxford, Blackwell, 1963).

Bultmann, Rudolf — *Jesus and the Word* (Louise Pettibone Smith and Erminie Huntress Lantero, transls.; London: Collins, 1958).

Chadwick, Henry — *The Church in Ancient Society: From Galilee to Gregory the Great* (Oxford: Clarendon Press, 2001).

Chadwick, Henry — *The Early Church* (London: Penguin, rev. ed. 1993).

Collins, John J. — 'The Works of the Messiah', *DSD* 1.1 (1994), 98–112.

De Jong, M.J. — 'Dominion through Obedience: Matt 1:21 among the Early Christian Characterisations of Jesus', in D. Senior (ed.), *The Gospel of Matthew at the Crossroads of Early Christianity* (BETL 243; Leuven: Peeters, 2011), 437–52.

Dodd, C.H. — *The Founder of Christianity* (London: Macmillan, 1970).

Duling, Dennis C. — 'Memory, Collective Memory, Orality and the Gospels', *HTS* 67.1 (2013), 1–11.

Dunn, James D.G. — *The Oral Gospel Tradition* (Grand Rapids/Cambridge, UK: Eerdmans, 2013).

Dunn, James D.G. — 'Kenneth Bailey's Theory of Oral Tradition: Critiquing Theodore Weeden's Critique', *Journal for the Study of the Historical Jesus* 7 (2009), 44–62.

Dunn, James D.G. — 'Social Memory and the Oral Jesus Tradition', in Stephen C. Barton, Loren T. Stuckenbruck and Benjamin G. Wold (eds.), *Memory in the Bible and Antiquity* (WUNT 212; Tübingen: Mohr Siebeck, 2007), 179–94.

Dunn, James D.G. — 'On History, Memory and Eyewitnesses: In Response to Bengt Holmberg and Samuel Byrskog', *JSNT* 26.4 (2004), 473–87.

Dunn, James D.G.	*Jesus Remembered* (Grand Rapids: Eerdmans, 2003).
Durkheim, Emile	*Les formes élémentaires de la vie religieuse: La système totémique en Australie* (Paris: Les Presses universitaires de France, 1968).
Durkheim, Emile	*The Elementary Forms of the Religious Life* (J.W. Swain, trans.; London: George Allen and Unwin, ET: 2nd ed., 1976 [1912]).
Esler, Philip F.	*The First Christians in their Social World: Socio-Scientific Approaches to New Testament Interpretation* (London: Routledge, 1994).
Faierstein, M.M.	'Why do the Scribes say that Elijah Must Come First?', *JBL* 100 (1981), 75–86.
Ferguson, Anthony	'The Elijah Forerunner Concept as an Authentic Jewish Expectation', *JBL* 137.1 (2018), 127–45.
Fitzmyer, Joseph A.	*Essays on the Semitic Background of the New Testament* (Grand Rapids & Cambridge, UK: Eerdmans, 1997).
Fitzmyer, Joseph A.	'More about Elijah Coming First', *JBL* 104 (1985), 295–96.
Flint, Peter W.	'The Qumran Scrolls and the Historical Jesus', in James H Charlesworth (ed.), *Jesus Research: New Methodologies and Perceptions* (Grand Rapids: Eerdmans, 2014), 261–82.
Focant, C.	'La Christologie de Matthieu à la Croisée des Chemins', in D. Senior (ed.), *The Gospel of Matthew at the Crossroads of Early Christianity* (BETL 243; Leuven: Peeters, 2011), 73–98.
France, R.T.	*The Gospel of Matthew* (Grand Rapids/Cambridge, UK: Eerdmans, 2007).
García Martínez, Florentino, and Eibert J.C. Tigchelaar,	*The Dead Sea Scrolls Study Edition* Vol 2 (Leiden/Boston, Köln/Brill, Grand Rapids /Cambridge UK: Eerdmans, 1997).
Gingrich, Wilbur,	*A Greek-English Lexicon of the New Testament* (Chicago/London: University of Chicago Press, 2nd ed., revised and augmented by F. Wilbur Gingrich and Frederick W Danker from Walter Bauer's 5th ed., 1979). 'BDAG'.
Hagner, Donald A.	*Matthew 1–13* (WBC 33A; Waco: Zondervan, 2000).
Halbwachs, Maurice	*Collective Memory* (Lewis A Coser, trans.; Chicago/London: University of Chicago Press, 1992).
Horbury, William	'The Jewish Dimension', in Ian Hazlett (ed.), *Early Christianity: Origins and Evolution to AD 600* (Fs. W.H.C. Frend; London: SPCK, 1991), 40–51.
Jeremias, Joachim	"Ηλ(ε)ίας', *Theological Dictionary of the New Testament* (Gerhard Kittel, Gerhard Friedrich, eds.; Geoffrey William Bromiley, ed. & trans.; Grand Rapids: Eerdmans, 1964), 2.928–41.
Keener, Craig S.	'Weighing T.J. Weeden's Critique of Kenneth Bailey's Approach to Oral Tradition in the Gospels', *JGRChI* (2017), 41–78.

Keith, Chris	'Social Memory Theory and Gospels Research: The First Decade (Part Two)', *EC* (2015), 517–42.
Keith, Chris	*Jesus' Literacy: Social Culture and the Teacher from Galilee* (London: Bloomsbury, 2011).
Kirk, Alan	'The Memory-Tradition Nexus in the Synoptic Tradition: Memory, Media and Symbolic Representation', in Tom Thatcher (ed.), *Memory and Identity in Ancient Judaism and Early Christianity: A Conversation with Barry Schwartz* (Atlanta: SBL Press, 2014), 131–59.
Kirk, Alan	'Memory', in Werner H. Kelber and Samuel Byrskog (eds.), *Jesus in Memory: Traditions in Oral and Scribal Perspectives* (Waco, Tx.: Baylor University Press, 2009), 155–72.
Kirk, Alan, & Tom Thatcher	'Jesus Tradition and Social Memory', in A. Kirk and T. Thatcher (eds.), *Memory, Tradition and Text: Uses of the Past in Early Christianity* (Leiden/Boston: Brill, 2005), 25–42.
Klausner, Joseph	*The Messianic Idea in Israel* (W.F. Steinspring, trans.; New York: Macmillan, 1955).
Kloppenborg, John S.	'Memory, Performance and the Sayings of Jesus', *JSHJ* (2012), 97–132.
Konradt, Mattias	'Die Rede von Glauben in Matthäusevangelium', in Jörg Frey, Benjamin Schleisser, & Nadine Ueberschaer (eds.), *Glaube: Das Verständnis des Glaubens im Frühen Christentum und in seiner jüdischen und hellenistich-römischen Umwelt* (Tübingen: Mohr Siebeck, 2017), 423–50.
Lieu, Judith	*Neither Jew nor Greek: Constructing Early Christianity* (London: T&T Clark, 2002).
Love, Stuart L.	'Jesus Heals the Haemorrhaging Woman' in Wolfgang Stegemann, Bruce J Malina and Gerd Theissen (eds.), *The Social Setting of Jesus and the Gospels* (Minneapolis: Fortress Press, 2002), 85–102.
Mowinkel, Sigmund	*He that Cometh* (New York/Nashville: Abingdon Press, 1954).
Nolland, John	*Matthew: A Commentary on the Greek Text* (Bletchley: Paternoster Press, 2005).
Nordhofen, Eckhard	'In der Spur-Gedächtnis als Ereignis', *StZ* (2018), 725–34.
Ollick, Jeffrey K., & Joyce Robbins,	'Social Memory Studies from "Collective Memory" to the Historical Sociology of Mnemonic Practices', *AnnRevSociol* 24 (1998), 105–40.
Puech, Emile	'Une Apocalypse Messianique (4Q521)', *Rev Q* 15.4 (1992), 475–522.
Quarles, Charles L.	*Matthew* (Nashville: B&S Academic, 2017).
Rodriguez, Rafael	'Textual Orientations, Written Texts, and the Construction of Social Identity in the Gospel of Luke', in J. Brian Tucker and Coleman A. Baker (eds.), *T&T Clark Handbook to Social Identity in the New Testament* (London: Bloomsbury, paperback ed., 2016), 191–210.

Scheffler, Eben — 'Putting Qumran, Jesus and his Movement into Relief', HTS 72.4 (2016), 1–10.

Schwartz, Barry — 'Christian Origins: Historical Truth and Social Memory', in A. Kirk and T. Thatcher (eds.), *Memory, Tradition and Text: Uses of the Past in Early Christianity* (Leiden/Boston: Brill, 2005), 43–56.

Strickland, Michael — 'The Integration of the Oral and Written Jesus Tradition in the early Church', *Journal of Early Christian History* 5.1 (2016), 132–43.

Strugnell, J. — 'Moses Pseudepigrapha at Qumran: 4Q375, 4Q376 and Similar Works', in L.H. Schiffman (ed.), *Archaeology and History in the Dead Sea Scrolls: The New York Conference in Memory of Yigael Yadin* (JSPSup 8; Sheffield: JSOT Press, 1990), 221–65.

Tabor, James D., & Michael O. Wise, — '4Q521. On Resurrection and the Synoptic Gospel tradition. A Preliminary Study', *JSP* 10 (1992), 140–62.

Theissen, Gerd — *The Miracle Stories of the Early Christian Tradition* (F. McDonagh, trans.; Edinburgh: T&T Clark, 1983).

Turner, David L. — *Matthew* (Grand Rapids: Baker Academic, 2008).

Van de Sandt, H. — 'Matthew 11:28–30: Compassionate Law interpretation in Wisdom Language', in D. Senior (ed.), *The Gospel of Matthew at the Crossroads of Early Christianity* (BETL 243; Leuven: Peeters, 2011), 313–38.

Weeden, Theodore J. — 'Kenneth Bailey's Theory of Oral Tradition: A Theory Contested by its Evidence', *JSHJ* 7 (2009), 3–43.

Wink, Walter — *John the Baptist in the Gospel Tradition* (Cambridge: Cambridge University Press, 1976).

Wise, Michael O., & James D. Tabor — 'The Messiah at Qumran', *BAR* (Nov-Dec 1992), 60–63.

Witherington, Ben, III — *Matthew* (Macon, Ga.: Smith & Helwys, 2006).

Chris Armitage
Sydney College of Divinity

'Put Your Sword Back into Its Place' (Matt 26:52)
The Rationale Behind Jesus's Sword Directive (and It Isn't Pacifism)

DAVID LERTIS MATSON

Abstract

Scholars typically construe Jesus's directive to 'put your sword back into its place' (Matt 26:52) as supporting a principled pacifism. Reading the Matthean arrest scene (Matt 26:47–56) from the standpoint of the Sermon on the Mount with its non-retaliation and enemy-love commands, they contend that Matthew is presenting a Jesus who practices what he preaches. Rarely, however, do these interpreters allow the immediate context to provide necessary hermeneutical controls while overlooking or ignoring altogether the fact that at least one disciple possesses a sword and uses it with dexterous precision. Giving due cognizance to such considerations, this article draws sharp attention to the immediate context of Matthew's arrest scene thus altering the common perception of Jesus as a pacifist in significant ways.

1. Introduction

One of the texts most often used to defend a pacifist Jesus is his warning to a sword-wielding disciple: 'Put your sword back into its place; for all who take the sword will perish by the sword' (Matt 26:52).[1] In commenting on this passage, Richard B. Hays pointedly declares: 'There is no foundation whatever in the Gospel of Matthew for the notion that violence in defense of a third party is justifiable. In fact, Matthew 26:51–52 serves as an explicit refutation of the idea'.[2] Employing the nomenclature of John Howard Yoder, one might classify Hays' declaration as a 'pacifism of absolute principle' that believes it is wrong to take a human life under any

---

1   That any principle-based pacifist movements existed in the Graeco-Roman world is doubtful, even among Jews, a number of whom actually served in the Roman imperial army 'from the beginning of the Pax Romana down to the days of the early fifth century' (Schoenfeld, 'Sons of Israel', 106). While it may be true then that the pacifism question is of 'no immediate relevance' to Matthew (Carson, *Matthew–Mark*, 613), it *is* of concern to later interpreters who base their absolute pacifism, at least partly, on Matt 26:52, an interpretive tendency stretching back at least as far as Origen. Unless otherwise indicated, all scriptural citations are from the New Revised Standard Version.
2   Hays, *Moral Vision*, 324.

circumstances.[3] The question thus comes sharply into focus: Does the Matthean Jesus at the point of his arrest advocate just such an absolute pacifism?[4]

The words of Jesus rejecting the use of the sword, highlighted rhetorically by Matthew, ostensibly agree with an earlier logion in the Sermon on the Mount: 'Do not resist an evildoer. But if anyone strikes you on the right cheek, turn the other also' (Matt 5:39).[5] Ulrich Mauser believes this command to non-resistance receives its 'authentic interpretation' later in Matthew when Jesus refuses to be defended at the point of a sword.[6] In Ulrich Luz's view, these two interlocking rationales open the door to 'absolute defenselessness and absolute rejection of violence. He [Jesus] himself offers no resistance at his arrest, and he also forbids the same to his disciples'.[7] So, too, Eduard Schweizer: 'Fulfilling the Sermon on the Mount, Jesus backs up his teaching by the actual deeds of his Passion'.[8]

With this interpretive marriage fully consummated in the minds of many interpreters, Matthew begets a pacifist Jesus who, when confronted by encroaching swordsmen, 'follows his own counsel for righteous behavior given at the Sermon on the Mount'.[9] According to Luz, Jesus demonstrates what non-retaliation means—'radical, uncompromising pacifism that has no room even for self-defense'.[10] Moreover, the five-fold structure of Matthew with its dynamic rhetorical interplay of deed and word appears to reinforce this picture of a Jesus who practices what he preaches: 'Jesus, in the First Gospel, embodies his sentences; the Lord lives as he speaks and speaks as he lives'.[11]

Closely conjoined with pacifistic non-retaliation is an interpretive twin: Jesus's teaching of enemy-love (Matt 5:43–48). Donald P. Senior, for example, asserts that both the fifth and sixth antitheses 'echo the same spirit as Jesus' rebuke to the disciples in 26:52b', thus producing a hermeneutical triumvirate with the same ideological DNA: Jesus refuses defense of the sword because he stands for non-retaliation and love of enemies.[12] Despite the nearly universal appeal to enemy-love to support a pacifist interpretation of Jesus, however, love as an explicit verbal theme surprisingly plays no appreciable role in Matthew's Passion narrative.[13] In fact, one could argue

---

3   See Yoder, *Nevertheless*, 32–37.
4   Yoder, *Nevertheless*, 36, recognizes that 'we need to weigh the pacifism of absolute principle against other absolutes, equally blunt and oversimplified' and nuances a number of pacifistic approaches, not all of which are absolutist. But why the need to resort to such variegated strategies unless all violence is morally wrong in principle? The 'transforming initiatives' of Stassen and Gushee, *Kingdom Ethics*, 147, for example, seem to presuppose and emanate from their absolute conviction that 'the kingdom of God consists of peace with justice, of life unmarred by killing'.
5   The τότε + historical present (λέγει) combination prefacing Jesus's statement at 26:52 serves to highlight what Jesus is about to say (see Runge, *Discourse Grammar*, 137). Runge also lists Matt 3:13,15; 4:5,10,11; 9:6,14,37;12:13; 15:1,12; 18:32; 22:8,21; 26:31,36[2x]; 38,45 [2x]; 27:13,38; 28:10.
6   Cited approvingly in Hays, *Moral Vision*, 322.
7   Luz, *Matthew 21–28*, 419.
8   Schweizer, *Matthew*, 496. According to Schweizer, Jesus becomes 'the prototype for his followers, who renounce violence and prefer to suffer injustice'.
9   Matera, *Passion Narratives*, 98. So also Sider, *Christ and Violence*, 24: 'But Jesus not only *lived* the way of non-violence. He also taught it', citing Matt 5:38–48 in particular (italics his).
10 Luz, *Matthew 21–28*, 419.
11 Allison, *Studies*, 154–55. Meier, *Matthew*, 328, too, sees Jesus practicing what he preaches at his arrest, citing Matt 5:38–48.
12 Senior, *Passion of Jesus*, 29. See also his *Passion Narrative according to Matthew*, 135. Harrington, *Matthew*, 375, ties both logia together as justification for Jesus's pacifism: 'Matthew presents Jesus as faithful to his own principle of non-violence (Matt 5:38–42) and love of enemies (Matt 5:43–48)'.
13 Only φιλέω (and the compound καταφιλέω) appears in Matthew's Passion and there with the specific meaning of 'kiss' (26:48). While one must guard against the word–concept fallacy, the striking lack of linguistic evidence calls into question Senior's assertion that Jesus 'would relentlessly proclaim in *word* and action his message of love, even to the point of death' (Senior, *Passion of Jesus*, 29, italics mine). Apart from generalized usages in Matt 6:24; 24:12 (ἀγαπάω/ἀγάπη) and Matt 6:5; 10:37 [2x]; 23:6 (φιλέω), love appears outside the Sermon on the Mount only in scriptural citations (19:19 [Lev 19:18]; 22:3 [Deut 6:5], 39 [Lev 19:18]).

that Matthew is guilty of massive inconsistency inasmuch as the Matthean Jesus does not seem to exhibit love towards enemies at all.[14]

This essay sharply contests the view that non-retaliation and enemy-love function as dual rationales for Jesus's refusal to be defended at his arrest.[15] One might just as well cite the sword saying in Matthew 10:34 to argue in the opposite direction: 'Do not think that I have come to bring peace to the earth; I have not come to bring peace, but a sword'. Such language is certainly more consistent in its ethos with Matthew's vision of the church militant (Matt 16:18).[16] Rather, as will become clear in the course of this discussion, Jesus's rejection of the sword emanates not from a principled stand against violence but from an unswerving commitment to the divine will in fulfillment of the prophetic scriptures. Negatively put, Jesus resists the sword because he 'did not desire the plans of His enemies to be thwarted'.[17] Why Jesus advocates such a non-obstructionist approach is the pivotal question in the Gethsemane arrest scene and provides a key clue for understanding the 'pacifism' of Jesus. Before getting to the rationale proper, however, two preliminary but extended textual matters confront the careful observer.

2. Possession of the Sword

The first observation is Jesus's often overlooked command to put the sword (μάχαιρα) back into its 'place' (Matt 26:52a).[18] Matthew removes the ambiguity from his Markan source by making the recipient of this command a disciple of Jesus.[19] The picture of a disciple equipped with a sheath or scabbard, even if concealed, is a jolting one, at least for those interpreters who care to notice.[20]

---

14 Allison, *Studies in Matthew*, 238, asserts that Jesus in Matthew 'does nothing but attack his enemies', and cites the observation of G.C. Montefiore: 'What one would have wished to find in the life-story of Jesus would be one single incident in which Jesus actually performed a loving deed to one of his Rabbinic antagonists or enemies. That would have been worth all the injunctions of the Sermon on the Mount about the love of enemies put together'. So, too, Luz, *Theology*, 145: 'The commandment to love one's enemy … seems in texts such as Matthew 23 to have vanished completely'. More recently, Nel, ('Not Peace but a Sword', 236: 'The non-violent Jesus of the Sermon on the Mount [...] seems annulled and dismissed by the rhetorically violent Jesus who argues with the religious leaders by denigrating motive and intention or by destroying character and integrity when he stereotypes them as exacting casuistry without practicing what they preach'.
15 While my approach in this essay is a narrative-critical reading of Matthew, I do not hesitate to employ historical-critical and redactional insights when those insights shed light on Matthew's textual meaning.
16 The imagery of the πύλαι ᾅδου implies the onslaught of the church against the gates of Hades, not the other way around. See the helpful discussion in Nolland, *Matthew*, 673–76. Moreover, if βιάζεται in Matt 11:12 is construed as a middle, the kingdom of God likewise takes on an aggressive rather than passive posture, 'forcefully advancing' (NIV [1984], NLT) rather than 'suffering violence' (NRSV, NASB, ESV, NAB, NET), in keeping with Jesus's sword imagery. This picture of the church is commensurate with Matthew's image of Jesus as the Son of God divine-warrior who conquers the forces of chaos (see Angel, '*Crucifixus Vincens*', 310).
17 Allen, *Matthew*, 281.
18 Matthew uses the more generalized τόπος for the sheath or scabbard whereas John uses the more technical θήκη (John 18:11). Mark and Luke are silent on the matter.
19 According to Suhl, the sword-wielder is 'eindeutig ein Gefolgsmann Jesu' ('Die Funktion', 313). While in Mark the sword-wielder is an ambiguous by-stander (εἷς δέ τῶν παρεστηκότων, Mark 14:47), Matthew redacts Mark to clarify that the wielder is a disciple. That the sword wielder is 'with Jesus' (μετὰ Ἰησοῦ) makes this identification probable inasmuch as association with Jesus in Matthew is a mark of true discipleship (26:38,40,69,71).
20 On the possible concealment of the sword, much depends on whether the Matthean narrator would consider swords to be contraband in Jerusalem. Osborne, *Matthew*, 983, thinks that the arresting party may well have concealed their weapons under their cloaks so as not to attract attention unnecessarily. See Jos. Asen. 23.6 for another example of weapon concealment.

Stanley Hauerwas, for example, remarks 'that anyone with Jesus, anyone who has listened to Jesus's preaching, would carry as well as use a sword seems odd'.[21] W.D. Davies and Dale C. Allison express similar perplexity: 'That a disciple of Jesus wears a sword is unexpected and unexplained'.[22] Raymond E. Brown acknowledges that Matthew 'seems to offer no reason why a disciple would be carrying his own (material) sword'.[23] In Luke, of course, Jesus expressly commands the disciples to procure swords (Luke 22:36–38), but Matthew's Jesus is silent about how the disciples come to possess swords.[24]

The rather surprising mention of both sword and sheath by Matthew is revelatory.[25] Marius Nel observes that Jesus does not renounce the sword but simply exhorts to return it to its proper place.[26] The Matthean reader can only wonder if at least some of the disciples may have carried swords as a matter of course, ostensibly with Jesus's approval. Thus the same question that Brown poses to the reader of John's Gospel he could also pose to Matthew's: 'Did Peter, the most prominent member of the Twelve, regularly carry a sword?'[27] In light of at least one sword-carrying disciple at Jesus's arrest, the question is a logical one and invites a re-reading of the Gospel of Matthew with this new information firmly in place.[28]

One initial place to look is in Jesus's missional instructions to the Twelve, where traveling with a sword might naturally be expected. In this, the second major discourse of Jesus in Matthew, Jesus instructs the apostles not to 'acquire' (κτάομαι) money, bag, coats, sandals or staff (10:9–10). Matthew's choice of verb here suggests that 'basic clothing and equipment are assumed' and that what Jesus is forbidding is engaging in a kind of fund-raising effort for the procurement of additional provisions for their journey.[29] Robert H. Gundry demurs somewhat, arguing that Matthew's redaction of Mark's αἴρω ('take') means that 'the prohibitions against taking money *for* the itinerant ministry become prohibitions against acquisition *from* the itinerant ministry'.[30] However one explains this exegetical detail, the pertinent question becomes: would Matthew's reader naturally expect the disciples to carry swords as part of their traveling attire?

---

21 Hauerwas, *Matthew*, 223.
22 Davies and Allison, *Matthew*, 3.511.
23 Brown, *Death*, 1:269.
24 As are Mark and John. For a recent non-pacifistic interpretation of this enigmatic Lukan text, see Matson, 'Double-Edged'. Filson, *Matthew*, 280, thinks that the disciple's possession of the sword was *ad hoc*, sensing the potential danger that they faced in Jerusalem. But Filson relies on data outside the Gospel of Matthew (Luke 22:38) to fill in this narrative gap.
25 One must not construe the sword here in too technical a fashion. As Fretz, 'Weapons', 893, observes, 'What distinguishes a butcher knife from a soldier's dagger is the context in which the implement is used'. Thus the extent to which the Roman imperial army controlled the circulation of weapons, including swords, does not apply here. Moreover, Brown observes that 'in a border area like Galilee sword-carrying would be necessary and almost the same as being clothed' (*Death*, 1:268). More important is the fact that in Matthew's story world a disciple expressly carries a sword and scabbard and has ready access to knives of some sort (Matt 26:17,19).
26 Nel, 'Not Peace but a Sword', 252: 'the disciples may still need the sword to protect themselves during and after the arrest'.
27 Brown, *Death*, 1:269. Matthew, of course, does not explicitly identify the sword-wielding disciple as Peter.
28 That we should assume a multiple implied reader of Matthew is evident in Jesus's closing instructions (28:20); so Allison, 'Anticipating the Passion', 703, and Scaer, *Discourses*, 67–68, who thinks that the catechetical nature of Matthew's Gospel implies that 'it might be reread and reviewed', particularly in a public setting. The term 'catechetical', however, is not sufficiently broad as a descriptor of Matthew's overall task (see Stendahl, *The School of St. Matthew*, 28–29).
29 France, *The Gospel of Matthew*, 384. France points out, for example, how footwear of some kind is already assumed in the injunction of Matt 10:14 (p.380). Contra Luz, *Matthew 8–20*, 76, who contends that the disciples were to travel defenseless and poor while dependent on their hosts for food.
30 Gundry, *Matthew*, 186, italics his. The use of αἴρω in Mark 6:8 has perhaps pushed translations such as the NRSV, CSB, NLT, NIV [1984] in a harmonistic direction in their rendering of κτάομαι in Matt 10:9.

A potentially helpful parallel exists in a comment from Josephus. Commenting on the Essenes, he writes:

> They occupy no one city, but settle in large numbers in every town. On the arrival of any of the sect from elsewhere, all the resources of the community are put at their disposal, just as if they were their most intimate friends. Consequently, they carry nothing whatever with them on their journeys, except arms as a protection against brigands (Josephus, *J.W.* 2.124–25 [Thackeray, LCL]).

Here exists a strategic role for weapons despite Essene reliance on the hospitality of their hosts. While it is difficult to know what type of weapons the Essenes may have employed, it seems likely that it involved swords of some kind.[31]

While a sword does not appear among the contraband listed in Jesus's missional instructions, Jesus does prohibit the acquisition of a 'staff' (ῥάβδος) that could well have served in a similar capacity.[32] A staff, of course, could function as a walking stick but also as a weapon to ward off robbers and wild animals, or both.[33] The potential use of such weaponry is not an insignificant detail when it comes to the question of a pacifist Jesus. Even more to the point, however: Is it plausible for readers of Matthew to envision at least some of the disciples carrying a sword in Essene-like fashion as part of their basic equipment as they travel hastily from one city to the next (Matt 10:23)?[34]

Three strokes are in play. First, the reader of Matthew, well-acquainted with the arrest scene at Gethsemane, knows that at least one of Jesus's disciples could readily produce a sword and use it in quasi-military fashion.[35] One simply has to be able to explain this stubborn narrative detail. Second, among the apostles sent out by Jesus was one 'Simon the Zealot' (Matt 10:4), who, if his title bears any of its later political connotations, could well be envisioned as carrying a sword. General agreement exists that Matthew's term for zealot (ὁ Καναναῖος), borrowed from his Markan source (3:18), derives from the Aramaic *qanna*, meaning 'zealous'.[36] The question is whether

---

31 France, *Gospel of Matthew*, 385, presumes that the Essenes travelled with staffs for weapons. Josephus, however, employs a compound form of ὅπλον for 'arms', which tends to carry military connotations (BDAG, 716, s.v. ὅπλον; see John 18:3; Rom 6:13; 13:12; ; 2 Cor 6:7; 10:4), suggesting that they may have carried daggers or swords.

32 Hays, *Moral Vision*, 333, seems practically to equate the two. France, *Gospel of Matthew*, 385, suggests that by forbidding the acquiring of a staff, Jesus is really forbidding the purchasing of a new staff in place of the old. In Mark (6:8), the requirement to carry a staff becomes explicit, unlike in Luke (9:3) where a staff is among the prohibited items.

33 In the LXX, a ῥάβδος could be used for walking/leaning (Gen 32:10; Exod 12:11; 21:19; Isa 36:6; Zech 8:4; cf. Heb 11:21) as well as for striking (Exod 21:20; 1 Kgms [1 Sam] 17:43; 2 Kgms [2 Sam] 7:14, often metaphorically). Paul threatens to discipline the Corinthians with a ῥάβδος (1 Cor 4:21), and the risen exalted Christ rules the nations with a ῥάβδος of iron (Rev 12:5; 19:15; cf. 2:27).

34 The lack of any actual narrated journey in Matt 10 is immaterial. If the aorist participle at Matt 10:5 (παραγγείλας) is temporal, then Jesus expressly sends out the Twelve *after* giving his missional instructions (so NASB, NAB, CSB). While the combination of an aorist main verb and participle usually denotes contemporaneous time, the participle can still at times be antecedent (e.g., Matt 4:2, though here underscored by ὕστερον ['afterwards']). Matt 10:5 more naturally reads as if the missional instructions precede the actual sending.

35 On Matthew's multiple implied reader, see n. 28 above.

36 BDAG, 507, s.v. Καναναῖος, pointing out that the term is not a toponym for either Cana (Jerome) or Canaan (KJV). Luke uses the more familiar ζηλωτής (Luke 6:15; Acts 1:13). Καναναῖος is a *hapax legomenon* in ancient Greek literature, no doubt due to its Semitic origin. Here a question of methodology comes to the fore. While Matthew's historical audience (especially if post-70) could well be assumed to be familiar with the zealot phenomenon, the question remains to what extent Matthew's implied reader could be, especially given the term's *hapax* status. The observation of Garrett, *Demise*, 6, is pertinent, that authors 'must rely on the culturally informed knowledge and beliefs of the readers to supplement the narrative world of a text, because the authors could no more explain every detail about every person or event in a narrative than could speakers define every word of every sentence spoken'. Is Simon's status as a Καναναῖος one of those details?

the term carries a political meaning as a designation for a member of a zealous nationalist sect, which instigated the outbreak of the Jewish war (e.g., Josephus *Ant.* 20.160–72). While such an identification is likely anachronistic, it seems reasonable that some degree of political significance attends Matthew's usage.[37] Craig L. Blomberg is correct in seeing Simon as zealous 'not yet in the sense of a member of the later, more formal political movement known as the Zealots but as one of the predecessors of that movement whose revolutionary aspirations for Israel against Rome perhaps led him to engage in terrorist activities against the government'.[38] Thus Matthew's reader could reasonably infer that Simon was a kind of proto-zealot adept in his use of the sword and could carry it with him on occasion.[39]

Third, Jesus reveals later in the same discourse that he has 'not come to bring peace, but a sword' (Matt 10:34). This statement, containing the only other use of μάχαιρα outside the Matthew's Passion narrative, refers specifically to the division within households, as the following verses make clear (10:35–37).[40] Few commentators, however, notice the juxtaposition of household division at Matt 10:34–37 and the earlier command to the disciples to enter into households with the message of peace at Matt 10:12–14. An exception is Luz: 'It is the disciples' greeting of *peace* that causes the split. […] And it is the rejection of the greeting of peace that seals the split with unheard-of sharpness'.[41] So construed, the withdrawal of peace should be seen for what it is—a violent act; the message of peace has become the sword of division.[42]

The sword then becomes an apt symbol for the divisive effects of the Jesus mission among households.[43] At the very least, it is difficult to see how one committed to non-violence and

---

37 Horsley with Hanson, *Bandits, Prophets, and Messiahs*, xiv–xvi, 190–243, contends that no unified nationalistic movement existed during the time of Jesus but rather an assortment of anti-imperial groups; contra Hengel, *Zealots*, 338, who claims that Simon 'the Zealot' is 'the first evidence that we have of the party name "Zealots"'. If the date of Matthew's composition is taken into consideration, the term may well carry socio-political overtones for Matthew's readers living closer to the outbreak of the Jewish War (see Harrington, *Matthew*, 376–77).
38 Blomberg, *Matthew*, 169. It would be anachronistic to assume that Simon was a Sicarius; I am simply arguing that Simon's nationalistic leanings might predispose him to carry a sword of some kind. That Simon would have put away his sword as a result of his 'conversion' to Jesus assumes, of course, what must be demonstrated, namely, that Jesus was a pacifist, committed to non-violence.
39 If Cullmann, *Jesus and the Revolutionaries*, 9, is correct that Peter and Judas Iscariot may have had zealot backgrounds, they, too, might be envisioned in Matthew as brandishing swords. Such identifications are unlikely.
40 Note the explanatory γάρ in v. 35 (so Black, 'Not Peace but a Sword', 287–88). See also Nel, 'Not Peace but a Sword', 246, who wisely connects this passage to Matt 26:52 as does Sim, 'The Sword Motif', 88–89.
41 Luz, *Matthew 8–20*, 112, italics his. One possible objection to Luz's view is that the household mission in Matt 10:12–14 assumes a united response (whether negative or positive) by the household. But if Matt 10:34–35 governs Matt 10:12–14, a rejecting household may still have believing recipients within it, a situation that pertains at Matt 10:21. A 'worthy' household is thus a united household that receives the message of salvific peace.
42 'Jesus brings the sword which cuts families in half' (Nel, 'Not Peace but a Sword', 241, relying on Sim, 'Sword Motif', 103). Windisch, 'ἀσπάζομαι', 499, sees the offer of peace as 'a power with which the disciples can spread blessing but the withdrawal of which has the force of a curse', noted by Marshall, *Luke*, 420. Storkey, *Jesus and Politics*, 83–84, misses the violent nature of this withdrawal due to his *a priori* commitment to peacemaking. So, too, Neville, *Vehement Jesus*, 35.
43 Is this division the purpose of the mission or the result? Unlike many commenters, Avalos, *Bad Jesus*, 94, argues for a purpose infinitive at Matt 10:34 (βαλεῖν εἰρήνην), stating that 'Jesus did not say that his mission would simply result in family strife. Jesus *is saying* that a primary *purpose* of his mission is to create violence within families, and the mention of the sword is consistent with that violent sentiment' (italics his). However, in view of the centrality of the house as the locus of the disciples' missionizing activity and the possibility of a unified positive reception there, the divisive effects of the sword appear to be a result of Jesus's mission rather than its purpose. Structurally, both purpose and result infinitives can utilize the 'naked' infinitive following an intransitive verb of motion (Wallace, *Greek Grammar*, 591–93). For a strenuous defense of an infinitive of result, see Neville, *Vehement Jesus*, 22–24.

enemy-love could describe the purpose or intended effects of his mission in such terms.[44] Even if Jesus's words are metaphorical, they contribute to a symbolic world in which adornment with a sword is not incongruous with the mission of Jesus.[45] Pacifist interpreters seek to mitigate this implication by relying on its metaphorical quality, but appeal to metaphor still does not explain Jesus's use of a *violent* metaphor and overlooks the very real effects of division perpetrated against the household.[46] This verse is not the only instance in which the Matthean Jesus resorts to violent imagery, sometimes graphically so.[47] Moreover, the intense eschatological expectation that attends the missionary discourse (Matt 10:23!) contributes to a story world in which the juxtaposition of peace and sword evokes 'struggle, conflict, war, violence, and death as elements of the establishment of God's empire'.[48]

3. Practice of the Sword

The evidence so far is admittedly speculative and suggestive. Momentum gains, however, with a second observation: not only does a disciple at Jesus's arrest possess a sword, he uses it, and seemingly in expert fashion. Matthew's depiction of a disciple 'drawing' (ἀπέσπασεν) his sword and 'striking' (πατάξας) the slave of the high priest (Matt 26:51) implies a fair degree of familiarity with the sword, and in an antagonistic context at that.[49] That the disciple executes his strike with pin-point accuracy, cutting off the ear of the slave of the high priest, is further evidence of his impressive dexterity with the sword.[50] While it is common among interpreters to think that the sword wielder intended a larger anatomical target, perhaps the slave's head or neck, nothing in Matthew's language suggests as much.[51] A straightforward reading of Matt 26:51, with its emphatic

---

44   Aslan, *Zealot*, 120, argues that a pacifist Jesus would hardly speak in this way. That Jesus can use the cutting effects of the sword as a descriptor of his ministry in Matt 10:34 suggests that the sword image here is positive. While positive imagery of the sword (Eph 6:7; Heb 4:12; Rev 6:4) outweighs the negative (Rom 8:35; Heb 11:37) in the New Testament, the neutral image of the sword predominates (Matt 26:51–52,55; Mark 14:43,47–48; Luke 21:24; 22:36,38,49,52; John 18:10–11; Acts 12:2; 16:17; Rom 13:4; Rev 13:10,14).

45   Avalos, *Bad Jesus*, 93–94, is not as quick to accept a metaphorical meaning assumed by most commentators, pointing to the literal directive in Deut 13:8–9 for violence against family members. Luke's use of διαμερισμός ('division') rather than μάχαιρα (Luke 12:51) in this Q passage argues for a metaphorical interpretation, at least on the part of Luke.

46   Hays, *Moral Vision*, 333, admits that Matt 10:34 taken in isolation 'would appear to contradict everything I have said so far about the [pacifistic] witness of the New Testament'. On Hays overlooking the destructive affects on the family, see Avalos, *Bad Jesus*, 92.

47   Jesus seemingly condones eschatological torture (Matt 18:34–35 [note οὕτως at v. 35!]; 24:51; and numerous references to weeping and gnashing of teeth [8:12; 13:42,50; 22:13; 24:51; 25:30]). I thank Bob Gundry for reminding me of these latter references. Jesus speaks of 'hell' (γέεννα) in Matthew more than all the other Gospels combined (Matt 5:22,29,30; 10:28; 18:9; 23:15; 23:33). The word appears only on the lips of Jesus in the New Testament with the exception of James 3:6.

48   Carter, *Matthew and the Margins*, 242. See also Sim, 'Sword Motif', 97–103.

49   Brandon, *Jesus and the Zealots*, 203 n.4, thinks that the re-sheathing of a drawn sword indicates 'a significant familiarity with the idea of a disciple's wearing a sword and scabbard'. For a recent historical analysis sympathetic to Brandon, see Rubio, 'Jesus and the Anti-Roman Resistance'. The instinctual ease with which a disciple draws his sword against a *human* target preempts any notion that the disciples possessed swords strictly for protection against, say, wild beasts.

50   Luke (22:50) and John (18:10) both indicate that it was the right ear of the high priest's slave.

51   Turner, *Matthew*, 636, for example, thinks that the disciple 'clumsily' wields his sword. Similarly, Keener, *Matthew*, 643, and, more vigorously, Gibbs, *Matthew 21:1–28:20*, 1452.

αὐτοῦ (*his* ear), makes an inadvertent strike unlikely.[52] Moreover, the disciple's swordplay is reminiscent of ancient Israelite military campaigns where 'striking with the edge of the sword' is a common Old Testament phrase for defeating an enemy in battle.[53] In other words, the wielder on this occasion is likely no novice but ably performs his duty as a would-be soldier of the Master.[54]

Possession and practice of the sword contain strong explanatory power. Whatever Jesus might have meant by non-retaliation and enemy-love, those twin ethical imperatives, embedded as they are in sermonic material profuse with hyperbolic language and eschatological significance, apparently do not rule out the bearing of arms.[55] Even if literally understood, the command to love one's enemies is unlikely to extend too far beyond Israel, if at all.[56] The parallel clauses in Matt 5:44 are mutually interpreting. The first clause (ἀγαπᾶτε τοὺς ἐχθροὺς ὑμῶν) is restated in the second clause (προσεύχεσθε ὑπὲρ τῶν διωκόντων ὑμᾶς), effectively defining 'enemies' as persecutors of Matthew's community, apparently the same antagonists envisioned in the beatitudes of 5:10–12.[57] That the ambiguous 'they' in Matt 5:11 refers to Jews soon becomes clear with the mention of 'prophets' in Matt 5:12, offering unmistakable evidence that Matthew has a particular referent in view.[58] It comes as no surprise then that the objects of enemy-love in Matthew are in fact non-Christian Jews with whom his Gospel is in dialogue, sometimes intensely so.[59]

The identification of Matthew's enemies/persecutors as unbelieving Jews finds further corroboration in Matthew's Gospel. Twice more Jesus will speak explicitly of persecutors of

---

52 Unless the αὐτοῦ is stylistic (cf. Josephus *Ant.* 14.13.10). Matthew inherits the sword strike from Mark (14:47), where it plausibly functions as an anti-temple statement (Viviano, 'High Priest's Servant's Ear', though he underestimates Mark's anti-temple polemic). Of the sword-wielding disciple in Matthew, Nel, 'Not Peace but a Sword', 250, writes: 'His use of the sword does not reflect an angry and impulsive attempt to kill the slave; it is a much more *deliberate act* of maiming the slave, instead of murdering him' (italics mine).

53 See, for example, Num 21:24; Deut 20:13; Josh 8:24,28,30,37,39; 19:47; Judg 1:8; 2 Kgdms [2Sam] 15:14; 23:10, using the same verb (πατάσσω) as Matthew. As Gundry, *Matthew*, 538–39, points out, Matthew's rather unique usage of ἀποσπάω in 26:51 for drawing the sword (cf. σπάω, Mark 14:47) likely owes to the ἀπ- correspondence with ἀπόστρεψον in 26:52 thus creating a high degree of literary irony: the disciple who 'drew out' his sword must in reality 'put it back in'. Brown, *Death*, 1.247, notes that the reference to a sheath would lead the reader 'to think of military or paramilitary arms'.

54 Peter's militaristic actions are thus somewhat analogous to the unlikely prospect of Jews serving in the Roman army, but which was in fact the case: 'The idea of the Jewish Roman soldier may strike one as odd. We naturally assume that Roman military service was incompatible with the Jewish religion, but [...] there does not seem to have been anything to prevent Jews from serving in foreign military forces in all Jewish units' (Roth, 'Jewish Military Forces', 89). Roth notes that Jews had a 'long tradition of military service, both at home and especially in foreign service' (p.81).

55 For example, Jesus categorically forbids the swearing of oaths in the fourth antithesis (Matt 5:33–36) but then later answers under oath when challenged by the high priest Caiaphas (Matt 26:63–64). If any equivocation exists here on Jesus's part, it is simply because Jesus is hesitant to affirm Caiaphas's own definitions of 'Christ' and 'Son of God', not because Jesus is hesitant to speak under oath (see Plummer, *Matthew*, 378–79). Contra Gundry, *Matthew*, 544–45, who thinks that Jesus is disavowing the adjuration imposed on him by the high priest (more recently, *Peter: False Disciple and Apostate*, 48). Yet Jesus seems to answer affirmatively (σὺ εἶπας) in the same way when not under oath (Matt 26:25; 27:11). For Jesus answering positively to Caiaphas's question, see Deines, *Die Gerechtigkeit der Tora*, 340.

56 Horsley, *Spiral*, 261–73, challenges the traditional interpretation of enemy-love as pacifistic. While this effort is a step in the right direction, he misses important evidence in Matthew that delimits enemy-love to a decidedly missional context. See the argument below.

57 Betz, *Sermon*, 312–13.

58 According to Betz, *Sermon*, 153, Matt 5:12 clearly envisions the persecutors as Jews since 'they' kill the 'prophets'. Matthew's three verbs in 5:11 have no expressed subject (ὀνειδίσωσιν, διώξωσιν, εἴπωσιν) nor does ἐδίωξαν in 5:12. So, too, Hare, *Theme*, 120–23 and Hagner, *Matthew 1–13*, lxxi, 95.

59 With Hagner ('Matthew: Apostate, Reformer, Revolutionary?'), 196–98, I see Matthew's community representing a form of Jewish Christianity separated from but still in contact with the synagogue. On the use of 'Jew/Jewish' to describe Matthew's opponents, see Matson, 'Should Ἰουδαῖος Be Translated "Judean"?'. For recent discussions on the place of Matthew within first-century Judaism, see Runesson and Gurtner, *Matthew within Judaism*.

God's people and both times in the context of an eschatological mission to Israel.[60] In the first, Jesus instructs his disciples: 'When they persecute [διώκωσιν] you in one town, flee to the next; for truly I tell you, you will not have gone through all the towns of Israel before the Son of Man comes' (10:23). Despite the ambiguous 'they' once again, the Jewish source of this persecution is clear from the mention of the cities of Israel and the scope of the disciples' mission: the lost sheep of the house of Israel (10:6). A thorough examination of Matthew's redactional activity in the missionary discourse leads Douglas R.A. Hare to conclude that 'it is with Jewish persecution, not persecution as such, that Matthew is primarily concerned'.[61] In the second, Jesus predicts persecution by the scribes and Pharisees: 'Therefore I send you prophets, sages, and scribes, some of whom you will kill and crucify, and some you will flog in your synagogues and pursue [διώξετε] from town to town' (23:34).[62] Once again persecution arises in the context of the church's mission to Israel.[63] Unbelieving Jews are the continuing object of the community's mission, not its scorn.[64]

This realization has important ramifications for Jesus's enemy-love directive, which Matthew plausibly intends as a missional ethic, not a generalized one. As Hare rightly observes, Matthew's enemy-love directive applies 'not to enemies in general but precisely to persecutors, who in this Gospel are almost exclusively Jewish persecutors'.[65] By loving and praying for their persecutors, Matthew's community hopes that its good deeds—being the salt of the earth (5:13) and the light of the world (5:14–15)—will result in the 'glorifying' of the disciples' Father in heaven (5:16).[66] As Betz puts it: 'Seeing the good deeds done by the insiders, the outsiders will be provoked to the praising of God. Converting the people to the awe and worship of God is, in Jewish terms, the whole purpose of doing good deeds'.[67] Loving one's enemies is one of those 'good deeds'. In an important sense, then, Jesus's command to 'pray' for persecutors is the Matthean equivalent to

---

60 While the word-concept fallacy guards against limiting the theme of persecution in Matthew to instances of διώκω alone (cf. its absence in Matt 24:9-14), the verbal connection between Matt 5:10-12 and 5:44 helps establish an important framework for understanding the Jewish identity of Matthew's 'enemies'.
61 Hare, *Theme*, 104. Moreover, this persecution arises precisely in a missional context. Matthew's insertion of Mark's persecution material (Mark 13:9-13) in a set of missionary instructions (Matt 10:17-22), for example, suggests that 'persecution arises *precisely on account of the Church's mission*' (p.100, italics his).
62 That Matthew has distinctly Christian messengers in view is apparent from the fact that the sender is Jesus himself. On the problematic reference to crucifixion, see Hare, *Theme*, 88–91.
63 According to Hare, *Theme*, 119, Matthew's meaning of διώκω includes 'those hostile activities which drive Christian missionaries out of a community' without ruling out legal action in some cases.
64 Though Matthew's community will expand its mission quite considerably, Israel remains among 'all' the nations discipled by the church (Matt 28:19; correctly, France, *Gospel of Matthew*, 1114; against Hare, *Theme*, 146-49, who thinks that Matthew's community has ceased evangelizing Jews). In my view the syntagmatic πάντα τὰ ἔθνη certainly includes Israel at Matt 25:32 and likely at Matt 24:9,14. The disciples engage the Jews in mission until the Son of Man returns (Matt 10:23), which explains why Matt 10 nowhere records the return of the Twelve from their mission to Israel (so Kingsbury, *Matthew as Story*, 71-72).
65 Hare, *Theme*, 162.
66 Here we see the focus and scope of the community's mission stretched considerably, since 'glorify' is a term used in Second Temple Judaism for the conversion of Gentiles (Jos.Asen. 20.8; cf. Phil 2:11; 1 Pet 2:12). Nonetheless, enemy-love of Jewish opponents still operates within this broader evangelistic scope (Matt 10:18; 24:14; 28:19; cf. 4:15; 12:18,21; 21:43; 25:32).
67 Betz, *Sermon*, 163-64.

Paul's praying for the conversion of unbelieving Israel (cf. Rom 9:3; 10:1).[68] For both Matthew and Paul, the conversion of Israel belongs to imminent end-time expectation.[69] Thus Jesus's 'pacifism' is a qualified pacifism, directly linked to evangelism.[70] Even Luz is careful not to push the ethical limits too far: 'National enemies in a war are hardly the major concern of Matthew'.[71]

Luz's observation finds immediate confirmation in the rhetorical structure of Matthew when Jesus commends the faith of the Capernaum centurion in the narrative section immediately following the Sermon on the Mount (Matt 8:5–13).[72] The narrative placement of this pericope is noteworthy and rarely appreciated. The backbone of the Roman army who led his soldiers in battle, the Roman centurion typically wore his short sword (*gladius*) in a scabbard strung from his left side in distinction from legionaries who wore their sword on the right.[73] He was particularly adroit in his use of sword and shield.[74] Striking in this pericope is the way that Matthew highlights the centurion precisely in his role as a military official: he, too, is a man 'under authority' (ὑπὸ ἐξουσίαν, Matt 8:9), a phrase that 'corresponds precisely to that of a junior officer who, in contrast to the commander of a cohort, has direct contact with the troops'.[75] Moreover, he has soldiers under his own authority (ὑπ' ἐμαυτόν) who are obedient to his every command (8:9). As Christopher Bryan comments, 'Surely, a clearer symbol of Roman power than a Roman centurion would be hard to conceive'.[76] Yet in commending this man's faith, Jesus says nothing about the problematic use of the sword; the Capernaum centurion, like all his comrades in the New Testament, is presumably free to continue his occupation as a Roman military official.[77] At the very least Jesus' favorable commendation casts doubt on Hauerwas' claim that the centurion's professed unworthiness was a recognition that 'his life and profession are antithetical to Jesus's life and work'.[78] Adorned as such, the sword may well have its proper sphere of action.[79]

---

68 Guelich, *Sermon*, 94,229, insightfully labels the prayers for persecutors in Matt 5:43 'intercessory'. Betz, *Sermon*, 313, points out that the prayers for Jewish persecutors would coincide with the liturgical prayers offered on behalf of Israel in the synagogue, particularly the thirteenth benediction of the *Shemoneh Esreh* (Eighteen Benedictions) in the Babylonian rescension. On the restriction of Jesus's enemy-love command to Israel, so too Aslan, *Zealot*, 122: 'His commands to "love your enemies" and "turn the other cheek" must be read as being directed exclusively *at his fellow Jews* and meant as a model of peaceful relations exclusively within the Jewish community' (italics mine).

69 Hence the Sermon on the Mount is truly an 'interim' ethic—in force until the Son of Man returns (Matt 4:17; 10:23; 24:29; 28:20).

70 Hare, *Theme*, 90, curiously still wants to speak of at least a qualified pacifism of Jesus, perhaps not realizing that his argument has significantly altered the category.

71 Luz, *Matthew 1–7*, 287, though he qualifies this statement somewhat in light of the experience of Matthew's community in the Jewish War. See also Horsley, *Spiral*, 262–63, who argues from the context that the conflict envisioned is personal and local, not political and foreign (à la Rome).

72 This centurion was likely employed in the service of Herod Antipas, who had a small force of auxiliary troops at his disposal (Josephus, *Ant.* 18.113–14).

73 See the marble statue of a centurion in battle from the National Museum in Naples (Stephens, *New Testament World*, 41). Also, *Roman Imperial Army*, 129–30.

74 Vegetius states that the centurion was 'chosen for his size, strength and dexterity in throwing his missile weapons and for his skill in the use of his sword and shield' (*De Re Militari* II, 14).

75 Luz, *Matthew 8–20*, 10.

76 Bryan, *Render to Caesar*, 46, who further notes that 'the very behavior in which Jesus sees such faith is explicitly presented to him by the centurion as modeled upon his behavior *as a military agent of imperial rule*' (emphasis his).

77 In this respect at least the centurion is not a liminal character in Matthew (cf. Duling, *A Marginal Scribe*, 49,125–29).

78 Hauerwas, *Matthew*, 94. Hays, *Moral Vision*, 335–36, concedes that the positive portrayals of soldiers offer the strongest evidence for non-pacifism in the New Testament.

79 Thus Avalos, *Bad Jesus*, 98, asks of the sword strike at Jesus's arrest: 'why could it not be that the disciple drew his sword precisely because he knew Jesus did not always object to defensive violence?'.

4. Perishing by the Sword

We now arrive at the rationale proper. The rationale stated by Jesus in Matt 26:52–54 is almost entirely Matthean, linked by grammatical connectives introducing one statement and two questions, each one building closely upon the former.[80] First, Jesus refuses defense by the sword 'for all who take the sword will perish by the sword' (Matt 26:52b). The γάρ here is explanatory, offering the reason for putting away the sword. R.T. France thinks that this chiastic statement, possibly proverbial in nature (cf. Gen 9:6; Jer 15:2; Rev 13:10; Tg. Isa. 50.11), offers *prima facie* evidence for a normative ethic of non-violence on the part of Jesus and his disciples.[81] Combining this statement of Jesus with his earlier commands, many interpreters imagine Jesus offering the following pacifistic rationale:

> 'Put your sword back into its place, for everyone who takes up the sword will perish by the sword. Or do you not know that God sends forth his rain on the righteous and the unrighteous? Love your enemy, I tell you. Love them, and do not harm them. Do good to those who persecute you. Renounce violence. Do not insist on an eye for an eye'.

Disappointingly, however, the narrative offers no such fanciful dialogue. In fact, very little verbal correspondence exists to link Matthew's arrest scene to Matt 5:38–48 in any significant way.[82] Moreover, the aphoristic quality of Jesus's words in verse 52 does not rule out a specific application, as the narrative context makes clear.[83] What that application is must await the discussion below. Suffice it here to say that such an aphoristic statement is not indicative of Jesus's attitude towards violence in any and all circumstances.[84]

If Jesus were renouncing violence in absolute terms, we might expect a clear and unambiguous statement such as occurs in the Hellenistic Jewish romance novel *Joseph and Aseneth* roughly contemporaneous with Matthew. Towards the end of the story when Pharaoh's first-born son plots to kill Joseph and steal the beautiful Aseneth away, Simeon 'intended to lay his hand on the handle of his sword and draw it from its sheath and strike Pharaoh's son', but Levi intervened and said to his brother, 'Why are you furious with anger with this man? And we are men who worship God, and it does not befit us to repay evil for evil' (Jos.Asen. 23.8–9). Later, when Pharaoh's son had suffered a near fatal blow at the hands of Benjamin, Levi implores his brother Benjamin, who has taken the sword from the fallen heir, with near-identical words:

---

80 The explanatory γάρ (Matt 26:52) establishes the reason, the particle ἤ (Matt 26:53) re-states the reason in a different form, and the inferential οὖν draws the necessary conclusion. This structure bears some similarity to the 'elaboration' pattern of argumentation characteristic of the *Progymnasmata* (see deSilva, *Introduction*, 762).
81 France, *Gospel of Matthew*, 1014). France qualifies this stance when he writes: 'Whether these words […] can be taken as the basis for a thoroughgoing pacifism will depend on a wider assessment of the relevant biblical material' (1015). Still, he writes of a violence that is 'wrong in principle' (1014).
82 Only high frequency words overlap, with the exception of ἀποστρέφω (Matt 5:42; 26:52). In this case, however, the semantic fields are decidedly different (see Louw and Nida, *Greek–English Lexicon*: 'help/care for' [1:460]; 'existence in space' [1:729]).
83 The future ἀπολοῦνται in verse 26:52 is likely gnomic, but Kosmala, 'Matthew 26:52', 3, questions the original proverbial nature of Jesus's statement. One thinks of Luther's application of Matt 26:52 to his nemesis Ulrich Zwingli upon learning of the latter's death on the battlefield in 1531 (Trueman, *Luther on the Christian Life*, 51). Paul is certainly a biblical example of one who can apply aphoristic statements to context-specific situations to great effect.
84 Witherington, *Matthew*, 495, reminds us that maxims are not always true but often true (see also Gibbs, *Matthew 21:1–28:20*, 1454). What is true in this case is that this saying of Jesus receives a decidedly *narrative* placement and must be judged accordingly.

By no means, brother, will you do this deed, because we are men who worship God, and it does not befit a man who worships God to repay evil for evil nor to trample underfoot a fallen (man) nor to oppress his enemy till death. And now, put your sword back into its place, and come, help me, and we will heal him of his wound (Jos.Asen. 29.1–4).[85]

If the Matthean Jesus were a thoroughgoing pacifist, one might expect a similar kind of self-conscious ethical reflection.

5. Precipitating Angelic Warfare

Instead of a clearly articulated pacifist ethic, however, we hear of an ominous military threat. According to Jesus, an imposing heavenly army stands ready and willing to defend him at the point of a sword: '[Or] Do you think that I cannot appeal to my Father, and he will at once send me more than twelve legions of angels?' (Matt 26:52–53).[86] Here occurs a second but related rationale, beginning with the particle ἤ ('or'), effectively re-stating the previous rationale in another way: if necessary, Jesus can avail himself of a host of heavenly warriors to decimate the temple police and preclude his arrest and eventual crucifixion.[87] The particular Greek construction (οὐ) expects a positive answer to Jesus's rhetorical question, thus underscoring Jesus's authority, a central concern for Matthew.[88] All authority *in heaven* and on earth has been given to Jesus (Matt 28:18).[89] If Jesus were to exercise that heavenly authority, all will perish.[90]

---

85   Cited from Charlesworth, *The Old Testament Pseudepigrapha*, 2. 246. Also noted by Nolland, *Matthew*, 1112. The two cases are not exact parallels, as noted by Burchard, 'Joseph and Aseneth', 247: 'Levi exhibits clemency toward a defeated enemy, as becomes a man in power, a deed both noble and sensible which serves the interests of both parties [...]. Jesus exacts love of one's persecutors from a subdued minority predicated upon God's boundless mercy'.

86   The use of λεγιῶνας ('legions') establishes the angels here precisely in their military role as heavenly warriors (Matt 13:39; 16:27; 25:31; cf. Ps 68:17–18; Isa 66:15; Jer 4:13; Zech 14:5; 2 Thess 1:7–8; Jude14–15; Rev 19:14). A λεγιών was approximately six thousand troops during the principate of Augustus, with an equal number of auxiliary troops (BDAG, 588, s.v. λεγιών). The number twelve would represent a legion each for Jesus and the eleven disciples (so Keener, *Matthew*, 643; Hagner, *Matthew 14–28*, 790; cf. Plato, *Phaedr.* 246e, where Zeus stands at the head of twelve companies of the heavenly host).

87   The particle ἤ (left untranslated by the NRSV) often introduces rhetorical questions (so BDAG, 432, s.v. ἤ), but *Thayer's Greek-English Lexicon*, 275, s.v. ἤ, notes that it can sometimes follow a declarative sentence 'to prove the same thing in another way', citing Matt 26:53 in particular; cf. Matt 7:4,9,10; 12:29; 16:26. In biblical thought angels often wield swords (e.g., Num 22:23; Josh 5:13; 4 Kgdms [2 Kgs] 6:15–17; 1 Chron 21:16,30; Ps 33[34]:7; Dan 10:13; 12:1; 2 Bar 63:5–7; 3 En. 22:6) and fight on behalf of Israel (2 Macc 2:21; 3:25–26; 10:30; 11:6–8; 3 Macc 6:18–21; 4 Macc 4:10–11; cf. 1QM 7:6; 12:8; 13:10). They are also the Lord's executioners (2 Kgdms [2 Sam] 24:16; 4 Kgdms [2 Kgs] 19:35; Acts 12:23).

88   See France, *Matthew: Evangelist and Teacher*, 307–08, who connects Jesus's authority to his ability to command angels.

89   This all-encompassing authority of Jesus is not simply a post-resurrection reality but extends to his earthly career. France, *Matthew: Evangelist and Teacher*, 307, rightly notes that Jesus's authority in Matthew's concluding scene (28:18) captures 'the impression which has been increasingly conveyed throughout the gospel'. See also Pennington, *Heaven and Earth*, 75: 'This post-resurrection universal authority consummates the authority that the Son of Man had *on earth* previously (9:6)'. The demarcation between heaven and earth in Matthew leads Pennington to observe that 'Jesus is clearly aligned with the divine side of the equation as compared to the human and earthly' (p.83). Pennington classifies the linguistic pairing in 28:18 as *antithetic* without denying that Jesus's universal authority is also in view (pp.203–04).

90   The question is, can the Matthean Jesus exercise that heavenly authority *now*, at a climactic moment in his earthly ministry? Pennington, *Heaven and Earth*, 204, speaks of the 'addition' to Jesus's earthly authority in Matt 28:18, but overlooks the πάντα ('all things') given to Jesus by his Father the Lord of heaven and earth (Matt 11:25) in the exercise of Jesus's earthly career or even before (Matt 11:27). At the very least, Jesus can appeal (παρακαλέω) to this same authority for heavenly support and achieve the same affect (Matt 26:53).

Whom does this 'all' include? Does it include the disciples or just members of the arresting party? If the magnitude of the heavenly army is taken seriously, Jesus would be envisioning the complete destruction of the arresting force, the 'all' who stand ready to take up swords at the instigation of Jesus's sword-bearing disciple.[91] Warren Carter's point is as serious as it is humorous, observing that 72,000 warring angels is 'more than enough to overwhelm the crowd with its swords and clubs, and more than enough to deal with the whole of the local Roman military!'[92] The potential for all-but-certain death on this occasion is even more impressive when one considers that in the Old Testament a *single* angel could account for the deaths of 70,000 Israelites (2 Kgms [2 Sam] 24:15) and 185,000 Assyrian deaths in a single night (4 Kgms [2 Kgs] 19:35; Isa 37:36; cf. 2 Bar 63.5–11).[93]

That the historical Jesus expected a frontal assault of the heavenly host upon the enemies of God at the end of time is a debatable point; that the Matthean Jesus thought that he had a host of warrior angels prepared to do just that is not.[94] Immediate access to these war-like beings is often lost on pacifistic interpreters. Why would a supposed thorough-going pacifist like Jesus even resort to such a threat? What does it say about the nature of the heavenly Father to whom Jesus appeals that more than 72,000 angels stand poised to defend Jesus at the point of the sword? Avalos makes the obvious point: 'the very remarks that God could send "twelve legions of angels" if Jesus so requested means that Jesus accepts the concept that God has a military force ready to take violent action at his command. If Jesus' theology is completely non-violent, then why does he envision God even having an angelic military force divided into legions in the first place?'[95]

Of course, this appeal is not the first time in Matthew's Gospel that Jesus is the object of divine aid. At his temptation, Jesus receives the assistance of angels, who 'wait' on him with continued heavenly protection (Matt 4:11).[96] These angels take on a far more aggressive role in Matthew in decidedly eschatological contexts, where they accompany the Son of Man as reapers of the eschatological harvest (13:30,39,41,49; cf. 16:27; 24:31; 25:31).[97] The connection to Matt 26:53 should not be overlooked.[98] The immediate availability of these eschatological warriors at Jesus's arrest (ἄρτι, 'at once') suggests that Jesus has his eyes on the present moment and intends his sword

---

91 See Konradt, *Matthew*, 400, who seems to support the interpretation offered here.
92 Carter, *Matthew and Margins*, 514. Restricting loss of life to the arresting party only becomes all the more apparent if the twelve legions *replace* the twelve disciples in the apocalyptic battle. See Crossan, 'Matthew 26:47–56', 182, who labels this replacement a 'possibility'.
93 One should also take note of the destroying angel who kills all of the Egyptian firstborn (Exod 12:13,23; 1 Cor 10:10; Heb 11:28).
94 For a recent treatment arguing the historical point, see Martin, 'Jesus in Jerusalem'. See also Matson, 'Double-Edged', 470–72. Despite identifying Peter as the sword-wielder, Osborne, *Matthew*, 984, is on the right track when he writes that Peter 'was thinking of Jesus as the conquering Messiah [...] and the twelve legions of angels [...] were going to appear and inaugurate the final battle'.
95 Avalos, *Bad Jesus*, 98.
96 Surely a component of this angelic service was physical protection.
97 The second petition of the Lord's Prayer ('your kingdom come') is decidedly eschatological in nature as recently argued by Mitchell, 'Your Kingdom Come', though he does not address angels as agents of the kingdom's arrival. Carter, *Matthew and Margins*, 514, acknowledges the angelic accompaniment at the Eschaton but does not comment on the potential violence that they inflict in the 'establishing' of God's empire. The eschatological function of the angels in Matthew invites comparison to Rev 14:15–16 and 19, where angels employ their sickles to reap the earth. While the first passage may possibly refer to the ingathering of the elect, the second results in eschatological destruction. Commenting on Matt 26:53, Horsley, *Spiral*, 298, states that Jesus thought of the role of angelic warriors as a future one. On the militaristic function of the Son of Man, see Sim, 'Sword Motif', 100–01.
98 Meier, *Vision*, 189, writes of Matt 26:53: 'The appearance of the Father, angels, and Jesus in the same verse raises the possibility that we have again the apocalyptic Jewish triad in which Jesus figures as the Son of Man'.

directive in Matt 26:52 to receive a temporal application. If the heavenly legions presently descend upon Jesus and assist him militarily, there will be blood, and the large arresting force will in fact perish. Jesus will win the battle but lose the war.

6. Prophesying Jesus's Death

The third and final rationale constitutes the upshot of the matter: 'But how then would the scriptures be fulfilled, which say it must happen in this way?' (Matt 26:54). The inferential οὖν ('then') broaches the unthinkable consequence of such dramatic angelic intervention: the non-fulfillment of Scripture, putting the divine plan at risk.[99] The fulfillment of Scripture is a strong Matthean theme as underscored by the evangelist's repeated use of a scriptural citation formula.[100] That events must happen in a certain way to fulfill Scripture's predetermined plan is a large component of Matthean determinism.[101] Scriptural fulfillment, not non-retaliation and enemy-love, is the reason for Jesus's refusal to be defended at the point of a sword. The idea that Jesus's earlier sermonic teaching meets the conditions of Jesus's arrest overlooks the unique and decisive role of divine sovereignty within the passage. Jewish persecutors in this instance are not objects of evangelism but tools in the hands of a sovereign God. As Donald A. Hagner observes, 'God has ordained that things should be thus and since αἱ γραφαί, "the scriptures", reflect the will of God, they must be fulfilled'.[102] Thus nothing less than divine faithfulness is at stake.[103]

What exactly does the Matthean Jesus have in mind when he speaks about the Scriptures being fulfilled at the time of his arrest? What is the 'it' that must happen a certain way (οὕτως δεῖ γενέσθαι)? The divine δεῖ here certainly looks back to Matthew's first passion prediction and the necessity of Jesus's suffering and death (16:21); yet, something even more specific and immediate is likely in view, namely, Jesus's arrest at the hands of the priestly authorities. Jesus's arrest must transpire in a certain way (οὕτως) in conformity with the predetermined will of God.

A reference to the arrest is all the more apparent when one considers the comprehensive outlook of verse 56: 'But all this has taken place, so that the scriptures of the prophets may be fulfilled'.[104] What particular scriptures Matthew may have in mind is not as germane as the theme

---

99 'Though he can gain the assistance of angelic warriors, he will not go against God's will revealed in Scripture' (Gundry, *Matthew*, 539). Meier, *Vision*, 190, considers v. 54 'not only the climax but also the main purpose of the Matthean insertion, 26:52-54'.

100 Ten of Matthew's sixteen usage of πληρόω ('fulfill') occur in fulfillment citations proper (Matt 1:22; 2:15,17; 2:23; 4:14; 8:17; 12:17; 13:35; 21:4; 27:9). Three more occur in connection with the fulfillment of Scripture minus the full formula (5:17; 26:54,56). See also 3:3 and 13:14-15 (using ἀναπληρόω). Even if πληρόω is nuanced at times, Matthew's determinism remains very much in play. On the use of γέγραπται to express a similar deterministic idea, see Matt 2:5; 11:10; and 26:31.

101 Matthew's determinism does not rule out so-called free decisions of human beings. The arresting force was acting 'freely' even though they were (unknowingly) fulfilling the will of God. Broer, 'Bemerkungen', 28, notes the paradox of both *Freiwilligkeit* and the *Notwendigkeit* in Matthew 26:53-54. Suhl, 'Funktion', 314, also observes in this connection: 'Die Einsicht in die Notwendigkeit der Schrifterfüllung ist nach Matthäus also nicht etwa ein zur Gethsemaneszene hinzukommendes Motiv, sondern ist ihr schon vorgegeben und führt zu ihr; denn nur wegen seiner Einsicht kann Jesus in Gottes Willen einwilligen'.

102 Hagner, *Matthew 14-28*, 790. Brown, *Death*, 1:278, concurs: 'For Matt, God has written from beginning to end what must be'.

103 Hagner, *Matthew 14-28*, 790, who further remarks, 'It is implied in v 54 that if the scriptures are not fulfilled, the very faithfulness of God could be called into question'.

104 Gundry, *Matthew*, 540, comments: 'As a whole, the first sentence in v 56 looks back on the events that will guarantee Jesus' death in fulfillment of Scripture'.

of scriptural fulfillment in general.¹⁰⁵ Matthew's particular construction τοῦτο δὲ ὅλον γέγονεν occurs in only one other place in his Gospel, in the first fulfillment formula cited in connection with Jesus's virginal conception: 'All this took place [τοῦτο δὲ ὅλον γέγονεν] to fulfill what had been spoken by the Lord through the prophet: "Look, the virgin shall conceive and bear a son, and they shall name him Emmanuel"' (1:22–23).¹⁰⁶ The verbal correspondence is exact, including the consummative use of the perfect γέγονεν, stressing completed action.¹⁰⁷ Thus what Hagner says of Jesus's miraculous birth could certainly be said of his arrest: 'All that had thus far transpired [...] was in exact accord with, indeed the very fulfillment of, God's sovereign purpose [...] as expressed through the prophet'.¹⁰⁸ By restraining (not renouncing!) the sword, Jesus is following the inscripturated plan of God, which necessitates that the Son of Man 'goes as it is written of him' (Matt 26:24), including betrayal into human hands (Matt 17:22; 20:18).¹⁰⁹ 'Jesus' path to the cross has been laid out in advance by the divine will', and an essential step in that direction is the events as they unfold in Gethsemane.¹¹⁰

7. Conclusion

So, is the Matthean Jesus practicing what he preaches? Schweizer answers in the affirmative, believing that Matthew 'has turned the story of Jesus's arrest into a fundamental statement about the use of force'.¹¹¹ Carter proceeds to a communal application: 'His [Jesus's] action again compels disciples after 70 still under Roman control to find alternate and nonviolent ways to resist the empire's definition of reality and control until Jesus' return'.¹¹² Both Schweizer and Carter assume a pacifist Jesus as a critical component in their reading of the text.¹¹³ A Jesus who practices what he preaches certainly appeals to many modern-day preachers, who endeavor to align themselves and

---

105 The plural 'prophets' may simply have a summary function as at Matt 2:23 (so Rydelnik, *Messianic Hope*, 108–110). If Matthew has specific passages in mind, Carter, *Matthew and Margins*, 514, suggests Zech 13:7 in light of Matt 26:31 or a conglomeration of texts centered around the theme of the righteous sufferer, perhaps Pss 42–43 in light of Matt 26:38 or the Suffering Servant of Isa 52–53. Gibbs, *Matthew 21:1–28:20*, 1453, likewise stresses the Zechariah text as encapsulating the divine plan. A more intriguing suggestion is the Aqedah of Gen 22 as argued by Huizenga, 'Obedience', 525.

106 And thus the two statements form an inclusio to Matthew's theme of scriptural fulfillment (Crossan, 'Matthew 26:47–56', 187). Matt 26:56 is different, of course, in that no actual quotation follows the scriptural fulfillment formula (Suhl, 'Funktion', 315).

107 Brown, *Birth*, 131, thinks of the perfect here as aoristic. Carter, *Matthew and Margins*, 515, argues that 'all this' in Matt 26:56 refers to all of the Passion events, not just the arrest.

108 Hagner, *Matthew 1–13*, 20. Davies and Allison, *Matthew*, 3.516, think that 'all this' goes beyond Judas's betrayal to 'the entirety of our pericope as well as to the events which flow to and from it. The passion narrative in its entirety stands under v. 56'. Deines, *Gerechtigkeit der Tora*, 264, expands Matt 26:56 to include the entire story of Jesus.

109 Thus Jesus's enigmatic statement to Judas (ἐφ᾽ ὃ πάρει) in Matt 26:50 ('Friend, do what you have come for', NRSV) may well be an elliptical idiom meaning something like 'let it [the arrest] take place'; Schweizer, *Matthew*, 495, who notes: 'Taken in this sense, it would express Jesus' readiness to meet the fate that stands before him; it would almost amount to a command setting the succeeding course of events in motion'. The meaning then is quite similar to the Lukan elliptical construction ἐᾶτε ἕως τούτου ('allow the arrest to happen') in Luke 22:51; see Matson, 'Pacifist Jesus?'.

110 Hagner, *Matthew 14–28*, 790.

111 Schweizer, *Good News*, 496.

112 Carter, *Matthew and Margins*, 514.

113 By contrast, Gibbs, *Matthew 21:1–28:20*, 1455–56, offers a much more nuanced appropriation of Matthew's text to the pacifism question.

their hearers with his non-violent way of life.[114]

This study slices the sword evidence a different way. Even if the sermonic directives of non-retaliation and enemy-love find alternative explanations, the important point of this essay is their severance from Jesus's stated rationale for rejection of the sword at his arrest.[115] The Matthean Jesus rejects the use of the sword not because he is a pacifist but because he acts supremely in accordance with his Father's will as revealed in Scripture. Since the Father's will is expressly that Jesus die, underscored in Jesus's prayerful struggle at Gethsemane (Matt 26:39,42), any attempt—human or angelic—to defend Jesus would prevent 'the working out of God's declared purpose'.[116] The Passion, not pacifism, is the all-controlling theme of Jesus's sermon.[117] In this way Jesus's directive to put away the sword receives a very specific context in the Gospel of Matthew, one that interpreters dare not miss nor ignore. Interpreters who ignore this context do violence to the text.[118]

---

114 Siker, 'Between Text and Sermon', 388, counsels preachers to see in Jesus's Gethsemane directive 'the portrait of a nonviolent Jesus who expects those who follow him to live a nonviolent life as well'.
115 See Carter, *Sermon on the Mount?*, 108–26, for various views of the relevance of the Sermon on the Mount for Christian ethics.
116 France, *Gospel of Matthew*, 1014.
117 Johnson, 'Passion according to David', 264–72, attempts to distinguish a Matthean non-violent Davidic Messiah from other types of Davidic (militant) messianisms in Second Temple Judaism but underplays the specific direction of the divine will in Matthew. The divine will to which Jesus submits is not pacifism *per se*, but the scripturally ordained plan of salvation.
118 Cf. E. Scheffler, 'Jesus' Non-Violence', 323, who states precisely the opposite.

Bibliography

Allen, Willoughby C. — *A Critical and Exegetical Commentary on the Gospel according to Matthew* (ICC; New York: Charles Scribner's Sons, 1907).

Allison, Dale C. Jr. — *Studies in Matthew: Interpretation Past and Present* (Grand Rapids: Baker Academic, 2005).

Allison, Dale C. Jr. — 'Anticipating the Passion: The Literary Reach of Matthew 26:47–27:56', *CBQ* 56 (1994), 701–14.

Angel, Andrew R. — '*Crucifixus* Vincens: The "Son of God" as Divine Warrior in Matthew', *CBQ* 73 (2011), 299–317.

Aslan, Reza — *Zealot: The Life and Times of Jesus of Nazareth* (New York: Random House, 2013).

Avalos, Hector — *The Bad Jesus: The Ethics of New Testament Ethics* (Sheffield: Sheffield Phoenix, 2015).

Betz, Hans Dieter — *The Sermon on the Mount: A Commentary on the Sermon on the Mount, including the Sermon on the Plain (Matthew 5:3–7:27 and Luke 6:20–49)* (Adela Yarbro Collins, ed.; Minneapolis: Fortress Augsburg, 1995).

Black, Matthew — '"Not Peace but a Sword": Matt 10:34ff; Luke 12:51ff', in Ernst Bammel & C.F.D. Moule (eds.), *Jesus and the Politics of His Day* (Cambridge: Cambridge University Press, 1984), 287–94.

Blomberg, Craig L. — *Matthew* (NAC; Nashville: Broadman Press, 1992).

Brandon, S.G.F. — *Jesus and the Zealots* (New York: Scriber's Sons, 1967).

Broer, Ingo — 'Bemerkungen zur Redaktion der Passionsgeschichte durch Matthäus', in Ludger Schenke (ed.), *Studien zum Matthäusevangelium. Festschrift für Wilhelm Pesch* (Stuttgart: Verlag Katholisches Bibelwerk GmbH, 1988), 25–46.

Brown, Raymond E. — *The Death of the Messiah: From Gethsemane to the Grave. A Commentary on the Passion Narratives in the Four Gospels* (Anchor Bible Reference Library; 2 vols.; New York: Doubleday, 1994).

Brown, Raymond E. — *The Birth of the Messiah: A Commentary on the Infancy Narratives in the Gospels of Matthew and Luke* (Anchor Bible Reference Library; New York: Doubleday, 1993).

Bryan, Christopher — *Render to Caesar: Jesus, the Early Church, and the Roman Superpower* (Oxford: Oxford University Press, 2005).

Burchard, C. — 'Joseph and Aseneth' in James H. Charlesworth (ed.), *The Old Testament Pseudepigrapha* (2 Vols.; New York: Doubleday, 1983, 1985), 2.177–247.

Carson, D.A. — *Matthew–Mark* (EBC; Grand Rapids: Zondervan, 2010 [rev. ed.]).

Carter, Warren — *Matthew and the Margins: A Sociopolitical and Religious Reading* (Maryknoll, NY: Orbis Books, 2000).

Carter, Warren — *What Are They Saying about Matthew's Sermon on the Mount?* (New York; Mahwah, NJ: Paulist, 1994).

Charlesworth, James H. (ed.) — *The Old Testament Pseudepigrapha* (2 Vols.; New York: Doubleday, 1983, 1985).

Crossan, Robert D. — 'Matthew 26:47–56: Jesus Arrested', in Fred O. Francis & Raymond Paul Wallace (eds.), *Tradition as Openness to the Future: Essays in Honor of Willis W. Fisher* (Lanham, MD: University Press of America, 1984), 175–90.

Cullmann, Oscar — *Jesus and the Revolutionaries* (Gareth Putnam, trans.; New York: Harper&Row, 1970).

Davies, W.D., & Dale C. Allison, Jr. — *A Critical and Exegetical Commentary on the Gospel according to Saint Matthew.* Vol. 3: XIX–XXVIII (ICC; Edinburgh: T&T Clark, 1997).

Deines, Roland — *Die Gerechtigkeit der Tora im Reich des Messias: Mt 5,13–20 als Schüsseltext der matthäischen Theologie* (Tübingen: Mohr Siebeck, 2004).

deSilva, David A. — *An Introduction to the New Testament: Contexts, Methods, and Ministry Formation* (Downers Grove, IL: IVP Academic, 2018 [2nd ed.]).

Duling, Dennis C. — *A Marginal Scribe: Studies in the Gospel of Matthew in a Social-Scientific Perspective* (Eugene, OR: Cascade, 2012).

Filson, Floyd V. — *A Commentary on the Gospel according to St. Matthew* (Harper's New Testament; San Francisco: Harper and Row, 1960).

France, R.T. — *The Gospel of Matthew* (NICNT; Grand Rapids: Eerdmans, 2007).

France, R.T. — *Matthew: Evangelist and Teacher* (Downers Grove, IL: InterVarsity Press, 1989).

Fretz, Mark J. — 'Weapons and Implements of Warfare', *ABD* 6:893–95.

Garrett, Susan R. — *The Demise of the Devil: Magic and the Demonic in Luke's Writings* (Minneapolis: Fortress, 1989).

Gibbs, Jeffrey A. — *Matthew 21:1–28:20* (ConC St. Louis: Concordia, 2018).

Guelich, Robert A. — *The Sermon on the Mount. A Foundation for Understanding* (Waco, TX: World Books, 1982).

Gundry, Robert H. — *Peter: False Disciple and Apostate according to Saint Matthew* (Eugene, OR: Wipf and Stock, 2015 [2nd ed.]).

Gundry, Robert H. — *Matthew: A Commentary on His Handbook for a Mixed Church under Persecution* (Grand Rapids: Eerdmans, 1994 [2nd ed.]).

Hagner, Donald A. — 'Matthew: Apostate, Reformer, Revolutionary?' *NTS* 49.2 (2003), 193–209.

Hagner, Donald A. — *Matthew 1–13* (WBC 33A; Dallas: Word, 1993).

Hagner, Donald A. — *Matthew 14–28* (WBC 33B; Dallas: Word, 1995).

Hare, Douglas R. A. *The Theme of Jewish Persecution of Christians in the Gospel according to St. Matthew* (SNTSMS 6; Cambridge: Cambridge University Press, 1967).

Harrington, Daniel J. *The Gospel of Matthew* (Sacra Pagina; Collegeville, MN: Michael Glazier/Liturgical Press, 1991).

Hauerwas, Stanley *Matthew* (Brazos Theological Commentary on the Bible; Grand Rapids: Brazos, 2006).

Hays, Richard B. *The Moral Vision of the New Testament: A Contemporary Introduction to New Testament Ethics* (San Francisco: HarperSanFrancisco, 1996).

Hengel, Martin *The Zealots: Investigations into the Jewish Freedom Movement in the Period from Herod I until 70 AD* (David Smith, trans.; Edinburgh: T&T Clark, 1989).

Horsley, Richard *Jesus and the Spiral of Violence: Popular Jewish Resistance in Roman Palestine* (San Francisco: Harper and Row, 1987).

Horsley, Richard, with John S. Hanson *Bandits, Prophets, and Messiahs: Popular Movements at the Time of Jesus* (San Francisco: Harper and Row, 1985).

Huizenga, Leroy Andrew 'Obedience unto Death: The Matthean Gethsemane and Arrest Sequence and the Aqedah', *CBQ* 71 (2009), 507–26.

Johnson, Nathan C. 'The Passion according to David: Matthew's Arrest Narrative, the Absalom Revolt, and Militant Messianism', *CBQ* (2018) 264–72.

Keener, Craig S. *A Commentary on the Gospel of Matthew* (Grand Rapids: Eerdmans, 1999).

Kingsbury, Jack Dean *Matthew as Story* (Philadelphia: Fortress, 1988 [2nd ed.]).

Konradt, Matthias *The Gospel according to Matthew: A Commentary* (M. Eugene Boring, trans.; Waco, TX: Baylor University Press, 2020).

Kosmala, Hans 'Matthew 26:52—A Quotation from the Targum', *NovT* 4 (1960), 3–5.

Louw, Johannes P., & Eugene A. Nida, *Greek-English Lexicon of the New Testament Based on Semantic Domains* (New York: United Bible Societies, 1988 [2nd ed.]).

Luz, Ulrich *Matthew 1–7: A Commentary* (James E. Crouch, trans.; Hermeneia; Minneapolis: Fortress, 2007).

Luz, Ulrich *Matthew 8–20: A Commentary* (James E. Crouch, trans.; Hermeneia; Minneapolis: Fortress, 2001).

Luz, Ulrich *Matthew 21–28: A Commentary* (James E. Crouch, trans.; Hermeneia; Minneapolis: Fortress, 2005).

Luz, Ulrich *The Theology of the Gospel of Matthew* (J. Bradford Robinson, trans.; Cambridge: Cambridge University Press, 1995).

Marshall, I. H. *The Gospel of Luke: A Commentary on the Greek Text* (NIGNT; Grand Rapids: Eerdmans, 1978).

Martin, Dale B.	'Jesus in Jerusalem: Armed and Not Dangerous', *JSNT* 37 (2014), 3–24.
Matera, Frank J.	*Passion Narratives and Gospel Theologies: Interpreting the Synoptics though their Passion Stories* (New York; Mahwah, NJ: Paulist, 1986).
Matson, David Lertis	'Double-Edged: The Meaning of the Two Swords in Luke 22:35-38', *JBL* 137 (2018), 463–80.
Matson, David Lertis	'Pacifist Jesus? The (Mis)Translation of ἐᾶτε ἕως τούτου in Luke 22:51', *JBL* 134 (2015), 157–76.
Matson, David Lertis	'Should Ἰουδαῖος Be Translated 'Judean'? The Challenge of 1 Thessalonians 2:14', in David Lertis Matson and K.C. Richardson (eds.), *One in Christ Jesus: Essays on Early Christianity and 'All that Jazz' in Honor of S. Scott Bartchy'* (Eugene, OR: Pickwick, 2014), 69–83.
Meier, John P.	*Matthew* (New Testament Message; Collegeville, MN: Glazier/Liturgical Press, 1990).
Meier, J.P.	*The Vision of Matthew: Christ, Church and Morality in the First Gospel* (Theological Inquiries; New York: Paulist, 1979).
Mitchell, Andrew	'Your Kingdom Come, Your Will Be Done: A Study of Matthew 6:10', *BBR* 30 (2020), 208–30.
Nel, Marius	'"Not Peace but a Sword": Jesus and the Sword in Matthew', *Neot* 49.2 (2015), 235–59.
Neville, David J.	*The Vehement Jesus: Grappling with Troubling Gospel Texts* (Eugene, OR: Cascade, 2017).
Nolland, John	*The Gospel of Matthew: A Commentary on the Greek Text* (NIGTC ; Grand Rapids: Eerdmans, 2005).
Osborne, Grant R.	*Matthew* (ZECT; Grand Rapids: Zondervan, 2010).
Pennington, Jonathan T.	*Heaven and Earth in the Gospel of Matthew* (Grand Rapids: Baker Academic, 2009; orig. published by Koninklijke Brill NV, Leiden, 2007).
Plummer, Alfred	*An Exegetical Commentary on the Gospel according to St. Matthew* (London: Robert Scott, 1915 [2nd ed.]).
Roth, Jonathan P.	'Jewish Military Forces in the Roman Service', in Christopher B. Zeichmann (ed.), *Essential Essays for the Study of the Military in First-Century Palestine: Soldiers and the New Testament Context* (Eugene, OR: Pickwick, 2019), 79–94.
Rubio, Fernando Bermejo	'Jesus and the Anti-Roman Resistance: A Reassessment of the Arguments', *JSHJ* 12. 3 (2014), 1–105.
Runesson, Anders, & Daniel M. Gurtner (eds.)	*Matthew within Judaism: Israel and the Nations in the First Gospel* (Early Christianity and Its Literature 27; Atlanta: SBL Press, 2020).
Runge, Steven E.	*Discourse Grammar of the Greek New Testament: A Practical Introduction for*

	Teaching and Exegesis (Peabody, MA: Hendrickson, 2010).
Rydelnik, Michael	*The Messianic Hope: Is the Hebrew Bible Really Messianic?* (Nashville: Broadman and Holman, 2010).
Scaer, David P.	*Discourses in Matthew: Jesus Teaches the Church* (St. Louis: Concordia, 2004).
Scheffler, E.	'Jesus' Non-Violence at His Arrest: The Synoptics and John's Gospel Compared', *Acts Patristica et Byzantina* 17 (2006), 312–26.
Schoenfeld, Andrew J.	'Sons of Israel in Caesar's Service: Jewish Soldiers in the Roman Military', in Christopher B. Zeichmann (ed.), *Essential Essays for the Study of the Military in First-Century Palestine: Soldiers and the New Testament Context* (Eugene, OR: Pickwick, 2019), 95–107.
Schweizer, Eduard	*The Good News according to Matthew* (David E. Green, trans.; London: SPCK, 1975).
Senior, Donald P.	*The Passion of Jesus in the Gospel of Matthew* (Collegeville, MN: Glazier/Liturgical Press, 1985).
Senior, Donald P.	*The Passion Narrative according to Matthew: A Redactional Study* (Gembloux; Leuven: Leuven University Press, 1975).
Sider, Ronald J.	*Christ and Violence* (Kitchener, ON: Herald, 1979).
Siker, Judy Yates	'Between Text and Sermon: Matthew 26:47–56', *Int* 58 (2004), 386–89.
Sim, David C.	'The Sword Motif in Matthew 10:34', *HTS* 56 (2000), 84–104.
Stassen, Glen H., & David P. Gushee	*Kingdom Ethics: Following Jesus in Contemporary Context* (Downers Grove, IL: InterVarsity Press, 2003).
Stendahl, Krister	*The School of St. Matthew and Its Use of the Old Testament* (Philadelphia: Fortress, 1968).
Stephens, William H.	*The New Testament World in Pictures* (Nashville: Broadman, 1987).
Storkey, Alan	*Jesus and Politics: Confronting the Powers* (Grand Rapids: Baker Academic, 2005).
Suhl, Alfred	'Die Funktion des Schwertstreiches bei der Gefangennahme Jesu: Beobachtungen zur Komposition und Theologie der synoptischen Evangelien [Mk 14,43–52; Mt 26,47–56; Lk 22,47–53]', in F. Van Segbroeck, et. al. (eds.), *The Four Gospels.* (Festschrift Frans Neirynck; BETL 100; Leuven: Leuven University Press, 1992], 1.295–323.
Thayer, Joseph Henry	*Thayer's Greek-English Lexicon of the New Testament* (Grand Rapids: Baker, 1977).
Trueman, Carl R.	*Luther on the Christian Life: Cross and Freedom* (Wheaton Il: Crossway, 2015).
Turner, David L.	*Matthew* (BECNT; Grand Rapids: Baker Academic, 2008).

Viviano, Benedict T.	'The High Priest's Servant's Ear: Mark 14:47', *RB* 96 (1989), 71–80.
Wallace, Daniel B.	*Greek Grammar Beyond the Basics: An Exegetical Syntax of the New Testament* (Grand Rapids: Zondervan, 1996).
Webster, Graham	*The Roman Imperial Army of the First and Second Centuries A.D.* (Norman, OK: University of Oklahoma Press, 1998 [3rd ed.]).
Windisch, Hans	'ἀσπάζομαι, ἀπασπάζομαι, ἀσπασμός, *TDNT* 1:496–502.
Witherington, Ben III	*Matthew* (Macon: Smyth & Helwys, 2006).
Yoder, John Howard	*Nevertheless: The Varieties and Shortcomings of Religious Pacifism* (Scottsdale, PA: Herald Press, 1992).

David Lertis Matson
Pacific Christian College of Hope International University, Fullerton CA, USA
dlmatson@hiu.edu

Casting Out Mountains (Mark 11:23)

CRAIG S. KEENER

Abstract

Although scholars generally agree that the promise in Mark 11:23 is a hyperbolically expressed invitation to faith, interpretations of particular elements diverge widely. Debate about the mountain's identity remains; the context of Jesus's challenge to the temple leads some to subsume Jesus's mountain-moving promise wholly under his teachings regarding eschatological, corporate judgment. Many others view the mountain as generic (i.e., *any* mountain), yet without explicating more specifically how Mark expects the faith to be addressed. This article contends that the mountain is generic (albeit perhaps using the Mount of Olives as an illustration), but that the wider Markan context qualifies how commands of faith should be expressed.

After discussing the mountain or mountains in view, I shall turn to the manner in which Mark expects hearers of the saying to express this commanding faith. Jesus has earlier illustrated such commands not only when cursing the fig tree but by stilling a storm, healing some illnesses, and casting out demons. Perhaps not coincidentally—although this connection is less secure than Jesus's model of commands more generally—the language of 'casting' applied to demons also appears here with respect to the removal of mountains. More critically, the context of Mark's Gospel envisions such commands of faith as expressions of delegated authority, hence for serving others rather than for personal ends.

1. Which mountain?

Although Coptic tradition does claim an emergency case of literally moving a mountain when Coptic Christians desperately prayed for this,[1] rarely have Jesus's followers otherwise seen a need to take his mountain–removing invitation literally. Scholars nevertheless debate the particular mountain to which Jesus referred. Jesus may have illustrated originally by pointing to a particular mountain in view (note '*this* mountain' in Matt 17:20; 21:21; Mark 11:23). Still, attempts to restrict the theological point to *only* the mountain in view mistakes an illustration for the principle. Jesus's followers probably applied his principle generically from the start (for acts of great faith; 1 Cor

---

[1] During the period of Al-Mu'iz Li Din Illah the Fatimid and Pope Abram in the tenth century. See e.g., Morgan, *History of the Coptic Orthodox People*, 235; Loubser, 'How Al-Mokattam Mountain was moved', 113–15.

13:2). On the level of the Evangelists, for example, certainly the mountain envisioned in Matt 17:20 (presumably the 'high mountain' of transfiguration, 17:1, 9) differs from any Judean mountain in view in Matt 21:21.

Since Jesus may have illustrated the point with a literal mountain, however, it seems worth exploring options for the mountain that may have served this function. Although scholars have offered other suggestions[2] related to, or within view of, Jerusalem, such as the Herodium,[3] scholars more commonly specify the mountain as either Mount Zion or the Mount of Olives.[4]

1.1 Casting Down the Temple Mount?

Many scholars view the mountain in Mark as the temple mount, identified with Mount Zion, and often see Jesus's reference to it as more than an illustration.[5] (The claim is rarely made for Jesus historically without the evidence of Mark. Given Mark's interest in the temple's judgment in the context, it is unlikely that Mark would neglect a prior application to the temple mount.) Mount Zion regularly appears as God's mountain in the OT, and already some ancient commentators thought that Jesus referred here to the temple mount (though they also thought that the sea represented the nations; cf. Rev 17:15).[6]

1.1.1 Inverting OT Images?

This view, which may be the most common one,[7] has definite appeal. It allows interpreters to connect the point of Mark's fig-tree-cursing sandwich around Jesus's demonstration in the temple (likely portending the temple's judgment) with the teaching on faith and prayer in 11:23–25. There is no *a priori* reason why this could not be the case. Even if not connected directly, in principle the command, like the fig tree cursing that it follows, could do double duty (applying both to the temple and faith).[8]

Some see Jesus's application to the temple mount as inverting biblical promises of the temple's eschatological exaltation (Isa 2:2; Mic 4:1).[9] In Hebrew, Ps 46:3 (ET 46:2; LXX 45:3) speaks of mountains being moved into the sea, as the earth melts in judgment on the nations (46:6; cf. 46:8–10). Meanwhile, by contrast, God is in the midst of Jerusalem, establishing and protecting them (46:4–7, 11). Likewise, Scripture declares that Mount Zion cannot ever be moved (Ps 125:1 [LXX 124:1]).[10] Jesus's promise, then, could offer a strong illustration: faith can move even the immovable!

---

2   Richardson, *Introduction*, 266, applies it figuratively to 'Jewish unbelief'; Schwarz, 'Pistin hōs kokkon sinapeōs', to the disciples' scribal adversaries; Marshall, *Faith*, 168–69, to overcoming 'institutionalized opposition' such as the temple establishment.
3   Edwards, *Mark*, 347; Beck, 'Lesson on Prayer', 408. Beck notes (p.411) that the Herodium's construction, which relocated earth from the adjacent mountain, involved 'the only mountain in view that had a history of being moved'.
4   Broadhead, *Mark*, 94–95, leaves both as options.
5   E.g., Dodd. *Parables*, 45n2; Telford, *Barren Temple*, 119; Hooker, *Message*, 84; Hooker, *Saint Mark*, 270; Wright, *Jesus and the Victory of God*, 334; Garland, *Mark*, 441; Such, *Abomination of Desolation*, 166; Watts, *New Exodus*, 333–37; Watts, 'Mark', 212; Evans, *Mark 8:27–16:20*, 188–89; Moloney, *Mark*, 227; Wright, *Mark for Everyone*, 153; Boring, *Mark*, 324; Healy, *Mark*, 231; Gray, *Temple*, 51–52; Marcus, *Mark 8–16*, 785, 787; Beavis, *Mark*, 172; Black, *Mark*, 240; Tan, *Mark*, 158; Ortlund, 'What Does It Mean to Cast a Mountain into the Sea?'.
6   Standaert, *Evangile*, 3:831.
7   So Watts, *New Exodus*, 333.
8   Watts, *New Exodus*, 337.
9   With e.g., Garland, *Mark*, 441; Marcus, *Mark 8–16*, 787, 794. For later rabbinic tradition about the event, see Jeremias, *Theology*, 165n1.
10 Likewise, God is in (Ps 48:3) his holy mountain (48:1–2), establishing her forever (48:8), smashing antagonistic nations (48:4–7).

But the wording differs too much to assume that Mark 11:23 responds to these psalms by hyperbolically transcending, refuting or inverting them. Claims of mountains being immovable (Ps 30:6–8 [LXX 29:7–8]; 76:4 [75:5]), and of God protecting his people even in the midst of mountains trembling (Isa 54:10), are not limited to Mount Zion. Even in the case of Ps 125:1, just noted, the psalmist seems to take confidence also in the firmness of *other* mountains surrounding Jerusalem (125:2).

If the great mountain that God's Spirit will make into a plain in Zech 4:7 is the temple, mountain-removal as temple-removal would make sense in light of that passage.[11] Elsewhere in Zechariah, the mountain is indeed Zion (3:11; 8:3). But in Zechariah 4, the context is not temple removal but temple building, and the mountain may refer to the heap of ruins that must first be cleared or to other obstacles to this mission.[12] Josephus also speaks of leveling ground in a later period to exalt the temple mount.[13] Jesus could envision the eschatological temple replacing the current one.[14] But would Mark's audience understand that point simply from 'this mountain'?

1.1.2 Eschatological Mountain Moving?

Jewish audiences and mature Gentile Christians familiar with the LXX might also think of future promise passages.[15] These could include the exaltation of Zion (Isa 2:2), mountains leveled to prepare the way for YHWH's new exodus (Isa 40:4; 45:2; 49:11), and the splitting of the Mount of Olives (Zech 14:4–5). In keeping with the new exodus, God could exalt his people to thresh mountains and make the hills like chaff (Isa 41:15). The trembling of mountains also fits poetic depictions of theophanies (e.g., Ps 18:7; 104:32; 144:5; Isa 5:25; 54:3; Jer 4:24), some of which many first-century hearers would construe eschatologically (Ps 97:4–5; Ezek 38:20; Mic 1:3–4; Nah 1:5; Hab 3:6, 10).[16]

Given the availability of mountains as massive, immovable structures, however, eschatological imagery is not necessary to make the saying's point about faith.[17] Moreover, the eschatological imagery can hardly limit a promise, associated both with Jesus's example of cursing the fig tree and an invitation to presently 'remove mountains', to an eschatological future. If the saying draws at all on biblical eschatological associations of God moving mountains eschatologically, which is possible, it might partly envision a realized eschatology of the kingdom, in which God's agents in the present could even move mountains as needed.

1.1.3 Tempering the Temple View

Eschatological questions aside, problems exist for the temple-removal view. Disciples are not called to seek the temple's physical destruction, and such a narrow application would in any case lose the connection between Jesus's cursing the fig tree and his followers' individual, continuing acts of faith.[18] This objection would not nullify the value of using the temple mount as an illustration for Jesus's more generic point about faith, but it would negate the proposed connection with judgment in the context, the primary reason for interpreters applying 'this mountain' to the

---

11   Marcus, *Mark 8–16*, 785, 787.
12   See discussion in Smith, *Micah–Malachi*, 206; Meyers and Meyers, *Haggai, Zechariah 1–8*, 244–48; Boda, *Zechariah*, 294–98.
13   Josephus *Ant.* 13.215-17; cf. the first temple in *Ant.* 8.97.
14   Cf. 1 En. 90:28–29; Jub. 1:17, 27–29; 11Q19 29.8–10; esp. Sanders, *Historical Figure*, 262.
15   Cf. Jeremias, *Theology*, 165–66, 191–92; Telford, *Barren Temple*, 118; Marshall, *Faith*, 166; Evans, *Mark*, 189.
16   Hab 3 poetically describes or complements the theophany at Sinai (3:3), but hearers of Mark 11 might also think of the fig tree that does not blossom in Hab 3:17. Cf. 1 En. 83:4.
17   Note Schnabel, *Mark*, 275–76.
18   Marshall, *Faith*, 169.

temple to begin with.

The most serious problem for applying 'this mountain' to the temple mount on the *Markan* level, where interpreters most often envision it, is one that I regard as decisive. This objection applies even to viewing the temple mount as the saying's illustration of faith in its Markan context. Apart from Jewish pilgrims, Mark's Diaspora audience would lack familiarity with Jerusalem's topography. Yet Mark *nowhere* informs his audience that the temple stands on a 'mount'.

Granted, those familiar with the LXX would surely know of the temple mount or city of David as the Lord's holy mountain.[19] This language continued in early Jewish sources, although somewhat less pervasively;[20] Josephus declares that visitors to Jerusalem's temple would view it from afar as a snow-covered mountain.[21] Such observations do support the credibility of the temple mount approach. But Mark chose not to make such a connection clear, when he easily could have identified the temple mount as a mountain somewhere in his context, even in his truncated quotation of a passage that, in the excluded lines, explicitly mentions it (Isa 56:7 in Mark 11:17).

Indeed, Jesus soon warns that Judean followers who discover the temple's desecration should 'flee to the mountains' (13:14), plainly distinguishing the temple from such mountains.

1.2 The Mount of Olives?

The only mountain that Mark specifies as such in this context is the Mount of Olives (11:1; 13:3; 14:26); none of the other mountains Mark mentions earlier is named. Many scholars thus view 'this mountain' as a reference to the Mount of Olives, which was visible and which, at this point in the narrative, Jesus and his disciples may be still traversing.[22] Although Mark's Diaspora audience would not know this, the historical Jesus's own disciples traveling with him presumably knew that a sea—the Dead Sea—was visible from the summit of the Mount of Olives[23] (though probably not at their presumed location near the fig tree on its lower slope).

One might discard something impure into the Dead Sea to get rid of it;[24] being cast into the sea also served as an image of punishment (Mark 9:42). Earlier Jesus expelled demons into pigs, which then rushed into the sea to their destruction (Mark 5:13), although commentators debate whether this was Jesus's intention. But 'cast into sea' is common vocabulary even for someone diving (John 21:7).

The image of moving the Mount of Olives would be particularly graphic, since Zech 14:4 envisioned its eschatological splitting (like a great earthquake, 14:5).[25] Granted, Zech 14 refers to the Mount of Olives being split, not removed or cast into the sea.[26] In the LXX, however, part of

---

19   E.g., the holy mountain or the Lord's mountain in Ps 47:2 [ET 48:1]; 98:9 [99:9]; Isa 2:2–3; 11:9; 25:6–7; 27:13; 30:29; 56:7; 57:13; 65:11, 25; 66:20; Ezek 20:40; Dan 9:16, 20; Joel 2:1; 4:17 [ET 3:17]; Mic 4:1; Obad 16; Zeph 3:11; Zech 8:3. For Mount Zion, see e.g., Ps 47:3, 12 [48:2, 11]; 73:2 [74:2]; Isa 4:5; 8:18; 10:12; 18:7; and *passim*.
20   Jub. 1:28–29; 4:26; 8:19; 18:7, 13; Josephus *Ant.* 1.226; 8.60, 97; 4 Ezra 2:42; 2 Bar. 13:1; 40:1; cf. 4Q180 f5–6.4; 4Q372 f1.8.
21   Josephus *War* 5.223. Nevertheless, Josephus applies mountain language more often to the Samaritans' holy site (*Ant.* 11.310, 346; 12.10, 257; 13.74; *War* 3.307), for which 'mountain' seems more often used in this period (as in John 4:20–21).
22   Gould, *Mark*, 215; Gundry, *Mark*, 649, 652; Pesch, *Das Markusevangelium*, 2:204; Witherington, *Mark*, 309; Keener, *Matthew*, 505; Schnabel, *Mark*, 275–76; cf. France, *Mark*, 449.
23   Witherington, *Mark*, 309; France, *Mark*, 449; Beck, 'Lesson on Prayer', 411.
24   Beck, 'Lesson on Prayer', 412, cites m. Abod. Zar. 3:3, 9; later, cf. y. Abod. Zar. 39b. Marcus, *Mark 8–16*, 787, compares the Cyclops hurling a piece of a mountain into the sea to try to harm his tormentors (Homer, *Odyssey* 9.644–50).
25   For this event's later association with the eschatological resurrection, see *Tg. Song* 8:5, noted in Evans, *Mark 8:27–16:20*, 401 (on Mark 14:26–31); the Dura synagogue panel in Grassi, "Ezekiel XXXVII.1–14," 163. Josephus applies Zechariah's description to the earlier earthquake Zechariah uses as an analogy (*Ant.* 9.225), but one of his false prophets may have tried to inaugurate God's kingdom there (*Ant.* 20.169; *War* 2.262).
26   Marshall, *Faith*, 168; Schnabel, *Mark*, 275–76.

this mountain would move toward the sea.[27] Some doubt reference to the Mount of Olives because it always appears positively in Mark's Gospel;[28] but if the mountain's removal functions only as an illustration for faith rather than as an act of judgment this objection becomes irrelevant.

1.3 Generic Mountains

Jesus need not have a particular mountain in view, but if he did (hence '*this* mountain'), whether the temple mount or (as I think more likely) the Mount of Olives, it may function merely as a visual illustration of a wider principle.

1.3.1 Ancient Mountain Hyperbole

Jesus's and Mark's audiences were familiar with hyperbole, including regarding mountains moving (see e.g., mountains skipping in Ps 29:6; 114:4, 6).[29] The following claim that whatever one says will come to pass is also hyperbole.[30] Such hyperbolic language stimulates imagination for readiness.[31]

Although, as a figure of speech, moving mountains may have been especially Jewish, Gentile writers also, probably independently, exploited such images for hyperbole. Lamenting those who squander their wealth on luxury, a pre-Christian Roman writer complains about those who 'have leveled mountains and built upon the seas'.[32] Desperate to maintain his paramour's favor, a wealthy Roman promises her 'seas and mountains'.[33] Ancients of course had many ways of speaking of accomplishing something next to impossible, such as 'shaving a lion'[34] or passing a large animal through a needle's eye.[35]

But as scholars often note,[36] later Babylonian rabbis speak of those who accomplished unimaginable feats of Torah exposition and debate as uprooters of mountains.[37] It is unlikely that the rabbis derived the image from Jesus, but it is certainly possible that Jesus adapted an image, already in circulation in his day, that they later attest. If so, the generic application of the image would have been evident immediately from the start, even if Jesus illustrated by gesturing toward a specific mountain. More graphically than his contemporaries, however, Jesus further envisions the mountains being buried beneath the sea.[38] And although the image of moving mountains is not limited to the early Christian movement, its specific association with faith is.

---

27 The 'sea' replaces the Hebrew text's sense of 'west', which of course is 'sea', referring to the Mediterranean.
28 Gray, *Temple*, 51.
29 The passage poetically depicts the theophany at Sinai. In the context of God's redemption, mountains can praise God (Isa 44:23; 49:13; 55:12; cf. Ps 114:4–6; 1 En. 51:4).
30 Cranfield, *Mark*, 361.
31 See Collins, *Mark*, 535. Cf. Huebenthal, *Reading Mark's Gospel*, 386–87, 414; also 389n125, noting Vena, 'Markan Construction', 82. Huebenthal argues that Jesus's ideal world of the kingdom effects reality in what others regard as the actual world, and he expects disciples also to embrace this higher reality (cf. 4:40; 8:33).
32 Sallust *Cat.* 13.1 (LCL 1:39); similarly, 20.11. In his note on 13.1, translator John T. Ramsey explains, 'Wealthy Romans in Sallust's day cut through hills to bring salt water into their fishponds (Plin. *NH* 9.170) and built villas on pilings sunk into the sea, especially on the Bay of Naples, at Baiae (Hor. *Carm.* 3.1.33–37)'.
33 Sallust *Cat.* 23.3. In the Loeb note (LCL 1:58n38), Ramsey suggests that the phrase was 'coined on the model of the proverbial expression of "promising mountains of gold" (e.g., Ter. *Phorm.* 68)'.
34 Philostratus *Vit. soph.* 1.14.497.
35 Mark 10:25; *b. Ber.* 55b; *b. B.M.* 38b; cf. Jeremias, *Parables*, 195; Yamauchi, 'Camels', 250.
36 E.g., Jeremias, *Theology*, 161; Nineham, *Mark*, 305; Marshall, *Faith*, 166 (drawing on Telford, *Barren Temple*, 109–19).
37 E.g., b. Ber. 63b–64a; Sanh. 24a; Ab. R. Nat. 6A; 12, §29B; others cite also *B. Bat.* 3b; *Lev. Rab.* 8:8. Cf. also (though possibly derivative and likewise late) a demon's claim to sufficient power as to move mountains in *T. Sol.* 23:1.
38 As noted by Gundry, *Mark*, 649.

1.3.2 OT Mountain Imagery

Yet Jesus's hearers and Mark's audience need be familiar with neither Roman engineering nor later-attested rabbinic figures of speech to understand his point. More generally, mountains may function as the epitome of height and the sea as the epitome of depth.[39] A mountain could be employed figuratively for something considered immovable.[40] Mountains were considered immovable because their roots were thought to descend deep (Deut 32:22; Ps 18:7 [LXX 17:8]; Sir 16:19; *Orphica* 35),[41] perhaps even beneath the seas themselves (Jon 2:5–6; cf. Jdt 16:15).

But God, who established the mountains (Ps 65:6; 90:2; Isa 40:12; Amos 4:13), rules mountains (Ps 95:4) and can move them.[42] Believers must thus trust God even if the mountains are moved into the heart of the sea (Ps 46:2; LXX 45:3; cf. Isa 54:10). Figuratively, God would someday level mountains before Cyrus (Isa 45:2) and turn mountains into a road for the new exodus (Isa 40:4; 49:11; Bar 5:7); perhaps most relevantly, he would also use his people to move mountains for him (Isa 41:15–16).[43]

Many scholars thus view the mountain in Jesus's original context and/or in Mark as generic.[44]

In Jesus's original context, he may well have illustrated by gesturing to a particular mountain; but by the time the saying reaches Mark, Christians already focused on the more generic principle that Jesus was emphasizing ('mountains' in 1 Cor 13:2; a northern mountain, or no mountain at all, envisioned in Q Matt 17:20//Luke 17:6). Jesus's dramatic hyperbole must have wider application, just as does the promise concerning 'all things' in Mark 11:24.

If mountain removal symbolizes the removal of any specific objects here, they may represent obstacles to the kingdom. Removing mountains could evoke preparing the way for the kingdom in Isa 40:4 (found in Luke 3:5).[45] This is part of a passage that functions programmatically in Mark's introduction,[46] although it should be noted that Mark 1:3 directly *quotes* only Isa 40:3. The recent spreading of cloaks and branches before Jesus (Mark 11:8) might also evoke preparing the way.

2. Invitation to faith

Jesus's original saying seems to have invited faith generically, without specific reference to judgment on the temple. This does not make the saying irrelevant to Mark's larger themes. Its specific expression in 11:23, namely, in the form of commands, follows a form modeled in the prophets and especially in Jesus's own authoritative actions in Mark's Gospel. By emulating Jesus's own faith in the Father, the disciples to whom Jesus delegates his authority may carry on his mission.

---

39 See e.g., Ps 36:6 [LXX 35:7]; Jer 46:18 [LXX 26:18]; Aristobulus 13:5; 4 Ezra 8:23; 2 Bar. 76:3). Note also the contrast between mountains and low places in Ps 95:4 [LXX 94:4]; Isa 44:23; cf. Josephus *War* 1.310, 405.
40 Ps 30:6–7 (MT 30:7–8; though the mountain of Ps 30:7 ET [30:8 MT] does not appear in LXX 29:8); Ps 125:1–2 [LXX 124:1–2]. Cf. possibly 'eternal mountains' in Hab 3:6; 'eternal hills' in Gen 49:26; Deut 33:15; Bar 5:7.
41 Mountains extended to the earth's foundations; overturning them at their roots (Job 28:9; Gundry, *Mark*, 649) hyperbolically depicts the extent to which miners could work (28:1–11).
42 Judg 5:5; Job 9:5; Ps 18:7; 97:5; 104:32; 114:4–6; 144:5; Isa 5:25; 64:1, 3; Jer 4:24; Nah 1:5; Hab 3:6, 10; 1 En. 53:7, though many of these references are figurative or hyperbolic. Babylon is figuratively a mountain (that God will destroy) in Jer 51:25 [LXX 28:25].
43 Cf. miners hyperbolically 'overturning mountains' in Job 28:9.
44 Telford, *Barren Temple*, 118 (for the original saying); Gnilka, *Evangelium*, 2:134; Evans, *Mark*, 188 (for the original saying); Donahue and Harrington, *Mark*, 329; France, *Mark*, 449; Collins, *Mark*, 535; Bock, *Mark*, 296–97.
45 Also Isa 45:2; 49:11; later, Bar 5:7; Ps. Sol. 11:4. Cf. Isa 42:15; mountains' personified celebration in Isa 44:23; 49:13; 55:12. Cf. also Healy, *Mark*, 230.
46 See esp. Watts, *New Exodus, passim*.

2.1 The Original Saying

Debate about the sense of the mountain-removing saying attaches more to Mark's usage than to its prehistory. Most scholars recognize that the original saying or sayings invited individual disciples' acts of faith rather than a corporate eschatological prayer (such as appears, for example, in Matt 6:9–10//Luke 11:2). The saying's different location in some other Gospel materials and its evocation in Paul focus on acts of faith without respect to the temple *per se*.

This saying, or sayings like this one, are so well-attested that most scholars accept the core saying's historical authenticity.[47] One miraculous removing saying appears in Matt 17:20//Luke 17:6, which most scholars (including myself) attribute to Q. If Mark has reworked the same saying in a new context, the saying is multiply attested in the Gospels. If, conversely, Jesus employed the image of faith removing mountains on more than one occasion,[48] the *image* is multiply attested and coheres with other reported sayings of Jesus. (The mustard seed image in the Q version certainly is consistent with Jesus's many 'seed' or sowing parables, including mustard seed [Mark 4:31; Matt 13:31–32; Luke 13:19].)[49]

Matt 17:20	Matt 21:21 (following esp. Mark 11:23)	Luke 17:6	Mark 11:23
Context of exorcism	Context of cursing the fig tree (explicit in 21:21)	Context of faith (Removal of sycamore fig tree in 17:6)	Context of cursing the fig tree
Faith as small as a mustard seed	--	Faith as small as a mustard seed	(Faith in God, 11:22)
	Do not waver		Do not waver
Say to this mountain	Say to this mountain	Say to this sycamore fig tree	Say to this mountain
Move	Be taken up	Be uprooted	Be taken up
From here to there	Be cast into the sea	Be planted in the sea	Be cast into the sea
It will move	It will happen	It will obey you	It will be (for you)
	Everything you request in faithful prayer you will receive (21:22)		For everything for which you pray and request, believe that you receive[50]

Besides these instances, Paul, probably writing earlier than any of our Gospels, knows of mountain-removing faith (1 Cor 13:2).[51] Two sayings about moving mountains also appear later in the *Gospel of Thomas* (§§40, 106), though Thomas omits mention of faith.[52]

---

47 See e.g., Perrin, *Rediscovering the Teaching of Jesus*, 137–39; Gnilka, *Evangelium*, 2:135; Collins, *Mark*, 532.
48 So Gundry, *Mark*, 652; Bock, *Mark*, 295n509.
49 Nor were seed or tree parables new; see e.g., Judg 9:8–15; Isa 5:1–2; Nitzan, '4Q302/302A (Sap. A)'.
50 Those who read the aorist temporally read, 'you *have* received'; I read it here as punctiliar or viewed from outside as a whole event ('Count it as done!'), though ultimately the meaning is roughly the same (cf. Donahue and Harrington, *Mark*, 330; Stein, *Mark*, 520; Marcus, *Mark 8–16*, 787; cf. Matt 6:8). It could have a futuristic sense (Gnilka, *Evangelium*, 2:135), as reworded in Matthew (Matt 21:22) or in the later textual variant here (see Metzger, *Textual Commentary*, 109–10).
51 Blomberg, 'Quotations, Allusions, and Echoes of Jesus in Paul', 138. Standaert, *Evangile*, 831, suggests that Paul learned the saying during his visit with Peter in Gal 1:18.
52 Evans, *Mark*, 185, 187.

The question as to which forms and contexts are most original is more debated than the core saying's authenticity. Since Matthew inserts 17:20 into a Markan context and Luke's saying (17:6) lacks links to its context apart from the disciples' request (17:5; cf. similarly 11:1), the Q saying was probably originally free-floating (or circulated only with the request in Luke 17:5). It is thus possible that the Q saying, with its original form closer to Luke, circulated independently from the Markan context, even if its use of the tree image may have evoked the account subsequently preserved in Mark.

Many scholars regard all the sayings in Mark 11:22–25 as originally circulated independently from the fig tree cursing.[53] A number argue that even the sayings themselves might be joined to each other loosely by catchwords: faith in 11:22, 23, 24; 'pray' in 11:24, 25.[54] Mark's arrangement does make sense, however. Although the topic of faith differs from Mark's sandwich application of the withered fig tree to Jesus's action in the temple,[55] it does relate to its preceding context of the fig tree.[56] When Peter marvels at Jesus's ability to destroy the fig tree (11:21), Jesus challenges the disciples to adjust their expectations regarding what God can do through him and through them, as he had earlier exhorted in 4:40; 8:17–21.

Matthew 17:20 might adjust the Q saying in light of Mark 11:23, so turning Q's tree (Luke 17:6) into a mountain. It would be going too far, however, to postulate that Mark has changed an original tree (fitting his own context with the cursed fig tree) into a mountain, since Paul undoubtedly echoes Jesus's saying about faith moving mountains (1 Cor 13:2). Alternatively, some suggest that Luke changed the original mountain (in the Q form preserved in Matt 17:20) into a sycamore fig tree (so *editorially* removing a mountain) to evoke the fig tree cursing context in Mark.[57] But then why change the mountain into a συκάμινος rather than the συκῆ of Mark's narrative? And Luke omits the fig tree cursing itself, obviating any narrative connection.

In any case, it seems likely that the earliest Christians did not restrict the saying to the context of Jesus's action in the temple. Rather, it expresses how faith can act more generically. Even if Jesus offered the saying only once and cursing the fig tree is its earliest context, scholars often regard as artificial Mark's sandwich construction around Jesus's temple sign (a construction circumvented in Matthew). And even if Mark's sequence of events with the fig tree, temple sign, and teaching on faith is exact (which I do regard as possible), in the short run Jesus may have addressed Peter's immediate question about faith without immediately addressing judgment on the temple.

Although this article's focus is on Mark's version rather than Luke's, it is noteworthy that later rabbis considered uprooting and relocating trees a dramatic sign.[58] Thus it was said that R. Eliezer, to prove his point, announced a rule miracle:[59] if his view of the Torah was correct, a carob tree present would prove it. The tree then uprooted and deposited itself one hundred or more cubits away. Unimpressed, his colleagues denied that a carob tree gives proof.[60] Neither R. Eliezer nor,

---

53 Lane, *Mark*, 409; Stein, *Mark*, 510.
54 Black, *Mark*, 244, comparing Mark 9:42–50; cf. Gundry, *Mark*, 654–55, though he accepts 11:23 as originally connected with what precedes. Mark links prayer and faith also in 9:23, 29; cf. Schenke, *Markusevangelium*, 270; Standaert, *Evangile*, 832.
55 Gnilka, *Evangelium*, 2:134, thinks it related in the sense that Israel's lack of faith is at the heart of the problem.
56 Some view the account of the cursed fig tree as probably a parable historicized (tentatively, Dodd, *Parables*, 45n2), but it makes no less sense as a symbolic prophetic act (e.g., Isa 20:2; Jer 13:1–7; 19:10; Ezek 4:1–17; 24:16–19; Hos 1:2; Acts 21:11; in this context, Mark 11:15–16), in which case it coheres with Jesus's fig tree parable in Luke 13:6–9.
57 Telford, *Barren Temple*, 117; cf. Marcus, *Mark 8–16*, 785. Telford also views Matt 17:14–20 as the saying's earliest context (*Barren Temple*, 117), but this position presumes that Matthew had access to an earlier version of the exorcism story now found in Mark 9:14–29.
58 Jeremias, *Theology*, 161.
59 On 'rule miracles', see e.g., discussion in Theissen, *Miracle Stories*, 107; Keener, *Miracles*, 63–64.
60 b. Baba Mesia 59b.

still less, this story precedes Jesus or the Gospels chronologically, but if it is independent from Christian influence (which is possible, though it could respond to the tradition of Jesus cursing the fig tree) it could illustrate contemporary perspectives.[61]

Still, Jesus's promise to all followers with faith is extraordinary, and most scholars feel that it meets the criterion of dissimilarity.[62] Not simply a particularly pious rabbi (right or not about a point of halakah), but ideally all disciples, can perform acts of great faith.

2.2 Mark's Context

Most scholars agree that, by sandwiching Jesus's action in the temple between the fig tree cursing and observation of the tree's withered state, Mark connects the withered fig tree with judgment on the temple. While this is likely the case, the withered fig tree also intersects with and illustrates Jesus's power illustrated throughout Mark's larger narrative. Sickness, storms and spirits remain subject to Jesus, even though people may choose to rebel. Jesus has delegated authority to his disciples (3:15; 6:7) and invited their faith (4:40; cf. 2:5; 5:34, 36; 9:23), and it is especially in this connection that Jesus's explanation of the withered fig tree occurs.

When Peter marvels at the power of Jesus's curse to destroy the fig tree (11:21), Jesus presents the present action with the fig tree as merely a small sample of what God can do with those who trust him (cf. John 1:50). If they adopt Jesus's model of faith, they can do even greater works than he had needed to do (cf. John 14:12).[63] Instead of merely drying a fig tree from its roots, they might uproot mountains.[64]

2.2.1 Faith in Mark 11:23[65]

Scholars debate how Mark construes the lesson on faith, presumably already attached to the fig tree cursing incident, in relation to Jesus's action in the temple that Mark uses the incident to frame. Although I have argued that the 'mountain' removed in 11:23 does not refer to the temple mount, that does not obviate all possible connections with the temple context. Thus some suggest that prayer in faith (11:23–25) may well replace or at least transcend the obstructed house of prayer (11:17).[66]

Yet Mark's theme of faith also goes beyond the most immediate context. Because Matthew rearranges Mark's fig tree cursing so that it no longer sandwiches Jesus's action in the temple, Matthew highlights the theme of faith more exclusively than does Mark (Matt 21:18–21).[67] This does not, however, minimize the emphasis of faith in Mark (who, according to the usual scholarly configuration of sources, precedes our current Gospel of Matthew). Mark, too, connects πίστις and its cognates with the language of healing and deliverance (2:5; 4:40; 5:34, 36; 9:23–24; 10:52), and, more broadly, faith in Jesus's message and mission (1:15; 9:42; cf. 11:32; 15:32).[68]

---

61 Tradition suggests that Eliezer himself was aware of Jewish Christian teaching; see Herford, *Christianity in Talmud and Midrash*, 137–45, 388; Moore, *Judaism*, 2:250.
62 Donahue and Harrington, *Mark*, 330. This criterion, however, is limited in its value; see e.g., Theissen and Merz, *Historical Jesus*, 115; Holmén, 'Doubts About Double Dissimilarity'; Holmén, *Jesus and Jewish Covenant Thinking*, 20–31; Dunn, *New Perspective on Jesus*, 57–78.
63 Cf. Collins, *Mark*, 536: 'A similar link between miracle-working and prayer is made in John 14:8–14'.
64 Cf. Gould, *Mark*, 215.
65 On faith in Mark, see esp. Marshall, *Faith*; on faith in Mark 11:23–24, see esp. Dowd, *Prayer*.
66 See Dowd, 'Whatever You Ask', esp. 96–98; Schenke, *Markusevangelium*, 270; Bayer, *Evangelium*, 408. Others apply it to prayer for justice (cf. Ouellette, 'Driving Out Injustice').
67 Telford, *Barren Temple*, 80, 83.
68 See Marshall, *Faith*, 57–74; for miracles as a summons to faith, cf. 59–61. For the historical Jesus, see Blackburn, 'The Miracles of Jesus', 375.

Faith certainly dominates the immediate passage (11:22–24):

Have trust in God (πίστιν θεοῦ, 11:22)
Believe that what you say (πιστεύῃ, 11:23)
Believe that you received it (πιστεύετε, 11:24)

Most scholars agree that these verses refer to trust in God. Although some noteworthy scholars contend that πίστιν θεοῦ in 11:22 reflects a subjective genitive, thus, 'Hold to God's faithfulness',[69] the invitation to trust in the following verses (11:23–24) suggests that in this context the expression is, with most scholars, an objective genitive with the sense, 'trust in God'.[70] The expression 'have faith' (ἔχετε πίστιν, 11:22) elsewhere in Mark addresses disciples' faith (4:40), not God's faithfulness. The conjunction of the two words in related contexts in Mark's earliest extant interpreters also refers to believers' faith, indicating that they understand Mark's expression as an objective genitive (Matt 17:20; 21:21; Luke 17:6). Other connections between this verb and noun in early Christianity also indicate believers' faith.[71]

Still, this observation does not undercut the theological contribution of the subjective genitive approach. The most common sense of πίστις is trust or dependence on its object, here God. Faith is only as reliable as its object. The unrelated forms of the English terms *faith* and *believe* lose some of this connection in a way that the Greek terms πίστις and πιστεύω do not; thus one may safely trust God who is absolutely trustworthy, rely on God who is absolutely reliable, have faith in God who is absolutely faithful. This understanding minimizes the theological difference between different views of the genitive's function.[72]

2.2.2 Without doubting?

In specifying the nature of this faith, Mark uses the verb διακρίνω. Earlier in this Gospel, the antithesis of πίστις and cognates is ἀπιστία (6:6; 9:24) or, less explicitly, φόβος and cognates (4:40; 5:36).[73] In 11:23, however, Mark contrasts πίστις with the verb διακρίνω. This verb is commonly rendered 'doubt',[74] but in classical usage and often in the NT (Matt 16:3; Acts 11:2, 12; 15:9; James 2:4; Jude 9),[75] the passive or middle form of διακρίνω has to do with differentiation, evaluation or disagreement rather than 'doubt' *per se*. NT scholarship largely adopted the sense 'doubt' because of Latin translators' interpretation of the Greek verb in the NT.[76]

Mark employs διακρίνω only in 11:23, but it does appear in contrast to trust in James 1:7 and Rom 4:20–21.[77] In Rom 4:20, διακρίνειν is effected by ἀπιστία. These and similar passages, however, probably also include the idea of division, namely in the sense of a divided self not

---

69 Bolt, 'The Faith of Jesus Christ', 210–14; Marcus, *Mark 8–16*, 785, 794.
70 Cranfield, *Mark*, 361; Jeremias, *Theology*, 161, suggesting Jewish parallels for the construction (including Josephus *Ant*. 17.179; cf. 4 Macc 15:24; 16:22); Dowd, *Prayer*, 60–63; Gnilka, *Evangelium*, 2:134; Donahue and Harrington, *Mark*, 329; France, *Mark*, 448. Omitting the most debated NT cases (treated in e.g., Bird and Sprinkle, *Faith of Jesus*), cf. e.g., Phil 1:27; Col 2:12; 2 Thess 2:13.
71 Acts 14:9; 1 Cor 13:2; Phlm 5; Jms 2:1, 14, 18; Ignatius *Eph*. 14.1; Hermas 14.5; 34.3; 43.9; probably Rom 14:22; 1 Tim 1:19; cf. 2 Cor 4:13; 1 Tim 3:9; Barnabas 1.5. LXX usage is less decisive; 4 Macc 16:22 refers to the believer having faith; Jer 15:18, however, may refer to a liar lacking faithfulness.
72 See similarly Hooker, *Mark*, 269.
73 With e.g., Beavis, *Mark*, 88–89, on 4:35–6:56. On πιστία, see Dowd, 'Whatever You Ask', 207–9.
74 On parallelism here, see Standaert, *Evangile*, 832.
75 Cf. also Diognetus 5.1; 8.7; similarly in the active: 1 Cor 4:7; 6:5; 11:29, 31; 14:29; Didache 11.7; Ignatius *Eph*. 5.3; Hermas 51.1.
76 See Spitaler, 'Διακρίνεσθαι'.
77 Dowd, 'Whatever You Ask', 205. Interpreters often view Rom 4:20 as the first occasion of the sense 'doubt' (e.g., Anderson, *Glossary*, 239n105).

exclusively decided on a single course. The concept of the divided self appears elsewhere in ancient thought;[78] early Christians perhaps adopted the specific language of διακρίνω in contrast to faith because of usage in the Gospel tradition (now extant in Mark 11:23; Matt 21:21).

The expression here might thus suggest wavering or uncertainty (cf. Rom 14:23; Hermas 27.6; perhaps Jude 22), in contrast to the sort of certainty on which one might act especially after some clear assurance from God (cf. Acts 10:20; Hermas 2.2). (Cf. unwavering faith in Ps 26:1, although LXX 25:1 does not use the same wording as Mark, the LXX rendering the Hebrew term in different ways in different passages.) Given desperate expressions of faith in Mark,[79] not wavering might also include an element of firm commitment and expectation as opposed to being nonchalant as to whether or not God will act, or certainty grounded in God's character.

In contrast to modern subjective understandings of faith, ancient trust could involve a strong certainty and confirmation based on knowledge; Stoics contrasted this with mere opinion or surmise.[80]

2.3 Command

Mark 11:23 expresses faith in divine authorization especially by commanding. Commanding expresses confidence in the object's consequent compliance (without which shame would surely ensue). Jesus's example with the fig tree in the nearer context and his other commands elsewhere in this Gospel model the nature of such commands.

The imperatives 'take up' and 'be cast' in Mark 11:23 develop the concrete illustration of Jesus's power of speech in the preceding context. In 11:14, Jesus's optative φάγοι typically should express merely a wish, but his wish is apparently nature's command.[81] Peter thus speaks of Jesus's words to the fig tree as a curse (11:21).[82] People in antiquity recognized the potential efficacy of curses, like that of blessings (cf. e.g., Gen 27:12; Matt 10:13).[83] When David blessed the people in YHWH's name (1 Chron 16:2), he was implicitly calling on YHWH to bless them. Such biblical blessings and curses functioned as 'wish-prayers', words directed grammatically to the addressee but implicitly invoking God as the one who could make the words efficacious.[84]

Jesus's curse (11:21), the invitation to command by faith (11:23), and the invitation to pray with faith (11:24) are all closely connected. Like blessings and curses, divinely authorized commands could function as indirect prayers invoking God. Thus, for example, when Joshua commands the sun directly, the narrator explains that he spoke to YHWH (Josh 10:12).

As God's representatives, prophets also sometimes commanded, speaking by the word of the Lord, and their words were fulfilled (e.g., Elijah and Elisha 2 Kgs 1:10; 2:14, 21–22, 24; 4:43; 5:10). Like blessings and curses, then, OT prophetic speech could prove effectual. Thus Jeremiah is called to uproot and plant kingdoms by his prophesying (Jer 1:10; cf. Sir. 49:7); the image of

---

78   See e.g., Meeks, *Moral World*, 44 (citing Plutarch *Flatt.* 20, *Mor.* 61DF); Stowers, 'Paul and Self-Mastery', 529, 538; Sorabji, *Emotion and Peace of Mind*, 303–05 (esp. on Plato's divided soul; more generally, 303–15).
79   See Mark 1:40; 2:4–5; 5:28, 34; 7:28; 10:48; on this subject further, Cotter, *The Christ of the Miracle Stories*.
80   Arius Didymus *Epit.* 2.7.11m, p. 94.19–25, 33–35; 96.2–14.
81   Cf. Gen. Rab. 74:4 and *Pesiq. Rab.* 3:4, where words not expressed as a curse in Gen 31:32 nevertheless functioned as such, because all a pious patriarch's words act like decrees.
82   Perhaps because it reflects his hunger (11:12) rather than, as with most of his miraculous commands, another's need.
83   For efficacious curses, see e.g., Aeschylus *Seven Ag. Thebes* 70, 656, 695–97, 709; *Libation-Bearers* 912; T. Jud. 11:3–5; b. Taan. 23b.
84   E.g., *Ab. R. Nat.* 8 A; Wiles, *Paul's Intercessory Prayers*, 25–29, 71. Earlier Egyptians also expected their priests, and increasingly in this period magicians, to bless and curse efficaciously (Frankfurter, 'Curses, Blessings, and Ritual Authority', noting continuity of practice even to later Coptic monks).

uprooting fits the fate of the fig tree's dried roots (Mark 11:20).[85] Ezekiel obeys God's command to prophesy to bones and to the winds, and in his vision of the future it happens just as he commands (Ezek 37:4, 7, 9–10). Closer to the specific image that Jesus employs in Mark 11:23, God summons Ezekiel to prophesy even to mountains (Ezek 6:2–3; 36:1, 6; cf. Mic 6:2), although this action functions figuratively. (The real point is about judgment on humans and about the people that God will settle there.)[86]

Prophetic actions such as Elisha's may have helped shape some subsequent Jewish depictions of commands. The verbal element of miracle-working was not uncommon, though it appears most often as words of assurance.[87] Although accounts of Jewish wonder workers more often depict miracles through prayer than by command,[88] a number of accounts of commands appear. Thus later Amoraim declared that R. Simeon ben Yohai could fill a valley with gold dinars by command.[89] Supernaturally recognizing that a Cuthean was trying to trick him, R. Simeon b. Yohai also 'decreed' the Cuthean's death, thereby killing him.[90] R. Isaac b. Eliashib reportedly would exclaim, 'May they become poor', and those he addressed would become poor.[91] R. Eliezer ben Hyrcanus could pronounce a word and a field would be filled with cucumbers, and another word and the abundance would be reversed.[92] Conversely, a sage too audacious in demanding a miracle could be viewed as having profaned the divine name.[93]

Closer to Jesus's example in Mark, other rabbis could, as already noted, command trees to uproot (b. B. Meṣi'a 59ab) or fig trees to bear fruit (b. Ta'an. 24a).[94] Although these reports, unlike Mark's, do not stem from within living memory,[95] they do suggest how some regarded the power of the pious (cf. Acts 3:12). Closer to Mark's time, though without success, one populist prophet promised to make the walls of Jerusalem collapse 'at his command' (Josephus Ant. 20.170), and another promised that his command would part the Jordan (Josephus Ant. 20.97). Developing OT models of prophetic commands, Josephus depicts Moses commanding his rod to become a serpent (Ant. 2.287; contrast Exod 7:9–10). Belief in efficacious speech appears in a range of cultures.[96]

Mark and the Jesus tradition associate the efficacy of such commands not with personal piety generically, however, but with faith in God. Jesus provides the model for commands in Mark's Gospel, almost always in the context of ministry. Sometimes, no explicit command even proves necessary (6:41–43, 51; 7:29; 8:6–8), but on many occasions Jesus commands efficaciously.

Providing deliverance, Jesus commands the wind and the sea, and they obey (4:39–41). Examples of efficacious commands abound for healing and related matters:

---

85   LXX Jeremiah's verb ἐκριζόω appears in a version of Jesus's command-with-faith saying (Luke 17:6).
86   Despite addressing mountains, requests for them to fall on supplicants to hide the supplicants from God's anger (Hos 10:8; cf. Rev 6:16) are not said to be fulfilled and are certainly not expressions of faith.
87   Theissen, *Miracle Stories*, 58–59 (citing Mark 2:5; 5:36; 6:50; 7:29; 9:23; 10:49; Philostratus *Vit. Apoll.* 3.38; 4.10, 45; 7.38; Lucian *Lover of Lies* 11; Hymn of Isyllus in *IG* 4.128). Pythagoras can also converse with a river as if animate (Iamblichus *Vit. pyth.* 28.134).
88   Aune, 'Magic in Early Christianity', 1533–34; cf. Anderson, *Mark*, 97.
89   Y. Ber. 4a (9:1, §3); cf. *Exod. Rab.* 52:3.
90   Pesiq. R. Kah. 11:16; *Eccl. Rab.* 10:8 §1. *T. Jud.* 11:3–5 also depicts cursing with death.
91   B. Ta'an. 23b.
92   Ab. R. Nat. 25 A.
93   E.g., *y. Taan.* 3:10, §1.
94   Cf. Bultmann, *History*, 235; Telford, *Barren Temple*, 187–89; Marcus, *Mark 8–16*, 789. Cf. further y. Moed Kat. 3:1, §6.
95   On this concept, see e.g., Bauckham, *Jesus and the Eyewitnesses*, 30–32; Keener, *Christobiography*, 476–83.
96   E.g., traditional African culture also attributes supernatural power to words, especially those spoken by a greater to a lesser (Mbiti, *African Religions and Philosophies*, 257–58).

- 'Be made pure!' (1:41)
- 'I tell you, get up, take up your mat and go to your house' (2:11)
- 'Stretch out your hand' (3:5)
- 'Go in peace, and be healed of your disease' (5:34; cf. 5:29–30)
- 'Girl, I tell you: get up!' (5:41)
- 'Be opened!' (7:34)
- 'Go, your faith has restored you!' (10:51)

Jesus also effectively commands demons:

- 'Be silent, and come out of him!' (1:25; cf. 3:12)
- 'Come out of the man, you unclean spirit!' (5:8; cf. 5:9–13)
- 'I'm ordering you, come out of him and don't enter him anymore!' (9:25)

Casting (using the verb βάλλω) the mountain might evoke Jesus recently casting out (using the verb ἐκβάλλω) people in the temple (11:15). But most often in Mark's Gospel, the latter verb appears in accounts regarding expulsion orders to demons (1:34, 39; 7:26; cf. 1:25; 3:22–23; 5:8). Jesus also delegates this ministry of demon expulsion to his disciples (3:15; cf. 6:7, 13; 9:38), though some spirits would exit only through prayer (9:18, 28–29). Although Jesus presumably is not authorizing his disciples to cast down cosmic powers (cf. Jude 8–10), through faith they could expel even massive demonic powers on earth (such as Legion in Mark 5:9). Human evil remains; like Jesus himself, disciples face suffering at the hands of others (13:9–13). But spirits, even those that seem as fixed as mountains, must submit.

With the possible exception of cursing the fig tree, all Jesus's commands concerning nonhuman entities serve others who are in need.[97] The model in Mark's Gospel to this point is normally benevolent: commanding healing, commanding the wind to be still, and, probably most relevant for commanding something to be removed, commanding impure, evil spirits to leave people. (It is an exorcistic context to which Matthew applies the saying in Matt 17:20.)[98] The commands envisioned involve acts of faith in the process of serving.

3. Qualifying Jesus's teaching

Although the hyperbole suggests that faith has access to virtually unlimited power—God's omnipotence—its immediate and Markan context circumscribe its application. The saying invites greater faith and encourages the faithful in the outcome, but context specifies faithfulness's character.

In the OT, it is God who moves mountains (Exod 19:18; Job 9:5; Ps 68:8; 90:2; 97:5; 114:4–7; 144:5; Jer 4:24; Nah 1:5).[99] Thus faith appears to enable a believer to act on divine authority;[100] Jesus invites his agents to speak with God's own authority.[101] Such authorization (cf. Matt 8:8–10//Luke 7:7–9) contrasts with the folly of the wicked king in 2 Macc 9:8, who thought that he could control

---

97 Even cursing the fig tree, apart from its illustrative value, addressed hunger (11:12) in preparation for strenuous action for God (11:15). But Jesus does not usually act even for his own hunger; cf. Matt 4:3–10//Luke 4:3–12.
98 Exorcistic texts could include commands, such as one for wombs to stop 'wandering', in the name of some deity (Faraone, 'New Light on Ancient Greek Exorcisms of the Wandering Womb').
99 Marshall, *Faith*, 166. See also (for God suspending Sinai over the Israelites) Mekilta Bahodesh 3.123–25 (Lauterbach, 3:219); Tg. Ps.-Jon. on Exod 19:17.
100 Marshall, *Faith*, 166.
101 Marshall, *Faith*, 167. Cf. Exod 16:8; 1 Sam 8:7; Matt 10:40//Luke 10:16//John 13:20; 2 Cor 5:20.

mountains and sea as if he were God.

In Mark's theology, God acts most fully for those who have a trusting relationship with him, but faith serves rather than replaces divine action. The command in Mark 11:23 is not, 'Take yourself up and cast yourself'; the passives are probably divine passives, indicating trust in God's action.[102] The invitation to faith *in God* (11:22) precedes the invitation to acts of faith in 11:23. Faith does not *force* God to act contrary to his will (cf. 14:35), since such an approach would not express faith in the real God.[103] As earlier in Scripture, one's speech does not function as efficacious commands apart from God (Lam 3:37);[104] the efficacious command here may therefore presuppose a measure of inspiration, as suggested in my earlier comparison with OT prophetic speech.

Because the faith is in God (11:22), it is limited to God's will, and because Jesus provides the model, it is limited to acting on God's behalf. Jesus shares with his followers his own relationship with his Father, to act at his Father's command. The absolute faith Jesus teaches is the absolute trust in his Father that he models, a trust that is expressed in fulfilling the Father's mission and purpose.

This is *delegated*, not independent, authority. As Christopher Marshall's monograph on faith in Mark's Gospel suggests, Markan conditions for this promise include being 'commissioned to exercise delegated authority (cf. 3:14f; 6:7, 12f)' and 'an implicit perception of God's will', which 'presupposes revelatory insight into the divine intention'.[105] As suggested in the sequel to Luke's Gospel (and in the later appendix to Mark's), Jesus's agents act in his name, for his purposes (Acts 3:6, 16; 4:10, 30; 9:34; 14:3; 16:18; Mark 16:17; cf. John 14:12–13; Acts 19:13).[106] Such acting in Jesus's name continues a trajectory already evident in Mark's Gospel (Mark 9:38–39). In Mark's Gospel, as already noted, Jesus delegates much of his own authority, especially over demons (1:27), to his disciples (3:15; 6:7).

We may observe the same pattern in Mark's following verse. The promise of answered prayer in 11:24 appears in a Gospel that contrasts honorable and dishonorable requests. Jesus addresses the words of Mark 11:23–24 to disciples being trained for mission, and Mark 11:24's 'Everything you pray and ask for' (πάντα ὅσα προσεύχεσθε καὶ αἰτεῖσθε) is informed by previous narratives.

Mark 11:24 presupposes Jesus's followers carrying out his agendas, not requests reflecting selfish desires as in 10:37. Jesus (and ultimately the Father) refuse the selfish request for exaltation in 10:35 (ὃ ἐὰν αἰτήσωμέν), where Zebedee's sons want (θέλομεν in 10:35) Jesus to do (ποιήσῃς in 10:35) for them what they ask. On the Markan level, their language may recall an earlier request in 6:22–25 (cf. ὅ τι ἐάν με αἰτήσῃς in 6:23). There Herod promises Herodias's daughter what she wants (θέλῃς in 6:22), which turns out to be John's head (cf. θέλω in 6:25).

In contrast to such selfish desires, Jesus, Mark's model agent of God, subordinates his own wish to the Father's (οὐ τί ἐγὼ θέλω ἀλλὰ τί σύ, 14:36). Positively, Jesus also invites Bartimaeus to request what he wants Jesus to do for him (τί σοι θέλεις ποιήσω; 10:51). Unlike the requests of Herodias's daughter or Zebedee's sons, Bartimaeus's plea does not come at another's expense.[107] Neither should the prayers or blessings of others with 'faith in God' (11:22).

---

102 With Donahue and Harrington, *Mark*, 330; Boring, *Mark*, 325.
103 Schenke, *Markusevangelium*, 270.
104 For limitations even on curses, see e.g., Num 22:12; Deut 23:5; 2 Sam 16:12; Neh 13:2; Prov 26:2.
105 Marshall, *Faith*, 168; cf. also Dowd, 'Whatever You Ask'; Gnilka, *Evangelium*, 2:135.
106 One of the senses of acting in another's name was acting as their representative (e.g., 1 Sam 25:9), authorized with their authority (e.g., Esth 3:12; 8:8).
107 Certainly the emphasis on forgiveness in 11:25 precludes imprecation against people, despite the cursed tree (Dowd, 'Whatever You Ask', 250–51).

4. Conclusion

Jesus expects his disciples to continue his prophetic mission, commanding with the faith and inspiration by which he himself commanded, and by the faithful relationship that breeds confidence in God's power when following Jesus's love for people. They will thus at times command sickness, storms and spirits, acting as Jesus's agents and in accordance with his leading, in ways similar to those detailed later in Acts. In so doing, they follow the model Jesus had provided both in cursing the fig tree and in his miracles elsewhere in the Gospel.

Bibliography

Anderson, Hugh — *The Gospel of Mark* (NCB; London: Oliphants, 1976).

Anderson, R. Dean Jr., — *Glossary of Greek Rhetorical Terms Connected to Methods of Argumentation, Figures, and Tropes from Anaximenes to Quintilian* (Leuven: Peeters, 2000).

Aune, David E. — 'Magic in Early Christianity', in H. Temporini & W. Haase (eds.), *ANRW* 23.1:1507–57 (Part 2, *Principat*, 23.1; Berlin: de Gruyter, 1980), 1533–34.

Bauckham, Richard — *Jesus and the Eyewitnesses: The Gospels as Eyewitness Testimony* (2nd ed; Grand Rapids: Eerdmans, 2017).

Bayer, Hans F. — *Das Evangelium des Markus* (Historisch-Theologische Auslegung 4; Witten: SCM R. Brockhaus, 2008).

Beavis, Mary Ann — *Mark* (Paideia; Grand Rapids: Baker Academic, 2011).

Beck, John A. — 'A Lesson on Prayer from the Landscape', in Barry J. Beitzel (ed.), *Lexham Geographic Commentary on the Gospels* (Bellingham, WA: Lexham, 2017), 408–13.

Black, C. Clifton — *Mark* (ANTC; Nashville: Abingdon, 2011).

Blackburn, Barry L. — 'The Miracles of Jesus', in Bruce Chilton & Craig A. Evans (eds.), *Studying the Historical Jesus: Evaluations of the State of Current Research* (NTTS 19; Leiden: Brill, 1994), 353–94.

Blomberg, Craig L. — 'Quotations, Allusions, and Echoes of Jesus in Paul', in Matthew S. Harmon & Jay E. Smith (eds.), *Studies in the Pauline Epistles: Essays in Honor of Douglas J. Moo* (Grand Rapids: Zondervan, 2014), 129–43.

Bock, Darrell — *Mark* (New Cambridge Bible Commentary; New York: Cambridge University Press, 2015).

Boda, Mark J. — *The Book of Zechariah* (NICOT; Grand Rapids: Eerdmans, 2016).

Bolt, Peter G. — 'The Faith of Jesus Christ in the Synoptic Gospels and Acts', in Michael F. Bird & Preston M. Sprinkle (eds.), *The Faith of Jesus Christ: Exegetical, Biblical, and Theological Studies* (Peabody, MA: Hendrickson, 2009), 209–22.

Boring, M. Eugene — *Mark: A Commentary* (NTL; Louisville: Westminster John Knox, 2006).

Broadhead, Edwin K.	*Mark* (Readings: A New Biblical Commentary; Sheffield: Sheffield Academic Press, 2001).
Bultmann, Rudolf	*The History of the Synoptic Tradition* (John Marsh, trans.; 2nd ed.; Oxford: Blackwell, 1968).
Collins, Adela Yarbro	*Mark* (Hermeneia; Minneapolis: Fortress, 2007).
Cotter, Wendy J.	*The Christ of the Miracle Stories: Portrait through Encounter* (Grand Rapids: Baker Academic, 2010).
Cranfield, C. E. B.	*The Gospel According to Saint Mark* (rev. ed.; CGTC; Cambridge: Cambridge University Press, 1966).
Dodd, C. H.	*The Parables of the Kingdom* (rev. ed.; New York: Charles Scribner's Sons, 1961).
Donahue, John R., & Daniel J. Harrington	*The Gospel of Mark* (SP 2; Collegeville, MN: Liturgical Press, 2002).
Dowd, Sharyn Echols	*Prayer, Power, and The Problem of Suffering: Mark 11:22–25 in the Context of Markan Theology* (SBLDS 105; Atlanta: Scholars Press, 1988).
Dowd, Sharyn Echols	'"Whatever You Ask in Prayer, Believe" (Mark 11: 22–25): The Theological Function of Prayer and the Problem of Theodicy in Mark (Magic, Miracles, Omnipotence)' (PhD diss., Emory University, 1986).
Dunn, James D. G.	*A New Perspective on Jesus: What the Quest for the Historical Jesus Missed* (Grand Rapids: Baker, 2005).
Edwards, James R.	*The Gospel According to Mark* (Pillar NT Commentary; Grand Rapids: Eerdmans, 2002).
Evans, Craig A.	*Mark 8:27—16:20* (WBC 34B; Nashville: Thomas Nelson, 2001).
Faraone, Christopher A.	'New Light on Ancient Greek Exorcisms of the Wandering Womb', *ZPE* 144 (2003), 189–97.
France, R. T.	*The Gospel of Mark: A Commentary on the Greek Text* (NIGTC; Grand Rapids: Eerdmans, 2002).
Frankfurter, David	'Curses, Blessings, and Ritual Authority: Egyptian Magic in Comparative Perspective', *JANER* 5 (2005), 157–85.
Garland, David E.	*Mark* (NIVAC; Grand Rapids: Zondervan, 1996).
Gnilka, Joachim	*Das Evangelium nach Markus* (2 vols.; EKK 2; Neukirchen-Vluyn: Neukirchener, 1994).
Gould, Ezra P.	*A Critical and Exegetical Commentary on the Gospel According to St. Mark* (ICC; Edinburgh: T. & T. Clark, 1912).
Grassi, J.	'Ezekiel XXXVII.1–14 and the New Testament', *NTS* 11.2 (1965), 162–164.
Gray, Timothy C.	*The Temple in the Gospel of Mark: A Study in its Narrative Role* (WUNT 2.242; Tübingen: Mohr Siebeck, 2008).

Gundry, Robert	*Mark: A Commentary on his Apology for the Cross* (Grand Rapids: Eerdmans, 1993).
Healy, Mary	*The Gospel of Mark* (Catholic Commentary on Sacred Scripture; Baker Academic, 2008).
Herford, R. Travers	*Christianity in Talmud and Midrash* (London: Williams & Norgate, 1903).
Holmén, Tom	*Jesus and Jewish Covenant Thinking* (BIS 55; Leiden: Brill, 2001).
Holmén, Tom	'Doubts About Double Dissimilarity: Restructuring the Main Criterion of Jesus-of-History Research', in Bruce Chilton & Craig A. Evans (eds.), *Authenticating the Words of Jesus* (NTTS 28.1; Leiden: Brill, 1999), 47–80.
Hooker, Morna D.	*The Gospel According to Saint Mark* (BNTC; Grand Rapids: Baker Academic, 1991).
Hooker, Morna D.	*The Message of Mark* (London: Epworth, 1983).
Huebenthal, Sandra	*Reading Mark's Gospel as a Text from Collective Memory* (Grand Rapids: Eerdmans, 2020).
Jeremias, Joachim	*The Parables of Jesus* (2d rev. ed.; New York: Charles Scribner's Sons, 1972).
Jeremias, Joachim	*New Testament Theology* (New York: Scribner's, 1971).
Keener, Craig S.	*Christobiography: Memories, History, and the Reliability of the Gospels* (Grand Rapids: Eerdmans, 2019).
Keener, Craig S.	*Miracles: The Credibility of the New Testament Accounts* (2 vols.; Grand Rapids: Baker Academic, 2011).
Keener, Craig S.	*The Gospel of Matthew: A Socio-Rhetorical Commentary* (Grand Rapids: Eerdmans, 2009).
Lane, William L.	*The Gospel According to Mark* (NICNT; Grand Rapids: Eerdmans, 1974).
Loubser, J. A. (Bobby)	'How Al-Mokattam Mountain was moved: the Coptic imagination and the Christian Bible', in Gerald O. West & Musa W. Dube (eds.), *The Bible in Africa: Transactions, Trajectories and Trends* (Leiden: Brill, 2000), 103–26.
Marcus, Joel	*Mark 8—16: A New Translation with Introduction and Commentary* (Anchor Yale Bible 27A; New Haven: Yale, 2009).
Marshall, Christopher D.	*Faith as a Theme in Mark's Narrative* (SNTSMS 64; New York: Cambridge University Press, 1989).
Mbiti, John S.	*African Religions and Philosophies* (Garden City, N.Y.: Doubleday, 1970).
Meeks, Wayne A.	*The Moral World of the First Christians* (LEC 6; Philadelphia: Westminster, 1986).
Metzger, Bruce M.	*A Textual Commentary on the Greek New Testament* (New York: United Bible Societies, 1975).

Meyers, Carol L., & Eric M. Meyers	*Haggai, Zechariah 1—8* (New Haven: Yale University Press, 1987).
Moloney, Francis J.	*The Gospel of Mark: A Commentary* (Peabody: Hendrickson, 2002).
Moore, George Foot	*Judaism in the First Centuries of the Christian Era* (3 vols.; Cambridge, Mass.: Harvard University Press, 1927–30; repr., 2 vols.; New York: Schocken, 1971).
Morgan, Robert	*History of the Coptic Orthodox People and the Church of Egypt* (Victoria, B.C.: FriesenPress, 2016).
Nineham, D. E.	*Saint Mark* (Philadelphia: Westminster, 1977).
Nitzan, Bilhah	'4Q302/302A (Sap. A): Pap. Praise of God and Parable of the Tree. A Preliminary Edition', *RevQ* 17 (1996), 151–73.
Ortlund, Dane C.	'What Does It Mean to Cast a Mountain into the Sea? Another Look at Mark 11:23', *BBR* 28.2 (2018), 218–39.
Ouellette, Dana Joseph	'Driving Out Injustice: A Socio-Economic Interpretation of Mark 11:11–25 in Light of Mark's Listening Audience' (MA thesis, Trinity Western University, 2005).
Perrin, Norman	*Rediscovering the Teaching of Jesus* (New York: Harper & Row, 1967).
Pesch, Rudolf	*Das Markusevangelium* (2 vols.; HTKNT; Freiburg: Herder, 2000).
Richardson, Alan	*An Introduction to the Theology of the New Testament* (New York: Harper and Brothers, 1958).
Sanders, E. P.	*The Historical Figure of Jesus* (New York: Penguin, 1993).
Schenke, Ludger	*Das Markusevangelium: Literarische Eigenart-Text und Kommentierung* (Stuttgart: W. Kohlhammer, 2005).
Schnabel, Eckhard J.	*Mark: An Introduction and Commentary* (TNTC; Downers Grove: IVP Academic, 2017).
Schwarz, G.	'Pistin hōs kokkon sinapeōs', *Biblische Notizen* 25 (1984), 27–35.
Smith, Ralph L.	*Micah–Malachi* (WBC 32; Grand Rapids: Zondervan, 1984).
Sorabji, Richard	*Emotion and Peace of Mind: From Stoic Agitation to Christian Temptation* (Oxford: Oxford University Press, 2000).
Spitaler, Peter	'Διακρίνεσθαι in Mt. 21:21, Mk. 11:23, Acts 10:20, Rom. 4:20, 14:23, Jas. 1:6, and Jude 22—the "Semantic Shift" That Went Unnoticed by Patristic Authors', *NovT* 49 (1, 2007), 1–39.
Standaert, Benoît	*Evangile selon Marc Commentaire* (Études Bibliques, n.s. 61; 3 vols.; Pendé: Gabalda, 2010).
Stein, Robert H.	*Mark* (BECNT; Grand Rapids: Baker, 2008).

Stowers, Stanley K.	'Paul and Self-Mastery', in J. Paul Sampley (ed.), *Paul in the Greco-Roman World: A Handbook* (Harrisburg, Pa.: Trinity Press International, 2003), 524–50.
Such, W. A.	*The Abomination of Desolation in the Gospel of Mark: Its Historical Reference in Mark 13:14 and its Impact in the Gospel* (Lanham, MD: University Press of America, 1999).
Tan, Kim Huat	*Mark* (New Covenant Commentary Series; Eugene: Cascade, 2015).
Telford, William R.	*The Barren Temple and the Withered Tree: A redaction-critical analysis of the Cursing of the Fig-Tree pericope in Mark's Gospel and its relation to the Cleansing of the Temple tradition* (JSNTSup 1; Sheffield: JSOT Press, 1980).
Theissen, Gerd	*The Miracle Stories of the Early Christian Tradition* (Francis McDonagh, trans.; John Riches, ed.; Philadelphia: Fortress Press, 1983).
Theissen, Gerd, & Annette Merz	*The Historical Jesus: A Comprehensive Guide* (John Bowden, trans.; Minneapolis: Fortress, 1998).
Vena, Osvaldo D.	'The Markan Construction of Jesus as Disciple of the Kingdom', in Nicole W. Duran, Teresa Okure, & Daniel M. Patte (eds.), *Mark: Texts @ Contexts* (Minneapolis: Fortress, 2011), 71–99.
Watts, Rikki E.	'Mark', in G. K. Beale & D. A. Carson (eds.), *Commentary on the New Testament Use of the Old Testament* (Grand Rapids: Baker Academic, 2007), 111–249.
Watts, Rikki E.	*Isaiah's New Exodus in Mark* (Grand Rapids: Baker Academic, 2000; reprint WUNT 2.88; Tübingen: Mohr, 1997).
Wiles, Gordon P.	*Paul's Intercessory Prayers: The Significance of the Intercessory Prayer Passages in the Letters of St Paul* (SNTSMS 24; Cambridge: Cambridge University Press, 1974).
Witherington, Ben III	*The Gospel of Mark: A Socio-Rhetorical Commentary* (Grand Rapids: Eerdmans, 2001).
Wright, N. T.	*Mark for Everyone* (Louisville, KY: Westminster John Knox, 2004).
Wright, N. T.	*Jesus and the Victory of God* (Minneapolis: Fortress, 1996).
Yamauchi, Edwin M.	'Camels', in Edwin M. Yamauchi & Marvin R. Wilson (eds.), *Dictionary of Daily Life in Biblical and Post-Biblical Antiquity* (3 vols.; Peabody: Hendrickson, 2014), 1.247–52.

Craig S. Keener
Asbury Theological Seminary, Wilmore, Kentucky, USA.

Luke–Acts as Prophetic Proclamation

JOHN A. DAVIES

Abstract

Luke's identification of his project as a λόγος *logos* (Acts 1:1) has not been fully explored as to its implications for how we read the Gospel of Luke, and Acts. Luke's use of λόγος *logos* throughout his two-volume work to denote the divine proclamation should inform our reading of Acts 1:1. Luke writes in the tradition of biblical prophetic literature with a message about the culmination of God's purposes in the Jesus story. The parable of the soils (Luke 8) is played out in the narrative of Luke–Acts, notably in the Athens pericope (Acts 17), and the prophetic message, the λόγος *logos*, calls on its hearers to repent and live in accordance with God's purposes.

1. Introduction

How are we to categorise the Gospel of Luke and its sequel, the book of Acts? What form of literature did Luke understand he was writing—biography, historical monograph, apology, epic, novel, or something else—and are Luke and Acts to be treated as a unified literary work, and are we restricted to just one genre? A further question, less often asked, is, should we look only to classical Graeco-Roman models, or is the Hebrew corpus also a potentially fruitful point of comparison? This article in no way denies the influence of Graeco-Roman genres on Luke's project on which much has been written, but sees Luke as standing in the tradition of the OT prophets (who used a variety of genres), proclaiming the message of the Lord.

Ancient prologues tended to inform the reader what to expect in the ensuing document, so Luke's prologues, particularly that of the Gospel, have received considerable attention over the last century or so.[1] While the prologue to Luke (1:1–4) is probably intended to cover both the Gospel and Acts, in the manner of Greek multi-volume works, Acts includes a recapitulatory prologue (1:1–5, or perhaps 1:1–11) in which the author refers to the former account that he wrote: τὸν μὲν πρῶτον λόγον ἐποιησάμην *ton men prōton logon epoiēsamēn* (v. 1). Though the formal expectation

---

1 For a sampling of scholarship on Luke's prologues and their relation to the question of genre, see Cadbury, 'Commentary'; Talbert, *Literary Patterns*; Dillon, 'Previewing Luke's Project'; Pervo, *Profit with Delight*; Alexander, *Preface*, and 'Preface'; Moessner, 'Lukan Prologue'; Schmidt, 'Rhetorical Influences'; Aune, 'Luke 1.1–4'; Burridge, *What Are the Gospels?*, 185–212; Adams, *Genre*; Smith and Kostopoulos, 'Biography'; Aletti, *Birth*; Keener, *Christobiography*, 221–39; Pitts, *History*.

set up by μέν *men* ('on the one hand') is not followed through (there is no balancing δέ *de* 'on the other hand'), by implication the sequel to the Gospel, Acts, is also to be identified as a λόγος *logos*. Where a prologue was included in Greek literature, it often identified the nature of the work (e.g. as βίος *bios*, biography, or ἱστορία *historia*, history), yet Luke's identification of his project as a λόγος *logos* has been largely glossed over in the commentaries, a curious omission in view of the fact that almost every other word in Luke's prologues has been scrutinised for what light it might shed on his method and purpose.[2] English translations for λόγος *logos* in Acts 1:1 include 'book' (NRSV, NIV, ESV, NLT), 'treatise' (AV), 'narrative' (HCSB), 'account' (NET), and 'volume' (Message), though we note that Luke elsewhere uses βίβλος *biblos* or βιβλίον *biblion* 'scroll, book' for the books of Isaiah, Psalms, and 'the prophets' (Luke 3:4; 20:42; Acts 1:20; 7:42–43; cf. also John 20:30).

At first glance, λόγος *logos* seems unpromising as an indicator of content, since it can be of such general meaning. Any first year Greek student will tell us that λόγος *logos* means 'word', though it is hard to find λόγος *logos* used in the singular with the unambiguous sense of a single word, a lexeme. A λόγος *logos* is a communication of indeterminate length. We might be better glossing it in the first instance more neutrally as 'utterance, expression, speech' if delivered orally, or 'text, document' if referring to a written account. If one needed specifically to designate a lexeme in Greek, one might do so with ὄνομα *onoma* (particularly for a noun) or ῥῆμα *rhēma* (particularly for a verb), though both ὄνομα *onoma* and ῥῆμα *rhēma* also have wider uses. Aristotle uses λόγος *logos*, in distinction from ῥῆμα *rhēma* and ὄνομα *onoma*, of a sentence-level utterance.[3] An instructive example from the NT is Matt. 12:36: 'I tell you, on the day of judgment you will have to give an account (λόγος *logos*) for every careless word (ῥῆμα *rhēma*) you utter' (NRSV).[4] A λόγος *logos* might then be a very brief communication, or it could be an extended speech or a long document. Depending on context, it could be a question, a request, a command, an oracle, an answer, a philosophical proposition, a wise maxim (BDAG 1aβ). If somewhat longer it could refer to a story or a lecture. If written, a whole philosophical treatise could be called a λόγος *logos* (BDAG 1b). λόγος *logos* might also refer to the matter that is the subject of discourse rather than the language used to describe it (Acts 8:21; 15:6).

More pertinently for our purposes, λόγος *logos* can have the special sense of a historical account, a narrative of things that are believed to have occurred. Herodotus uses it a number of times to refer to his history, for example, 'The part of it which had reference to the Argives I will record when I reach that place in the history (λόγος *logos*)'.[5] Or λόγος *logos* could be used for a section of a longer historical work.[6] Plato uses λόγος *logos* in opposition to μῦθος *mythos*; history in distinction from legend. He has Socrates say in the *Timaeus* (26e): 'the fact that it is no invented fable but genuine history (ἀληθινὸν λόγον *alēthinon logon*) is all-important'.

2. The Prophetic λόγος *logos* of God

Andrew Pitts notes that the prologue to Acts (like that of the Gospel) is an 'outline of the subsequent discourse', the progress of the gospel.[7] It would then be worth asking, how does

---

2   Keener, for example, has no discussion of the word, other than to gloss it as 'volume', in his extensive treatment of the opening verse: *Acts*, 646–60.
3   Aristotle, *De interpretatione* 16b. Cf. Louw and Nida, *Greek-English Lexicon* §33.98.
4   Unless otherwise indicated, all Bible translations are my own.
5   Herodotus, *Histories* 6.19; cf. 2.123; 7.152.
6   Herodotus, *Histories* 2.38; 6.39.
7   Pitts, *History*, 81.

Luke use the word λόγος *logos* elsewhere? Luke uses λόγος *logos* in the singular twenty times in the Gospel, and fifty-six times in Acts. I am restricting the scope to the singular because λόγοι *logoi* in the plural is commonly used to refer to the content of any speech event and it is not possible from such usage to determine the extent of an individual component λόγος *logos*. Jesus says, for example, in Luke 6:47, 'I will show you what someone is like who comes to me, hears my utterances (λόγοι *logoi*), and acts on them'. Some of these plurals may well fit within Luke's idiomatic nuance of λόγος *logos* discussed below.

Luke uses λόγος *logos* in varied ways like those just mentioned. It can denote a question (Luke 20:3), a proposal (Acts 6:5), a report (Luke 5:15; 7:17; Acts 7:29; 11:22), a command (Luke 7:7), a complaint (Acts 19:38), or a speech act in general (Luke 1:29; 12:10; 20:20; Acts 14:12). But Luke uses λόγος *logos* in one particular way far more than any other NT writer as a designation for the gospel message, the proclamation of Jesus himself and then of his agents. One of Luke's common expressions (fourteen times) is ὁ λόγος τοῦ θεοῦ *ho logos tou theou*, traditionally 'the word of God' (Luke 5:1; 8:11, 21; 11:28; Acts 4:31; 6:2, 7; 8:14; 11:1; 13:5, 7, 46; 17:13; 18:11), or ὁ λόγος τοῦ κυρίου *ho logos tou kyriou*, 'the word (or proclamation) of the Lord', a further nine times (Acts 8:25, 13:44, 48, 49; 15:35, 36; 16:32; 19:10, 20). In the Gospel examples the expression is not found in the synoptic parallels, so it is Luke's own contribution. It is what crowds came to hear from Jesus (Luke 5:1). It is what the twelve understood to be their primary endeavour after the ascension of Jesus and the coming of the Spirit (Acts 6:2). It is what the apostles proclaimed in synagogues or in homes or before Roman officials or practically an entire city (Acts 13:5, 7; 13:44; 16:32). It is what Paul taught the believers in Corinth for eighteen months (Acts 18:11). To these we could add 'your λόγος *logos*' when addressed to God in prayer (Acts 4:29), or 'his λόγος *logos*', or 'this λόγος *logos*', referring to the teaching of Jesus (Luke 4:32, 36; 10:39; 24:19). The high usage of such an idiom is notable in view of the fact that the other Gospels each have only one reference to the λόγος *logos* of God / the Lord (Matt. 15:6 // Mark 7:13; John 10:35).

What is meant by the λόγος *logos* of God? It is widely recognised that Luke is immersed in and imitates the language of the Septuagint (LXX), where 'the λόγος *logos* of God / the Lord' is an expression for a prophetic oracle (e.g. 2 Sam. 16:23; 24:11; 1 Kgs 12:22).[8] A number of the writing prophets with their more extended proclamations declare their works to be the λόγος κυρίου *logos kyriou* 'the message of the Lord' (Hos. 1:1; Amos 5:1; Mic. 1:1; Joel 1:1; Zeph. 1:1; Hag. 1:1; Zech. 1:1; Mal. 1:1).[9]

We should ask, what sort of genitive is in Luke's use of ὁ λόγος τοῦ θεοῦ / κυρίου *ho logos tou theou / kyriou*? A possible construal of the λόγος *logos* of somebody is as a subjective genitive. If that were the case, it would mean that God, or the Lord, had spoken those very words. That would be claiming too much for most of the uses of λόγος *logos*, as when it refers to apostolic preaching. For an actual quote, or direct revelation, Luke uses either the plural λόγοι *logoi* or else he uses ῥῆμα *rhēma* rather than λόγος *logos* (Luke 3:2; 22:61; Acts 11:16; 20:35). This usage is consistent with the LXX preference for ῥῆμα κυρίου *rhēma kyriou* when recounting direct divine revelation to prophets in the historical books (e.g., Gen. 15:1; Num. 22:18; 1 Sam. 3:1, 7; 15:10; 1 Kgs 2:27; 15:29; 1 Esd. 2:1).

A better understanding of the genitive in the 'λόγος *logos* of God' in Luke-Acts is a genitive of origin and relationship in a more general sense.[10] God is the originator of the proclamation in that it gives expression to God's saving plan. This would seem to fit Luke's use where no immediate divine

---

8   See Sparks, 'Semitisms'; Fitzmyer, *Luke*, 107–27; Smith, 'When Did the Gospels Become Scripture?'.
9   See Shead, *A Mouth Full of Fire*.
10 Blass and Debrunner, *Greek Grammar* §162, 89–90.

revelation is said to be involved. Since λόγος *logos* can designate the referent of a speech act—the matter under discussion—as well as the speech act itself, there may be a suggestion that God's λόγος *logos* is the account of the events of which God is the agent. This is the implication of Luke's use of the phrase περὶ τῶν πεπληροφορημένων *peri tōn peplērophorēmenōn* in Luke 1:1, 'the events that have been fulfilled' (NRSV). This suggests there has been a plan, and indeed Luke speaks a number of times of ἡ βουλὴ (τοῦ θεοῦ) *hē boulē (tou theou)* '(God's) plan', as it comes to fruition in Jesus (Luke 7:30; Acts 2:23; 4:28; 13:36; 20:27).[11] While by no means alone among NT writers, Luke repeatedly draws attention to the fact that what is happening in the life and death of Jesus, his resurrection, and the coming of the Spirit, is just as the prophets foretold (Luke 4:17–21; 18:31; 22:37; 24:25–27, 44–47; Acts 2:16–21; 3:18, 24; 8:30–35; 10:43; 13:27; 15:15–18; 26:22; 28:23; 28:25–27).

A third possibility for the genitive in ὁ λόγος τοῦ κυρίου *ho logos tou kyriou* is a genitive of content: 'the proclamation concerning the Lord'.[12] Given the ambiguous referent of κύριος *kyrios*, 'Lord', as either God or Jesus, the λόγος of the Lord, in the context of Acts, could mean the message that has Jesus and his ministry as its subject matter. Perhaps a combination of genitive of origin and genitive of content is appropriate for the proclamation that both stems from Jesus and concerns him.

Prophetic speech in the name of the Lord purports to give God's perspective of how things are, how they ought to be, and how they will be when God accomplishes his purpose. Isaiah and Jeremiah, for example, include in their prophetic works historical narrative, as well as warning, exhortation, encouragement, and prediction. Their proclamations concern the destiny of Israel and through them the nations. They concern God's governance of the world, particularly in the face of the threat posed by empires, or God's use of those empires for his purposes. The prophets' proclamations of God's message come with an imperative, expressed or implied by references to a coming judgement, a call for a response of faith and faithfulness (Isa. 31:6; 45:22; Jer. 5:3; 7:28; 18:11; Ezek. 14:6; 18:30; Hos. 4:1; 5:1; 6:1; Joel 1:15; 2:12; Amos 5:4, 14; Mic. 3:9; Zeph. 2:3). There is also an eschatological expectation that in a coming age of salvation, 'the proclamation of the LORD' would issue forth from Jerusalem (Isa. 2:3).

Luke uses λόγος *logos* in a way that closely reflects LXX usage. When the crowds came to hear the λόγος *logos* of God from Jesus' lips (Luke 5:1), it was because they saw him as a prophet in the biblical tradition (Luke 7:16; cf. 4:24; 5:1; 24:19; Acts 3:22–23; 7:37).[13] Jesus' proclamation, like that of his prophetic predecessors, concerns God's coming kingdom and the appropriate response to it: one of hearing, with the Hebraic nuance of heeding, of repentance and persevering faith. Joel Green writes, 'the Lukan narrative is an invitation to embrace an alternative worldview and to live as if the reign of God had already revolutionized this age'.[14] The prophecy from Isa. 2 cited above would appear to lie behind Jesus' commission to his disciples in Luke 24:47–48 that their witness was to begin in Jerusalem, and his further instruction to wait in Jerusalem for the Spirit (Acts 1:4), and so to set the agenda for the Book of Acts, the journey of the victorious λόγος *logos* from Jerusalem to Rome (Acts 1:8; 28:16).[15]

Besides his frequent use of the prophetic phrase 'the λόγος *logos* of God / the Lord', Luke has

---

11 Luke also uses πληροῦν for the fulfilment of prophecy in the ministry of Jesus (Luke 4:21; 24:44; Acts 1:16; 3:18; 13:27). For the theme of the outworking of God's plan in Luke-Acts as the fulfilment of prophecy, see Squires, *Plan*, 121–54; Tannehill, 'Story'.
12 Blass and Debrunner, *Greek Grammar* §167, 92.
13 Patterson, 'Old Testament Prophecy', adopts 'proclamation' as the overarching prophetic genre of the Hebrew Bible.
14 Green, *Luke*, 11.
15 See O'Reilly, *Word and Sign*; Pao, *Acts*, 156–59; Hill, 'God's Speech', 209–12.

other affinities with prophetic literature.[16] As with biblical prophecy (e.g. Num. 24:2, 13; 1 Kgs 22:5, 24; 2 Sam. 23:2), there is a close connection between the proclamation of the prophetic message and the work of the Spirit.[17] When Jesus read from the scroll of Isaiah, beginning with the words 'The Spirit of the Lord is upon me' (Luke 4:18), and declared that it was being fulfilled in the hearing of the synagogue attendees (v. 21), he identified himself with the prophets (v. 24). When that same Spirit fell upon the church on the day of Pentecost (Acts 2:4) the effect was to enable prophetic speech on the part of all (Acts 2:17–18) and a lengthy proclamation (λόγος logos) from Peter (Acts 2:41). In Acts 4:31 we read that the members of the gathered community of believers 'were all filled with the Holy Spirit and spoke the λόγος logos of God with boldness'. The Spirit is also an agent of the reception of the λόγος logos: 'While Peter was still speaking, the Holy Spirit fell upon all who heard the proclamation (λόγος logos)' (Acts 10:44; cf. 15:7, 8). And the Holy Spirit can at times redirect the proclamation of the λόγος logos, as when the Spirit (for the moment) prevented Paul and his group going to Asia, and they went instead to Phrygia and Galatia (Acts 16:6).

Like the OT prophets, Luke sets the coming kingdom of God in the context of the dominant world power of the day. The message has clear political implications. Mary declares, '[God] brings down the mighty from their thrones, and lifts up the lowly' (Luke 1:52), and Zechariah rejoices in the prophecies, now coming to fruition, that 'we would be saved from our enemies and from the power of all who hate us' (Luke 1:71). The Jesus story is explicitly set against the backdrop of the reigns of the Roman emperors Augustus and Tiberius (named only in Luke: Luke 2:1; 3:1). Not only does Jesus constantly proclaim the kingdom (or empire) of God, but he deals with the interaction of God's sovereignty with that of the emperor (Luke 20:20–26). From the outset of the book of Acts (1:6–7), the reader, like the disciples, is given cause to ask when the announced kingdom will be restored to Israel and what this might mean. Jesus' followers gained a reputation for 'turning the world upside down' and 'acting contrary to the decrees of Caesar, saying that there is another emperor, namely Jesus' (Acts 17:6–7). After numerous interactions with Roman officials, the story of Acts ends with the proclamation of the kingdom of God in the capital city itself (Acts 28:31). While many have puzzled over this ending (we are left wondering what happened to Paul), if the purpose of Acts is to recount the progress of the λόγος logos from Jerusalem to Rome, it is the perfect ending.[18] There is no overt anti-imperial polemic such as a dirge for the emperor (cf. Ezek 28:11–19), but the message of a time of alleviation, a universal restoration at the coming of messiah as foretold in the prophets (Acts 3:20–21), signals the end of all oppressive regimes.

There may be no 'thus says the Lord' or 'the word of the Lord came to Luke'. Luke prefers to let his characters do the talking, pre-eminently Jesus, the Prophet *par excellence*. We ought not think that exactly the same formulae need to be employed, as the biblical prophets themselves use a variety of modes of expression. But if the believing community has now been endowed with the Spirit, and after a long absence the promised age of prophetic inspiration has dawned (Acts 2:17–18), it is no surprise that Luke (along with others) should think there ought now to be a written account (Luke 1:3) of the climax of salvation history in the spirit of the biblical prophets.[19] Israel's

---

16 Johnson notes the 'prophetic structure' of Luke-Acts and the centrality of the portrayal of Jesus as Prophet: *Luke*, 17–21, 119–20. See also O'Reilly, *Word and Sign*, 30–32, for Jesus' baptism as his prophetic anointing. Borman outlines Luke's interest in and extensive treatment of the revival of prophecy: 'Rewritten Prophecy'.
17 See Marguerat, *The First Christian Historian*, 109–28.
18 Marguerat, *The First Christian Historian*, 205–30.
19 For the belief that prophecy had ceased in the Second Temple period but was expected to return, see Psa. 74:9; 1 Macc. 9:27; 14:41; Keener, *Acts*, 886–911. For the idea that Luke was consciously writing in continuity with Scripture, see Barrett, 'The First New Testament?'; Hill, 'God's Speech'; Kruger, *Question*, 47–78. It would seem that Luke was regarded as Scripture at least from the time of the writing of 1 Tim. 5:18 (cf. Luke 10:7).

story, as read in synagogues in the Second Temple period, was 'a story in search of a conclusion'.[20] The coming of the one who announced 'the kingdom of God has reached you' (Luke 10:11) brings that story to its goal. The sufferings and subsequent glory of Jesus are the fulfilment of all that the prophets foretold (Luke 24:25–27, 44–47).[21] In particular, Luke stresses the long-foretold inclusion of Gentiles in the people of God (Luke 24:47; Acts 2:39; 3:25–26; 10:34–43; 13:47; 15:16–18).[22] And God's redemptive acts, as they have always done, call for prophetic proclamation.

Luke is also not lacking in predictive prophecy designed both to warn and to encourage. In this regard, Jesus reinforces the things that stand written (τὰ γεγραμμένα *ta gegrammena*, Luke 21:22). In particular, the prophetic message of eschatological judgement and blessing reaches its climax in the teaching of Jesus and the apostles concerning the role Jesus is to have in calling the world to account (Luke 9:26, 27; 10:11–15; 11:30–32; 12:8–12; 13:29–30; 14:14; 17:22–31; 21:7–28; Acts 1:11; 17:31). Likewise the numerous references in Luke-Acts to the fulfilment of prophecy are a feature of the historical books of the Hebrew Bible ('Former Prophets' in Jewish tradition) with such phrases as 'according to the declaration of the Lord' (e.g. 1 Kgs 14:18; 15:29; 17:16).

Like a biblical prophet, Luke is notable for his appeals for repentance. The verb μετανοεῖν *metanoein* and noun μετάνοια *metanoia* are found twenty-three times in Luke-Acts which account for almost half of the uses in the NT. Jesus declares: 'I have come to call not the righteous but sinners to repentance' (Luke 5:32; the words 'to repentance' are Luke's additions to Mark's wording, Mark 2:17). In his final resurrection appearance, Jesus commissions his disciples with these words (only in Luke), 'Thus it is written, that the Messiah is to suffer and to rise from the dead on the third day, and that repentance and forgiveness of sins should be proclaimed in his name to all nations' (Luke 24:45–47). In the NT, only in Acts is the verb μετανοεῖν *metanoein* 'repent' found in the imperative in apostolic proclamation (Acts 2:38; 3:19; 8:22; cf. Isa. 46:8 LXX). The prophets link their call for repentance for failing to heed the proclamation of God with judgement (Jer. 8:6–9; Ezek. 18:30; Zech. 1:6). So also Luke: 'The people of Nineveh will rise up at the judgement with this generation and condemn it, because they repented at the proclamation of Jonah, and see, something greater than Jonah is here!' (Luke 11:32; cf. 10:14; 13:3, 5; 22:30; Acts 10:42; 17:30–31; 24:25).[23] As in the prophets, repentance is no mere volitional reorientation, but a changed lifestyle (Luke 3:8; Acts 26:20).

3. The Parable of the Soils

Luke presents a paradigmatic account of the λόγος *logos* of God and its reception in his treatment of the parable of the soils (Luke 8:5–15; cf. Mark 4:3–20). This proclamation, represented by the seed sown in different soils (Luke 8:11), meets with a range of receptions by those who hear it. Some hear, but have the message snatched away from their hearts by the devil (v. 12); some receive it with joy, but lacking root, 'they believe for a while and in a time of testing fall away' (v. 13); some 'are choked by life's worries and riches and pleasures, and their fruit does not mature' (v. 14). But a final group responds to the λόγος *logos* by holding it fast 'with a noble and good heart,

---

20 Wright, *New Testament*, 217.
21 Luke has a greater interest in the fulfilment of prophecy than the other Gospels; see Aune, *New Testament*, 133–34; Peterson, 'Motif'.
22 Jervell, 'Future'.
23 While the focus is on a different literary background, there are points of contact between this prophetic reading of Luke and that of Moles, 'Luke's Preface', who sees the Greek decree as the model for Luke's project.

and bear fruit with patient endurance' (v. 15). The parable of the soils is the first extended parable. Prior to this there are only two single-verse sayings identified as parables (Luke 5:36; 6:39). With its explanation, the parable is programmatic for the response to all of Jesus' teaching and the community of faith he gathers around himself.[24] In his pre-crucifixion exhortation to his disciples, Jesus echoed the parable's call for perseverance with the words, 'By your endurance you will gain your lives' (Luke 21:19). Following (only in Luke) and closely associated with the parable of the soils is the pericope about Jesus' mother and brothers (Luke 8:19–21) which concludes with Jesus' words: 'My mother and my brothers are those who hear the proclamation (λόγος logos) of God and do it' (v. 21; wording unique to Luke).[25] Hearing is the 'better part', chosen by Mary of Bethany (Luke 10:42). It is what brings blessing (Luke 11:28).

4. Luke's Absolute Use of λόγος *logos* as Gospel Proclamation

In the parable the seed that is sown is initially identified as the λόγος *logos* of God (Luke 8:11) where 'of God' is a Lukan addition (cf. Mark 4:14), but thereafter it is simply ὁ λόγος *ho logos* 'the proclamation' (Luke 8:12, 13, 15), so providing the key to our understanding of this absolute expression elsewhere in Luke-Acts. There are at least a further ten absolute uses of ὁ λόγος *ho logos* in Luke-Acts, that is, without further qualification. It is simply the account, the proclamation, or perhaps the Proclamation. Just as Luke uses ἡ ὁδός *hē hodos* 'the Way' (Acts 9:2; 19:9, 23; 22:4; 24:14, 22) as a shorthand for 'the Way of the Lord / God' (Acts 18:25, 26), so ὁ λόγος *ho logos* serves as a shorthand and semi-technical expression for God's story, God's proclamation.[26]

The prologue to the Gospel incorporates just such an absolute use of ὁ λόγος *ho logos*. Luke makes reference to 'those who from the beginning were eyewitnesses and servants of the λόγος *logos*' (Luke 1:2), that is, those who told their account of the ministry and message of Jesus as they had observed it. This is the only occurrence of λόγος *logos* used absolutely ahead of the parable of the soils, so the elaboration of the phrase awaits that parable and its explanation. We might compare the phrase 'servants of the λόγος *logos*' with a somewhat parallel expression in Acts 6:4 where the twelve identify their role as being 'in the service of the λόγος *logos*'. Luke also refers to the twelve as 'witnesses' in Luke 24:48, forming a conceptual *inclusio* around the Gospel, and also has Paul identify himself as one who has been appointed as a 'servant and witness' (Acts 26:16). So Luke undoubtedly at least intends to include the apostles among his eyewitnesses.

> Further absolute uses of ὁ λόγος *ho logos* are as follows:
> 'But many of those who heard the proclamation believed' (Acts 4:4).
> 'Now those who were scattered went from place to place, proclaiming the message' (Acts 8:4).
> 'You know the proclamation he sent to the people of Israel, gospeling peace by Jesus Messiah—he is Lord of all' (Acts 10:36).
> 'While Peter was still speaking, the Holy Spirit fell upon all who heard the proclamation' (Acts 10:44).
> 'They spoke the proclamation to no one except Jews' (Acts 11:19).
> 'When they had spoken the proclamation in Perga, they went down to Attalia' (Acts 14:25).
> 'They went through the region of Phrygia and Galatia, having been forbidden by the Holy

---

24 Johnson, *Luke*, 133–35.
25 Marshall, *Luke*, 317–18.
26 See Pao, *Acts*, 59–68; Keener, *Acts*, 1626–27.

Spirit to speak the proclamation in Asia' (Acts 16:6).

'These Jews were more receptive than those in Thessalonica, for they welcomed the proclamation very eagerly and examined the scriptures every day to see whether these things were so' (Acts 17:11).

'When Silas and Timothy arrived from Macedonia, Paul was occupied with proclaiming the message, testifying to the Jews that the Messiah was Jesus' (Acts 18:5).

A few times the word λόγος *logos* has further descriptors added. Paul tells those in the synagogue at Pisidian Antioch: 'to us the proclamation of this salvation has been sent' (Acts 13:26). At Iconium the Lord 'testified to the proclamation of his grace by granting signs and wonders to be done' through Paul and Barnabas (Acts 14:3; cf. 20:32).

λόγος *logos* is also closely tied to the gospel. Twice it is the object of the verb εὐαγγελίζεσθαι *euangelizesthai*: 'Now those who were scattered went from place to place, gospeling the proclamation' (εὐαγγελιζόμενοι τὸν λόγον *euangelizomenoi ton logon*, Acts 8:4; cf. 15:35). Speaking the λόγος *logos* is also found in parallel with gospeling (Acts 8:25; 10:36). Once we have the expression 'the proclamation of the gospel' (τὸν λόγον τοῦ εὐαγγελίου *ton logon tou euangeliou*, Acts 15:7), where τοῦ εὐαγγελίου *tou euangeliou* is best taken as a genitive of apposition—the proclamation that is the gospel.[27] It is noteworthy that Luke only uses the noun εὐαγγέλιον *euangelion* twice (unless we read the Western text at Acts 1:2), each time from the mouth of one of his characters, Peter or Paul.[28] The phrase 'the message of the gospel' (τὸν λόγον τοῦ εὐαγγελίου *ton logon tou euangeliou*) is spoken by Peter at the Jerusalem Council. The other instance of εὐαγγέλιον *euangelion* is found at Acts 20:24 where Paul is farewelling the Ephesian elders: 'But I do not count my life of any value to myself, if only I may finish my course and the ministry that I received from the Lord Jesus, to testify to the gospel (εὐαγγέλιον *euangelion*) of God's grace'. Where other NT writers use εὐαγγέλιον *euangelion*, Luke prefers λόγος *logos*, seemingly avoiding εὐαγγέλιον *euangelion* even when his source uses it (cf. Mark 1:14–15 // Luke 4:14–15; Mark 8:35 // Luke 9:24; Mark 10:29 // Luke 18:29). Where Mark introduces his Gospel with 'The beginning of the good news (εὐαγγέλιον *euangelion*)', Luke has the word λόγος *logos* twice in his introduction (Luke 1:2, 4). In his two uses of εὐαγγέλιον *euangelion* then, Luke is probably reflecting his understanding of Petrine and Pauline idiom; in 1 Pet. 4:17 obedience to God's εὐαγγέλιον *euangelion* is the criterion for the final judgement, while in Paul's letters it is the characteristic word for the message he proclaims (e.g. Rom. 1:1; 1 Cor. 4:15; 2 Cor. 2:12; Gal. 1:6; Phil. 1:5; 1 Thess. 1:5; 2 Thess. 1:8). So for Luke, the constitutive noun for the proclamation of the early church is not εὐαγγέλιον *euangelion* but λόγος *logos*.

Over half of Luke's uses of λόγος *logos* in the singular are in this specialised sense of the prophetic proclamation by and concerning Jesus. This does not include those uses where there is room for ambiguity or *double entendre*. Acts 20:7 tells us that Paul 'continued speaking until midnight', or did he 'extend the proclamation' (τὸν λόγον *ton logon*)? Peter asks the centurion Cornelius, 'Now may I ask why (τίνι λόγῳ *tini logō*) you sent for me?' (Acts 10:29). Or, in view of the fact that Cornelius speaks by way of explanation of 'all that the Lord has commanded you to say' (Acts 10:33), is the reader to perceive a hidden nuance in Peter's question, 'for what proclamation ...'? Luke's high usage of ὁ λόγος *ho logos* to refer to the gospel proclamation may be contrasted with its far less frequent use elsewhere in the NT (Gal. 6:6; Phil. 1:14 (some mss); 2 Tim. 4:2; Jas 1:22, 23; 1 Pet. 2:8).

---

27 Blass and Debrunner, *Greek Grammar* §167, 92.
28 The Western Text (D) adds και εκελευσε κηρυσσειν το ευαγγελιον 'and commanded to preach the gospel'.

Luke uses an array of verbs with λόγος *logos* as object. Most commonly, it is simply spoken (λαλεῖν *lalein*, the verb commonly used in the LXX with λόγος κυρίου *logos kyriou* 'the message of the Lord'; Acts 4:29, 31; 8:25; 11:19; 13:46; 14:25; 16:6, 32). As noted above, it can be 'gospeled' (εὐαγγελίζεσθαι *euangelizesthai*, Acts 8:4; 15:35). It can also be sent out (ἐξαποστέλλειν *exapostellein*, Acts 13:26), or announced (καταγγέλλειν *katangellein*, Acts 13:5; 15:36; 17:13), or taught (διδάσκειν *didaskein*, Acts 15:35; 18:11). One can testify to the λόγος *logos* (μαρτυρεῖν *martyrein* + dative; Acts 14:3) or be wholly occupied in it (συνέχειν *synechein* + dative, Acts 18:5).

The λόγος *logos* can itself also be an active player, so much so that it is possible to regard the λόγος *logos* as the principal character in the plot of Acts.[29] A refrain runs through that book telling of the continued progress of the proclamation. Like a living organism, it grows and spreads, advances and becomes strong (αὐξάνεσθαι *auxanesthai*, Acts 6:7; 12:24; 19:20; πληθύνειν *plēthynein*, Acts 12:24; διαφέρεσθαι *diapheresthai*, Acts 13:49; ἰσχύειν *ischyein*, Acts 19:20). One is put in mind of the hundredfold increase of the seed sown in good soil (Luke 8:8). People are described as being eyewitnesses of the λόγος *logos* (Luke 1:2) and in the service of the λόγος *logos* (Luke 1:2; Acts 6:4). Like the powerful creative speech acts of God in Genesis 1, this λόγος *logos* comes with authority (Luke 4:32, 36) and brings life (Acts 13:46, 48). It is powerfully active in building up a community of believers and giving them an inheritance among all who are sanctified (Acts 20:32). The λόγος *logos* of the Lord itself becomes the object of praise (Acts 13:48; elsewhere only God or Jesus receives praise). Such hypostatised usages may be seen as a step along the road to John's more developed theology of the incarnate λόγος *Logos* (John 1:1, 14) and were so regarded in the early church.[30]

For Luke, the proclamation of Jesus and of his agents is in continuity with and fulfilment of the story and message of Israel's Scriptures, the sacred history that points to and culminates in the death, resurrection, and ascension of Jesus (Acts 1:4).[31] There is consistently a strong narrative component to the proclamation of the early church. Luke uses the noun διήγησις 'narrative' in the prologue to the Gospel (Luke 1:1), by implication applying it to his own work as well as that of his predecessors, and he uses the cognate verb διηγεῖσθαι *diēgeisthai* several times. He equates 'proclaiming' (κηρύσσειν *kēryssein*) with 'telling the story' (διηγεῖσθαι *diēgeisthai*) in the account of Jesus' healing of the demon-possessed man (Luke 8:39; cf. 9:10; Acts 8:33; 9:27; 12:17).[32] The apostolic proclamation in Acts consists largely of narrating the Jesus story in the context of the Israel story and ultimately the world's story (Acts 2:14–40; 3:12–26; 7:2–53; 10:34–43; 13:16–41; 17:22–31; 26:23). Even the barest summary account of apostolic preaching, 'The messiah is Jesus' (Acts 18:5, 28), situates the gospel proclamation within the context of Israel's narrative.

The prominence given to the parable of the soils in the Gospel makes Luke's agenda clear. The parable sets the tone of warnings against failing to heed the proclamation, or having a shallow commitment to it. To reject the proclamation is to prove oneself 'unworthy of eternal life' (Acts 13:46). Luke gives examples of unbelief: the members of the Nazareth synagogue (Luke 4:28–29); Samaritans (Luke 9:51–52); some from the synagogue at Ephesus (Acts 19:9); some of the Jews in Rome (Acts 28:24); and has Paul cite Isaiah 6:9–10, a prophecy concerning those who refuse to pay heed to the proclamation (Acts 28:26–27). But Luke's emphasis is to provide positive models of the

---

29 Pao, *Acts*, 147–80.
30 Cadbury, 'Commentary', 500.
31 Rosner focuses on the links between Luke and the historical component of Israel's Scriptures: Rosner, 'Acts'; cf. also Uytanlet, *Luke-Acts*.
32 Dillon, 'Previewing Luke's Project', 208–09.

response he desires for his readers. People show their confidence in Jesus: the four who carried a paralysed man (Luke 5:20); a centurion (Luke 7:9); the woman who anointed Jesus (Luke 7:50); the woman suffering from haemorrhaging (Luke 8:48); a Samaritan leper (Luke 17:19); and a blind beggar (Luke 18:42). The Book of Acts contains multiple examples of positive responses to the proclamation: the three thousand (Acts 2:41); the five thousand (Acts 4:4); large numbers of men and women (Acts 5:14); a large number of priests (Acts 6:7); Samaritans (Acts 8:14); Cornelius and his household (Acts 10); Gentiles at Pisidian Antioch (Acts 13:48); a great number of both Jews and Greeks (Acts 14:1); Jews and Greeks, men and women from Thessalonica (Acts 17:4); Athenians (Acts 17:34), to name a few. The final recorded instance, by its use of the imperfect, may suggest the ongoing effect of the proclamation on those who 'were being convinced' (Acts 28:24).

5. Paul as Seed-picker or Message-sower? (Acts 17:18)

The outworking of the parable, with its focus on what happens when people hear (ἀκούειν *akouein*) the message (λόγος *logos*), is nowhere more evident in Acts than in the Athens pericope (Acts 17:16–34). The varied responses to Paul's preaching at Athens echo the varied responses anticipated in the parable and its explanation.

First, Luke informs us, 'listening' (ἀκούειν *akouein*) is a preoccupation of the residents of Athens: 'Now all the Athenians and the foreigners living there used to spend their time in nothing other than telling or hearing something new' (Acts 17:21). So what sort of listeners will the Athenians prove to be? What will be their response when they hear Paul's message? The verb ἀκούειν *akouein* occurs twice in v. 32 in connection with describing the different responses of two groups at hearing Paul's proclamation, neither of whom is said to believe, though the second shows some initial interest, suggesting a second hearing. The third and final group are those who respond by believing (v. 34).

The Athens pericope is the only account in Acts where, as in the parable, more than two nuanced responses of those who hear apostolic preaching are identified, with the following structure:

> ἀκούσαντες *akousantes* ... οἱ μὲν *hoi men* ... οἱ δὲ *hoi de* ... τίνες δὲ *tines de*... ἐπίστευσαν *episteusan*

> 'On hearing ... some ..., while others ... But some ... believed' (Acts 17:32–34).

This echoes the structure of the parable's explanation. In the explanation, we have some who hear but fail to respond positively, other groups who hear and show initial or superficial interest, while a final group holds onto the message:

> οἱ δὲ *hoi de* ... οἱ ἀκούσαντες *hoi akousantes* ... οἱ δὲ *hoi de* ... ὅταν ἀκούσωσιν *hotan akousōsin* ... οὗτοί εἰσιν οἱ ἀκούσαντες *houtoi eisin hoi akousantes*... οὗτοί εἰσιν οἵτινες *houtoi eisin hoitines* ... ἀκούσαντες τὸν λόγον κατέχουσιν *akousantes ton logon katechousin*

> 'Some are those who hear ..., while others are those who hear ... Still others are those who hear ... These are those who hear and retain the message' (Luke 8:12–15).

In the parable the final batch of seed which results in a good crop is distinguished from the earlier batches simply by ἕτερον *heteron* 'other' (Luke 8:8) and it is ἕτεροι *heteroi* 'others' who, along with two named individuals, respond positively to Paul's message (Acts 17:34).

With this in mind, we note the designation of Paul as a σπερμολόγος *spermologos*, a *hapax* in biblical literature, often translated as 'babbler' (Acts 17:18). On the lips of the Athenian philosophers who hear his message of Jesus and the resurrection, it is an unflattering term. The word suggests the image of a bird pecking at seeds or scraps (BDAG). In a city with a long history of avian metaphors and jibes (notably Aristophanes, *The Birds*), the word was used of those who scrounged around for second-hand ideas but had nothing useful to contribute to intellectual discussion.[33] The first element σπερμ- *sperm-* is cognate with the verb σπείρειν *speirein* 'sow' used three times in Luke's version of the parable, where the very image of birds pecking at seeds is employed (Luke 8:5). However, a label used by one group as a pejorative can be adopted as a badge of honour by or on behalf of those so designated, as is the case, for example, with the term 'Christian' (Acts 11:26). Luke is known to enjoy wordplay,[34] so we may detect his smile as he contemplated the appropriateness of the designation of Paul as a σπερμολόγος *spermologos*. While the second element of the compound word -λόγος *-logos* is etymologically connected with λέγω *legō* (B) 'pick out' (LSJ), it is readily heard as Luke's *Leitwort* λόγος *logos* 'proclamation, message', cognate with λέγω *legō* (C) 'say, speak', which in the parable's explanation is the reality behind the image of the seed (Luke 8:11; cf. vv. 12, 13, 15). If the designation of Paul as a σπερμολόγος *spermologos* is not a Lukan invention, Luke's most likely source is Paul himself as Paul appears to be without companions at this point. Paul may have recalled this rare word in later recounting the incident—there is further scoffing after the Areopagus address without the actual words used then being recorded or possibly even remembered (Acts 17:32)—because he saw it as ironically apt. If so, this would suggest Paul's familiarity with the parable in some form. It is not Paul who is the dilettante or scrounger, pecking away at scraps. It is the philosophers with their incessant quest for novelty. Rather, Luke invites us, with a twinkle in his eye, to envisage Paul as a prime example of one who acts as an agent of God in propagating God's message to a range of hearers, including those who 'have ears to hear' (Luke 8:8) in a demonstration of the parable. Paul is a 'message-sower'.

6. Luke's Project as a Prophetic λόγος *logos*

We return to Luke's use of λόγος *logos* to refer to his own project in Acts 1:1. While at one level it may refer to the earlier 'volume', the Third Gospel, this would appear not to exhaust its meaning when Luke has given careful thought to the wording of his prologues. We do need to avoid the fallacy of illegitimate totality transfer—importing all the force of λόγος *logos* as used elsewhere into this one occurrence. But there is good reason to suggest that Luke's prevalent and distinctive usage of λόγος *logos* elsewhere has informed his decision to use it in Acts 1:1 to refer to his project.[35] For English readers, the connection is obscured by the fact that translations invariably use different English words for λόγος *logos* in Acts 1:1 and everywhere else. But Luke has enthusiastically adopted a word current in early Christian circles (Gal. 6:6; Col. 4:3; 1 Pet. 3:1) for the proclamation of Jesus and has found it the ideal word to use for his two-part written account of Christian origins, an account that is in continuity with and fulfilment of God's story and God's proclamation as recorded in Israel's Scriptures.[36] We should note the verb Luke uses in Acts 1:1. His λόγος *logos*

---

33 See Keener, *Acts*, 2595–96.
34 See Reich, *Figuring Jesus*, e.g. 141.
35 See, e.g., Silva, *Biblical Words*, 25–26.
36 For the Gospel of Luke as a continuation of Israel's story, see Tiede, *Prophecy*; Evans, 'Luke'; Wright, *Scripture*, 47–59.

was not something he 'wrote' (γράφειν *graphein*) but something he 'did, accomplished' (ποιεῖσθαι *poieisthai*), echoing the words of Jesus about those who hear and *do* his λόγος *logos* (Luke 8:21), the only other place in the NT where λόγος *logos* is object of the verb ποιεῖν *poiein* ('do, accomplish').[37]

This use of λόγος *logos* in the opening verse of Acts echoes its use in the prologue to the Gospel ('eyewitnesses and servants of the λόγος *logos*') where λόγος *logos* refers to earlier narrative accounts of the ministry of Jesus. Some of the primary versions of the Jesus story to which Luke refers were doubtless more fragmentary, perhaps largely oral, accounts of miracles, parables, and other teaching, as well as reports of Jesus' death and resurrection. These were arranged in an orderly narrative account (ἀνατάξασθαι διήγησιν *anataxasthai diēgēsin*, Luke 1:1). Luke does not so much see himself in competition with these previous accounts as in solidarity with them.[38] We may get a glimpse of the activity of one whom Luke may have had in mind. In Acts 13:5, we read: 'When they arrived at Salamis, they declared the proclamation (λόγος *logos*) of God in the synagogues of the Jews. And they also had John as their assistant'. The John here is John Mark (Acts 12:25). How did he assist Barnabas and Saul? Perhaps he carried the bags. But it is at least possible that Mark is directly assisting in what the apostles were engaged in, namely the promulgation of God's λόγος *logos*. Did Mark's supportive role even at this early stage involve the beginnings of gathering and recording and arranging something of the Jesus narrative which Luke later came to use as one of his sources?[39]

We should note Luke's description of his own work in Luke 1:2–4. He is operating with a tradition he has received from eyewitnesses (v. 2).[40] He maintains that he has been thorough and detailed in his investigation (παρηκολουθηκότι ἄνωθεν πᾶσιν ἀκριβῶς *parēkolouthēkoti anōthen pasin akribōs*, v. 3) and in writing an orderly account (καθεξῆς *kathexēs*, v. 3). The Gospel of Luke is not merely a narrative of events, but itself has affinities with a prophetic type of proclamation. It aims to be persuasive, in the first instance to Theophilus, that in this work he might experience the 'safety' (ἀσφάλειαν *asphaleian*) of the λόγοι *logoi* he has been taught (v. 4), though clearly the work is intended for a wider audience.[41] While λόγοι *logoi* here is generally translated 'things' or 'events', it could just as easily be the 'accounts' or 'stories', the 'proclamations' Theophilus has heard and which Luke now sets down in what he regards as a compellingly persuasive style.[42] Luke's account is no mere chronicle of events, no mere biography of a great man to be admired. There is much to be said for the comparison of Luke with classical academic writing—technical, apologetic, and especially biographical and historiographical, as long as this is qualified by reference to the historical narratives of the OT in the Former and Latter Prophets. Luke not only recounts the progress of the λόγος *logos*, but his project is itself a λόγος *logos*, a proclamation of

---

37 The idiom ποιεῖσθαι + the plural of λόγος is common in wider Greek usage, but also occasionally ποιεῖσθαι with the singular of λόγος is found with senses such as 'pay attention to', 'take account of', or 'make mention of', e.g., Herodotus, *Hist.* 7.218 line 17; Thucydides, *Hist.*, 1.37.1 line 2; Isocrates, *Plataicus* 39 line 3.
38 Brown, 'Role', 104–05; Dillon, 'Previewing Luke's Project', 207–08; Du Plessis, 'Once More', 201–02. Luke's only point of comparison with the work of predecessors is that his is more appropriately arranged for his audience (Luke 1:3): Keener, *Christobiography*, 229–31, 238.
39 For a discussion of orality and literacy in early Christianity and the transition from oral tradition to text, see Kruger, *Question*, 79–118.
40 While some have suggested Luke's knowledge of events is third-hand (eyewitnesses > servants of the λόγος > Luke), it is more natural to understand the eyewitnesses and servants of the λόγος to be identical since they share the definite article. For treatments of the role of eyewitnesses in the formation of the Gospel narratives, see Bauckham, *Jesus*; Hengel, 'Lukan Prologue'.
41 Marshall, *Luke*, 39–40.
42 For this understanding of ἀσφάλεια as a technical term known from Greek writers on literary style to describe a style designed to present an argument that will not be subject to contradiction, see Strelan, 'Note'.

how things are as God wants them to be understood, a proclamation to be heeded and persevered in. We might then paraphrase the opening words of Acts, read in the light of what follows, as 'The earlier prophetic Proclamation I accomplished'.

7. Conclusion

Luke's characterisation of his work as a λόγος *logos* in Acts 1:1 may be too general a word in isolation to identify its literary affinities, but given Luke's enthusiastic adoption of an early Christian shorthand expression for the proclamation of God's purposes in Jesus, it would seem that, along with other technical vocabulary in his prologues, Luke has used λόγος *logos* to mean something like a narration of events which have a divine origin and significance and which call for a response of heeding. That is to say, along with our comparisons of Luke-Acts with Graeco-Roman literary models, we should include the Jewish category of prophecy in our discussions of the character and purpose of Luke-Acts.

Bibliography

Adams, S. A. — *The Genre of Acts and Collected Biography* (SNTSMS; Cambridge: Cambridge University Press, 2013).

Aletti, J.-N. — *The Birth of the Gospels as Biographies: With Analyses of Two Challenging Pericopae* (tr. P. M. Meyer; Analecta Biblica Studia; Rome: Pontifical Biblical Institute, 2017).

Alexander, L. C. A. — 'The Preface to Acts and the Historians', in B. Witherington III (ed.), *History, Literature, and Society in the Book of Acts* (Cambridge: Cambridge University Press, 1996), 73–103.

Alexander, L. C. A. — *The Preface to Luke's Gospel* (Cambridge: Cambridge University Press, 1993).

Aune, D. E. — 'Luke 1.1–4: Historical or Scientific Prooimion?', in A. Christophersen, et al. (eds.), *Paul, Luke and the Graeco-Roman World: Essays in Honour of Alexander J. M. Wedderburn* (JSNTSup; Sheffield: Sheffield Academic, 2002), 138–48.

Aune, D. E. — *The New Testament in its Literary Environment* (Philadelphia, PA: Westminster, 1987).

Barrett, C. K. — 'The First New Testament?', *NovT* 38 (1996), 94–104.

Bauckham, R. — *Jesus and the Eyewitnesses: The Gospels as Eyewitness Testimony* (Grand Rapids, MI: Eerdmans, 2006).

Blass, F. and A. Debrunner — *A Greek Grammar of the New Testament and Other Early Christian Literature* (R. W. Funk, trans.; Cambridge: Cambridge University Press, 1961).

Borman, L.	'Rewritten Prophecy in Luke-Acts', in J. T. Nielsen and M. Müller (eds.), *Luke's Literary Creativity* (London: T. & T. Clark, 2016), 121–43.
Brown, S.	'The Role of the Prologues in Determining the Purpose of Luke-Acts', in C. H. Talbert (ed.), *Perspectives on Luke-Acts* (Edinburgh: T. & T. Clark, 1978), 99–111.
Burridge, R. A.	*What Are the Gospels: A Comparison with Graeco-Roman Biography* (Grand Rapids, MI: Eerdmans, 2004 [2nd ed.]).
Cadbury, H. J.	'Commentary on the Preface of Luke', in F. J. Foakes-Jackson and K. Lake (eds.), *The Beginnings of Christianity* 1/2 (London: Macmillan, 1922), 489–510.
Dillon, R. J.	'Previewing Luke's Project from his Prologue (Luke 1:1–4)', *CBQ* 43 (1981), 205–27.
Du Plessis, I. I.	'Once More: The Purpose of Luke's Prologue [Lk 1:1–4]', *Novum Testamentum* 16 (1974), 259–71.
Evans, C. A.	'Luke and the Rewritten Bible: Aspects of Lukan Hagiography', in J. H. Charlesworth and C. A. Evans (eds.), *The Pseudepigrapha and Early Biblical Interpretation* (Sheffield: JSOT Press, 1993), 170–201.
Fitzmyer, J. A.	*The Gospel according to Luke (1–9): Introduction, Translation, and Notes* (Garden City, NY: Doubleday, 1985 [2nd ed.]).
Green, J.	*The Gospel of Luke* (NICNT; Grand Rapids, MI: Eerdmans, 1997).
Hengel, M.	'The Lukan Prologue and its Eyewitnesses: The Apostles, Peter, and the Women', in M. F. Bird and J. Maston (eds.), *Earliest Christian History: History, Literature, and Theology: Essays from the Tyndale Fellowship in Honor of Martin Hengel* (Tübingen: Mohr Siebeck, 2012), 533–87.
Hill, C. E.	'God's Speech in These Last Days: The New Testament Canon as an Eschatological Phenomenon', in L. G. Tipton and J. C. Waddington (eds.), *Resurrection and Eschatology: Theology in Service of the Church* (Phillipsburg, NJ: P & R, 2008), 203–54.
Jervell, J.	'The Future of the Past: Luke's Vision of Salvation History and its Bearing on his Writing of History', in B. Witherington III (ed.), *History, Literature, and Society in the Book of Acts* (Cambridge: Cambridge University Press, 1996), 104–26.
Johnson, L. T.	*The Gospel of Luke* (Sacra Pagina; Collegeville, MN: Liturgical, 1991).
Keener, C. S.	*Christobiography: Memory, History, and the Reliability of the Gospels* (Grand Rapids, MI: Eerdmans, 2019).
Keener, C. S.	*Acts: An Exegetical Commentary*. 4 vols. (Grand Rapids, MI: Baker Academic, 2012).
Kruger, M. J.	*The Question of Canon: Challenging the Status Quo in the New Testament*

	Debate (Downers Grove, IL: Intervarsity, 2013).
Louw, J. and E. Nida	*Greek-English Lexicon of the New Testament Based on Semantic Domains* (New York: United Bible Societies, 1988).
Marguerat, D.	*The First Christian Historian: Writing the 'Acts of the Apostles'* (Cambridge: Cambridge University Press, 2002).
Marshall, I. H.	*Commentary on Luke* (NIGTC; Grand Rapids, MI: Eerdmans, 1978).
Moessner, D. P.	'The Lukan Prologue in the Light of Ancient Narrative Hermeneutics: παρηκολουθηκότι and the Credentialed Author', in J. Verheyden (ed.), *The Unity of Luke-Acts* (Louvain: Leuven University Press, 1999), 399–417.
Moles, J.	'Luke's Preface: The Greek Decree, Classical Historiography and Christian Redefinitions', *NTS* 57 (2011), 461–82.
O'Reilly, L.	*Word and Sign in the Acts of the Apostles: A Study in Lucan Theology* (Rome: Pontificia Università Gregoriana, 1987).
Pao, D. W.	*Acts and the Isaianic New Exodus* (Grand Rapids, MI: Baker Academic, 2002).
Patterson. R.	'Old Testament Prophecy', in L. Ryken and T. Longman III (eds.), *A Complete Literary Guide to the Bible* (Grand Rapids, MI: Zondervan, 1993), 296–309.
Pervo, R. I.	*Profit with Delight: The Literary Genre of the Acts of the Apostles* (Philadelphia, PA: Fortress, 1987).
Peterson, D.	'The Motif of Fulfilment and the Purpose of Luke-Acts', in B. W. Winter and A. D. Clarke (eds.), *The Book of Acts in its First Century Setting*. Vol. 1: *Ancient Literary Setting* (Grand Rapids, MI: Eerdmans, 1993), 83–104.
Pitts, A. W.	*History, Biography, and the Genre of Luke-Acts: An Exploration of Literary Divergence in Greek Narrative Discourse* (Leiden: Brill, 2019).
Reich, K. A.	*Figuring Jesus: The Power of Rhetorical Figures of Speech in the Gospel of Luke* (Leiden: Brill, 2011).
Rosner, B.	'Acts and Biblical History', in B. W. Winter and A. D. Clarke (eds.), *The Book of Acts in its First Century Setting*. Vol. 1: *Ancient Literary Setting* (Grand Rapids, MI: Eerdmans, 1993), 65–82.
Schmidt, D. D.	'Rhetorical Influences and Genre: Luke's Preface and the Rhetoric of Hellenistic Historiography', in D. P. Moessner (ed.), *Jesus and the Heritage of Israel: Luke's Narrative Claim upon Israel's Legacy* (Harrisburg, PA: Trinity Press International, 1999), 27–60.
Shead, A.	*A Mouth Full of Fire: The Word of God in the Words of Jeremiah* (Leicester: Apollos, 2012).
Silva, M.	*Biblical Words and their Meaning: An Introduction to Lexical Semantics* (Grand Rapids, MI: Zondervan, 1983).

Smith, D. L. and Z. L. Kostopoulos 'Biography, History and the Genre of Luke-Acts', *NTS* 63 (2017), 390–410.

Smith, D. M. 'When Did the Gospels Become Scripture?', *JBL* 119 (2000), 3–20.

Sparks, H. D. F. 'The Semitisms of St Luke's Gospel', *JTS* 44 (1943), 129–38.

Squires, J. T. *The Plan of God in Luke-Acts* (Cambridge: Cambridge University Press, 1993).

Strelan, R. 'A Note on ἀσφάλεια (Luke 1:4)', *JSNT* 30 (2007), 163–71.

Talbert, C. H. *Literary Patterns, Theological Themes, and the Genre of Luke-Acts* (Missoula, MT: Scholars, 1974).

Tannehill, R. C. 'The Story of Israel within the Lukan Narrative', in D. P. Moessner (ed.), *Jesus and the Heritage of Israel: Luke's Narrative Claim upon Israel's Legacy* (Harrisburg, PA: Trinity Press International, 1999), 325–39.

Tiede, D. L. *Prophecy and History in Luke-Acts* (Philadelphia, PA: Fortress, 1980).

Uytanlet, S. *Luke-Acts and Jewish Historiography: A Study on the Theology, Literature, and Ideology of Luke-Acts* (WUNT; Tübingen: Mohr Siebeck, 2014).

Wright, N. T. *Scripture and the Authority of God* (London: SPCK, 2005).

Wright, N. T. *The New Testament and the People of God* (Christian Origins and the Question of God; Minneapolis, MN: Fortress, 1992).

John A. Davies
Sydney College of Divinity
john.a.davies@optusnet.com.au

The Fourth Gospel and a Fourth Quest of the Historical Jesus

CRAIG L. BLOMBERG

Abstract

The quest of the historical Jesus has comprised a significant percentage of the study undertaken in Gospels research over the last two centuries. Has it accomplished all that it can? Or has its current phase, often called the Third Quest, played itself out? Will there be a Fourth Quest? Has it already begun? What is the role of the Gospel of John, if any, in an ongoing quest, since the Synoptics have almost totally dominated historical Jesus research for almost two hundred years? This study surveys where we have come from, where we are today, and where we might still make good headway in the years to come.

1. The Quest(s): An Overview

Albert Schweitzer's summary of key nineteenth-century efforts remains the standard for that time period,[1] even if we better recognize now how he assessed everything in terms of thoroughgoing apocalyptic and assembled his narrative so that it would lead to the opposition between William Wrede's literary-critical approach and his own, as the climax of the quest to date and the fundamental choice that scholars had to make.[2] N. T. Wright's delightful sketch of the *Schweitzerstrasse* and the *Wredebahn* in his *Jesus and the Victory of God* shows how that fundamental opposition still colored historical Jesus study a century later.[3]

Wright, in his editing and updating of Stephen Neill's classic history of New Testament interpretation, set out the schematization that has been used more than any other over the last thirty-five years.[4] In broad strokes, it observes that the 'first quest' or 'old quest' that Schweitzer summarized, and brought to something of an end, gave way to a period of reduced research (a reduction exacerbated by two world wars), which Wright with conscious exaggeration dubs the

---

1 Schweitzer, *The Quest*.
2 Gathercole, 'Critical and Dogmatic Agenda'; Blanton, *Displacing Christian Origins*, 164.
3 Wright, *Jesus and the Victory of God*, 16–82.
4 Neill and Wright, *Interpretation*, 379–403; systematized in *Jesus and the Victory of God*, 16–27, 83–124. For even further systematization, see Witherington, *Jesus Quest*.

period of 'no quest'. Rudolf Bultmann's influence was at its zenith during this period, including his well-known skepticism about how much we can know of the historical Jesus.[5] French and English scholarship was less affected than German and American New Testament studies, and Dale Allison prefers to call it not a period of 'no quest' but of 'no biography'.[6]

After World War II, however, things would change. Employing the language of Ernst Käsemann and James Robinson in the 1950s, we see that a 'new quest of the historical Jesus' emerged, of which Günther Bornkamm's book-length treatment of *Jesus of Nazareth* became the most famous and influential exemplar.[7] Compared to Bultmann, these three former students of his were downright optimistic about how much could be recovered of Jesus, especially of his sayings or teachings. Later scholarship would look back and focus more on how much they still rejected, along with discerning the remnants of the anti-Semitism that raged in Europe before and during the Third Reich, which was also bound up with the popularity of the double dissimilarity criterion.[8] Of course Jesus was Jewish, but he was a Jew 'with a difference', as it were, with the result that he was more compatible with Gentile Christianity.[9]

The mid-1970s through the mid-1980s saw another comparative reduction of historical Jesus research, with some key protests against some of the criteria of authenticity that the 'new quest' had honed.[10] At least by 1985, however, what is now widely called the 'third quest' was underway with E. P. Sanders' *Jesus and Judaism*.[11] Like Schweitzer and Bornkamm in the first two quests, Sanders penned major works that set the tone for much scholarly conversation about both Jesus and Paul, though in Sanders' case, his big work on Paul preceded his study of Jesus.[12] No one accused Sanders of his Jesus not being sufficiently Jewish; fitting Jesus squarely within the mainstream Judaism of his day, in fact, became one of the hallmarks of the third quest. Others included rethinking some or all of the criteria of authenticity, an unprecedented use of later non-canonical sources, especially among the literature of the Gnostics (or at least of *Nag Hammadi*), interdisciplinary studies (especially in the social sciences), and a secularizing of the discipline in the sense that overtly theological motives did not dominate the enterprise to the same extent that they had in earlier eras.[13]

All historiography inevitably schematizes and oversimplifies. The extent to which the taxonomy of 'first quest, no quest, new quest, and third quest' distorts reality continues to be debated. Stanley Porter's iconoclastic tendencies are on full display in his monograph, *The Criteria of Authenticity in Historical-Jesus Research*, as he rejects this periodization, argues for just one ongoing quest, and proposes three new criteria of authenticity that have found little support over the past two decades since their proposal.[14] But he is certainly correct that things are not nearly as simple as Wright's attractive narrative makes them seem to be.

There are a few generalizations, nevertheless, that do not seem as susceptible to easy contradiction. First, in the last ten years there has been a notable dearth of historical Jesus studies

---

5   Bultmann, *Jesus and the Word*, 14; a position that has to be interpreted in light of the minority of the Synoptics he did salvage for the Jesus of history, throughout his *History of the Synoptic Tradition*.
6   Allison, 'Secularizing', 137.
7   Käsemann, 'Problem'; Robinson, *A New Quest*; Bornkamm, *Jesus of Nazareth*.
8   Winter, 'The Dissimilar Jesus'; cf. Weaver, *The Historical Jesus*, 256.
9   Cf. even the conservative German Lutheran Jeremias, *New Testament Theology*, vol. 1.
10 See esp. Stein, 'The "Criteria" for Authenticity'; and Calvert, 'An Examination'.
11 Sanders, *Jesus and Judaism*.
12 Sanders, *Paul and Palestinian Judaism*.
13 Cf. Evans, 'Assessing Progress'.
14 Porter, *Criteria*. Cf. also Rubio, 'Fiction'.

of book-length nature.[15] Certainly, nothing with the detail or impact of works such as those by Vermes, Sanders, Crossan, Borg, Wright, Theissen and Merz, Ehrman, Fredriksen, Dunn has appeared.[16] To be sure, John Meier continues his enormous project on Jesus as a 'marginal Jew', and we hope he will live long enough to see it to completion. But his first four volumes were completed before 2010, while the one that appeared in the past decade moved in a much more skeptical direction than all the others.[17] Arguably the two most important historical Jesus studies of this period appeared at the same time in 2009—Craig Keener's *The Historical Jesus of the Gospels* and the Institute of Biblical Research's Historical Jesus Study Group's volume on *Key Events in the Life of Jesus*.[18] Yet neither has received the attention it deserved. It remains to be seen if the 2019 English-language translation of Hengel and Schwemer will generate more discussion,[19] but increasingly scholars seem to think that the third quest has just about played itself out.

2. The Problem of Criteria of Authenticity

One surprising reason for that perception stems from a comparatively small study, edited by Chris Keith and Anthony LeDonne and published in 2012, ambitiously entitled *Jesus, Criteria and the Demise of Authenticity*.[20] The thesis of the editors and of several of the contributors to the volume is that the use of criteria of authenticity, however refined or chastened, is a cul-de-sac. Intriguingly, they build on two articles by Morna Hooker in the 1970s, which were important cautions about the abuse of the standard criteria of the day, and which went largely ignored at that time.[21] But Hooker never called for the overthrow of all criteria, nor do some of the other contributors who seem, therefore, to be at least partially at odds with the editors. Most significant is the essay by Dagmar Winter, who builds on her previous work with Gerd Theissen and Annette Merz in proposing a four-part plausibility criterion.[22]

The results, though expressed in different terminology, are remarkably similar to Wright's double similarity and double dissimilarity criterion,[23] and it is a criterion to be used only positively. In short, when a portion of the Gospel tradition is completely credible in an early first-century Palestinian Jewish context (i.e., there is no hint of anachronism) but shows Jesus teaching or doing something highly distinctive for that context, *and* when that same portion demonstrates at least some continuity with subsequent early church activity, especially in the rest of the New Testament, but not to the same degree that one suspects Christian invention, then we quite likely have a detail

---

15 The two most important exceptions were both translations into English of German works penned in the previous decade: Schröter, *Jesus of Nazareth*; and Hengel and Schwemer, *Jesus and Judaism*. The *Journal for the Study of the Historical Jesus*, however, keeps a lively conversation going among those who produce article-length works.

16 Vermes, *The Authentic Gospel*; Sanders, *Jesus and Judaism*; Crossan, *The Historical Jesus*; Borg, *Meeting Jesus Again*; Theissen and Merz, *The Historical Jesus*; Ehrman, *Jesus*; Fredriksen, *Jesus of Nazareth*; Dunn, *Jesus Remembered*.

17 Meier, *A Marginal Jew*, 5 vols. to date. His fifth volume cast doubt on the authenticity of most of the parables (due to so many of them being singly attested), despite their generally being viewed as among the bedrock of historical Jesus tradition.

18 Keener, *The Historical Jesus*; Bock and Webb, *Key Events*.

19 Hengel and Schwemer, *Jesus and Judaism*.

20 Keith and LeDonne, *Jesus*.

21 Hooker, 'Christology and Methodology'; Hooker, 'On Using the Wrong Tool'.

22 Winter, 'Saving the Quest for Authenticity'; Theissen and Winter, *The Quest for the Plausible Jesus*. Cf. Theissen and Merz, *The Historical Jesus*, 116–18.

23 Wright, *Jesus and the Victory of God*, 131–33.

that is historically plausible. Put differently, if we combine the old double dissimilarity criterion with Tom Holmén's continuum approach, illustrated also by Dale Allison,[24] one has what the Germans call *die Plausibilitätskriterium*.[25] Moreover, as Wright has shown in detail, this need not result in the atomistic analysis practiced by the new quest or the Jesus Seminar but can and should be combined with larger questions about the aims or goals, symbols and conceptualizations, deeds and practices of Jesus more generally.[26] That Keith and LeDonne included Winter's essay in their book may suggest that they did not entirely think that there was no way ahead for the historical Jesus quest or the use of criteria of authenticity.[27]

3. The Fourth Gospel and a 'New Look on John'

One glaring omission characterizes all the various phases of the quest and it is very intentional. Almost entirely missing from the 'database' of what we can fairly claim to know about Jesus using historical methods is the Gospel of John. In an age when scholarship is fully aware of just how different the Fourth Gospel is from the Synoptics, this hardly causes any surprise. Even evangelicals like Keener and Wright play it safe by sticking with the Synoptics in doing their historical Jesus research. So does the IBR anthology edited by Bock and Webb. Darrell Bock and Ben Simpson, representing a slightly more conservative position, in their commentary on a synopsis of the Gospels, still separate John off and treat him after their exposition of all the Synoptic texts.[28] What is less well known is that, up until and including the writings of Friedrich Schleiermacher, John was often considered the most reliable Gospel, and the material from the Synoptics was fit into a chronology established by the Fourth Gospel.[29] A decent smattering of book-length treatments of the historicity of large parts of John also appeared from the middle of the nineteenth through the middle of the twentieth centuries, particularly in England.[30]

The liberal Anglican bishop of Cambridge, John A. T. Robinson, nevertheless surprised the scholarly world with his article in 1959 entitled, 'The New Look on the Fourth Gospel'.[31] His interest in the Fourth Gospel continued to grow until his posthumously published book, *The Priority of John*, brought all of his arguments together.[32] Not only was there a significant minority of the details in John's Gospel that could satisfy the criteria of authenticity, there were numerous places, Robinson believed, where information in John should be preferred to that of the Synoptics. Moreover, John may have been the first of the Gospels to be written but, if not, much of the conceptual framework he utilizes should at least receive priority over its Synoptic counterparts.

---

24 Holmén (ed.), *Jesus from Judaism to Christianity*; Allison, *Constructing Jesus*.
25 Theissen and Winter's original German title was *Die Kriterienfrage in der Jesusforschung: Vom Differenzkriterium zum Plausibilitätskriterium* ('The Question of Criteria in Jesus Research: From the Dissimilarity Criterion to the Plausibility Criterion').
26 Wright, *Jesus and the Victory of God*. More briefly, cf. his *The Challenge of Jesus*.
27 Picking up on the same tension among the contributors to the volume, esp. Winter vs. Keith and Le Donne, and coming to similar conclusions as me, is Licona, 'Is the Sky Falling?'. Cf., more generally, Hägerland, 'The Future of Criteria'.
28 Bock and Simpson, *Jesus according to Scripture*.
29 Westerholm and Westerholm, *Reading Sacred Scripture*, 298–326, citing Friedrich Schleiermacher's *Life of Jesus*, which was based on German lectures delivered in 1832.
30 See esp. Sanday, *Authorship*; Robinson, *Historical Character*; Askwith, *Historical Value*; Holland, *Fourth Gospel*; Headlam, *Fourth Gospel*; and Higgins, *Historicity*; and, to a lesser degree, Dodd, *Historical Tradition*.
31 Robinson, 'New Look'.
32 Robinson, *Priority of John*.

An ever-growing stream of studies adopting a significant part of this new look flowed steadily after Robinson's final work.[33] They didn't always agree with every detail or incident Robinson found historically credible, but sometimes they discovered others. Since the late 1990s, the scholar who has written more in this area than anyone else is Paul Anderson,[34] and his establishment and chairing of the 'John, Jesus, and History' seminar at the Society of Biblical Literature has proved highly significant. To date three large volumes of essays from their proceedings have appeared; volume 2 in particular contains essays by a wide swath of scholars internationally in support of certain aspects of almost every major passage in the Fourth Gospel.[35] Later papers not included in those volumes are being collected and edited for what are projected to be another three volumes, while others have appeared elsewhere in print.[36]

In 2001, I published *The Historical Reliability of John's Gospel: Issues and Commentary*.[37] Because N. T. Wright and the trio of German authors (Theissen, Merz, and Winter) had developed the double similarity and double dissimilarity criterion (or the criterion of historical plausibility) already in the mid-to-late 1990s, it struck me as worthwhile to try it out on a pericope-by-pericope analysis of the Fourth Gospel. In almost every instance, I showed there were elements of each pericope that well satisfied the criterion. To be sure, how much similarity and how much dissimilarity is needed, and in what combination, can prove highly subjective, so I was particularly grateful to be invited to participate in the IBR Historical Jesus Study Group and to write for that anthology, which tried to utilize all of the major criteria of authenticity in their most responsible fashion. But it limited itself to twelve key events or themes in the Synoptics. Still, I was able to use the historical plausibility criterion in my analysis of Jesus' meals with sinners and break what I believe was a little bit of some new ground there.[38]

Paul Anderson began to ask questions already in the 2000s about whether it was time to speak of a fourth quest of the historical Jesus, one that would give John parity with the Synoptics.[39] By that he did not mean that the same amount of authentic material should be drawn from each corpus, merely that both should be treated as legitimate and viable quarries for historical Jesus research, without presupposing in advance how much or how little might emerge. In his writings in the 2010s, he began to stop asking the question and started just to affirm that a fourth quest has begun.[40] He has more than once told me over the years that he is engaged long-term in the research for and writing of a major fourth quest book on Jesus, but if and when that will appear remains uncertain. He has, however, summarized some of the key incidents and themes distinctively emphasized by the Fourth Gospel, which he believes will need more treatment in such a book than the three previous quests of the historical Jesus have given them: 'Jesus' simultaneous ministry alongside John the Baptist and the prolific availability of purifying power',

---

33 See esp. Hengel, *The Johannine Question*; Barton, 'The Believer'; Thompson, 'The Historical Jesus'; Ensor, *Jesus and His Works*; Berger, *Im Anfang war Johannes*; Wenham, 'The Enigma'; Wenham, 'A Historical View'; Moloney, 'The Fourth Gospel'; Lierman (ed.), *Challenging Perspectives*; Bauckham, *The Testimony*, 137–206; van Belle, 'The Return of John'; Porter, *John*.
34 See esp. Anderson, *Fourth Gospel*; and *Riddles*.
35 Anderson, Just, and Thatcher, (eds.), *John, Jesus, and History*. Vol. 2 is subtitled *Aspects of Historicity in the Fourth Gospel*.
36 For just one example, see Blomberg, 'The Sayings of Jesus in Mark'.
37 Blomberg, *Historical Reliability of John's Gospel*.
38 Blomberg, 'Authenticity and Significance'. Cf. also my 'Jesus, Sinners and Table Fellowship'. For a minority view that rejects this approach wholesale, see Wassen, 'Jesus' Table Fellowship'.
39 E.g., Anderson, *Fourth Gospel*, 192; Anderson, *Riddles*, 237. Painter, 'Fourth Gospel', 279, argues that Dodd anticipated this approach in his final book, *The Founder of Christianity*.
40 Anderson, 'Incidents', 200; Anderson, 'Why the Gospel of John is Fundamental', 46.

'Jesus' cleansing of the temple as an inaugural prophetic sign', 'Jesus' travel to and from Jerusalem and his multi-year ministry', 'early events in the public ministry of Jesus', 'the Judean ministry and archeological realism', 'the Last Supper as a common meal and its proper dating', and 'Jesus' teaching about the way of the Spirit and the reign of truth'.[41] James Charlesworth has also endorsed the idea that a fourth quest is already underway and compiled a large volume of disparate studies using a variety of approaches that support the probability of considerable historical information available from the Fourth Gospel.[42]

4. The Struggles of Gospel Source Criticism

Perhaps unfortunately, scholarship, especially in the humanities, does not always advance in a linear, evolutionary fashion, with each successive critical methodology developing as a clear improvement on past ones. Many reasons explain why one method or one set of conclusions about a certain issue in biblical studies becomes popular at a given point in the history of the discipline and not at another. One that has only recently begun to receive the attention it deserves in the history of biblical scholarship has to do with the factor of power.[43] Who are the major powerbrokers in the guild at any given moment and how did they gain that power? What institutions' faculty or academic societies carry more credibility, not by virtue of the compelling logic of all their publications but due to the prestige of the colleges and universities that employ them or the makeup of the societies? What about the reputations of the publishers or journals in which the scholarship appears? Which individual scholars or schools of thought that might disagree with one's own position can be ignored without one's work being viewed as deficient by many in the guild(s)? These kinds of issues may ultimately determine if a fourth quest ever really gets off the ground and, if it does, if it is recognized as such.

Then there are the more benign trends of what catches on and simply proves more interesting than preceding approaches. During the nearly fifty years of my academic career in religious studies, of all the higher-critical tools in New Testament criticism, Gospel source criticism (esp. with the Fourth Gospel) has fallen out of favor more than any other, not because all the important issues have been solved (or have been proved to be insoluble), but because other forms of analysis have come to be perceived as more exciting or relevant.[44] Then again, the passing of a major champion of a certain perspective can lead to remarkable shifts of allegiance to competing theories. From the publication of his doctoral dissertation in 1964 on the Synoptic problem to his death in 2000, William Farmer tirelessly and enthusiastically championed the Griesbach hypothesis with extensive files of the comparisons of parallel texts to back him up.[45] Almost

---

41   Anderson, *Fourth Gospel*, 154–72.
42   Charlesworth, 'Historical Jesus'; Charlesworth, *Jesus as Mirrored*.
43   To date, almost all attention has been devoted to issues of discrimination and underrepresentation among scholars based on gender, race, ethnicity, and/or sexual orientation. Still to receive comparable attention are the identical issues based on one's position on controversial issues within one's discipline. To take just one example, scholars have been (illegally) fired from their academic posts for having either too 'conservative' or too 'liberal' a view on pseudonymity in the Bible, despite nothing in any contract or agreement specifying that as a requirement of employment.
44   Literary criticism, particularly narrative criticism, at the latest by the 1990s was overshadowing older source, form, and redaction criticism. With the flourishing of social-scientific analysis, the hermeneutics of advocacy movements, and new developments in linguistics, interest in the older trio of methods waned even further, arguably more in source than in form and redaction criticism.
45   See initially Farmer, *Synoptic Problem*. Then cf. esp. Farmer (ed.), *New Synoptic Studies*; and his *The Gospel of Jesus*.

singlehandedly, he convinced a small group of similarly vocal proponents in what Christopher Tuckett already in the late 1980s dubbed 'the revival of the Griesbach hypothesis'.[46] But since Farmer died, the popularity of Griesbach has plummeted, while the Farrer hypothesis, as nuanced by Michael Goulder and his student Mark Goodacre, has grown so that it now stands second only to Markan priority combined with the Q-hypothesis in the amount of support it has garnered.[47] It is not clear that either Griesbach or Farrer merited as much or as little support as they received at either the zenith or nadir of their popularities based on the evidence alone.

A similar problem has bedeviled Johannine source criticism. As long as Robert Fortna was still producing major works, particularly on a Signs Source, the dominant view was that John used sources, even if they were harder to detect than with the Synoptics.[48] More recently, with the burgeoning of literary criticism's focus on the final form of the text, and Richard Bauckham's attempts to debunk redaction criticism's focus on an original audience for which each Gospel highlighted situation-specific themes,[49] it is much less common to find studies that try to separate redactional from traditional material in Johannine exegesis. Still, and in keeping with the criterion of cutting against the grain of an evangelist's redaction,[50] it would seem that a fruitful appropriation of the Fourth Gospel for historical Jesus research would include a return to a cautious form of bracketing the most theologically dominant themes in each Johannine pericope, seeing what remains, and then looking for whatever patterns or motifs might recur within those potentially authentic cores, even if they are somewhat submerged.[51] None of this is to suggest that what is more demonstrably redactional is unhistorical, merely that other criteria will have to come into play in assessing that material. The approach suggested here could complement Anderson's in a fourth quest that mined the Fourth Gospel as well as the Synoptics. The rest of this article will sketch out the contours of what such a study might look like.

5. Cutting against the Grain in John's Gospel

The new look on John has regularly pointed to the role of John the Baptist in John 1 and 3 as a good example of probably historical details in the Fourth Gospel not found in the Synoptics.[52] Only John discloses that several of Jesus' closest followers came originally from John's orbit. Only John narrates some of those individuals' earliest encounters with Jesus and the remarkable cluster of titles with which they address him—Rabbi, Messiah, King of Israel, even Son of God. Most intriguingly, only John contains the enigmatic saying of the Baptist about Jesus that 'he must become greater; I must become less' (3:30).[53] Even if one does not go as far as John Meier to suggest that Jesus, too, was originally a disciple of John, the Baptist's initially greater popularity than Jesus is not a detail readily invented.[54] Neither is the passing reference to Jesus as a baptizer,

---

46 Tuckett, *Revival*.
47 Farrer, 'On Dispensing with Q'; Goulder, *Luke*; Goodacre, *The Case against Q*.
48 The two most important works were Fortna, *The Gospel of Signs* and Fortna, *The Fourth Gospel*.
49 Bauckham (ed.), *Gospels for All Christians*. Cf. also van Belle, 'The Return of John'.
50 For explanation, see Stein, 'The "Criteria for Authenticity"', 247–48, under the heading of 'divergent patterns from the redaction'.
51 See the frequent practice of Meier throughout the volumes of *A Marginal Jew*.
52 Robinson, *Priority of John*, 168–89; Anderson, *Fourth Gospel*, 154–58.
53 All Scripture quotations are from the NIV unless otherwise noted.
54 Meier, *A Marginal Jew*, 2.19–233.

even when it is clarified that he did so through his followers.[55] It is certainly not a recurring feature of Jesus' ministry depicted in either John or the Synoptics. In its historical context, the Baptist's movement appears to have been a purity movement,[56] whereas the key Johannine theme about the Baptist is the testimony or witness he provides for Jesus. Many think his twofold reference to Jesus as Lamb of God is part of another important redactional theme, though how big its role is seems often to have been exaggerated.[57] For the sake of the exercise, nevertheless, let us bracket these themes. Still, the topics of Jesus the Baptist and several of Jesus' disciples as original followers of the Baptist during the height of his popularity remain as probably authentic artifacts to be taken seriously in any full-orbed historical Jesus study.[58]

John 2:1–12 introduces Jesus' first miracle, in Cana, which by virtue of its literary form adds to the complexity of the analysis. For John, Jesus' miracles are 'signs', which is the most basic redactional emphasis for him here (see v. 12). Also important is the introduction of the theme of Jesus' 'hour' in his interchange with his mother. But in a passage with such economy of narrative as to omit even the statement that at some point Jesus turned the water into wine (it just refers to the action after the fact in a two-word adjectival clause in verse 9—οἶνον γεγενημένον), it is remarkable that an entire verse is taken up with describing the kinds of jars containing the water that was transformed (v. 6). Of course, the number and size magnify the greatness of the miracles, but why should it matter that they were 'the kind used by the Jews for ceremonial washing'? Is this an unmotivated historical detail?[59] Or does it have significance, but more for Jesus than for anything John might wish to stress?[60]

The new look on John regularly appeals to the placement of the temple clearing incident in 2:13–22 as a potentially historical datum.[61] The reference to 46 years for the rebuilding of the temple in verse 20 squares only with a date of about A.D. 28, not 30 or 33 (the major contenders for the year of the crucifixion). Whether that means one opts for the Johannine chronology *rather* than the Synoptic one or that one dares to suggest what some find preposterous that Jesus framed his ministry with similar incidents,[62] it does mean that historical Jesus research needs to reckon with the possibility of an early temple clearing event. Nothing in the theological emphases of the passage requires that, however, since John is keen on showing Jesus as the fulfillment of the Temple (vv. 19–22), *whenever* this occurred. Verses 14–16, nevertheless, read just a little more like an attempt at 'cleansing' rather than the prediction of destruction of the literal temple that the Synoptics highlight,[63] so perhaps the incident fits an early period on Jesus' ministry more than is often acknowledged.

The dialogue between Jesus and Nicodemus that occupies at least John 3:1–15, and perhaps verses 16–21 as well, illustrates several key Johannine themes—the role of signs, new birth, the contrast between Spirit and flesh, another between heavenly and earthly things, the lifting up of the Son of man, and belief leading to eternal life. Tucked into this conversation is the 'explanation' of new birth as being 'born of water and the Spirit'. The number of proposals as to

---

55 Twelftree, 'Jesus the Baptist'.
56 Murphy, *John the Baptist*, 141–43.
57 Witetschek, 'The Hour of the Lamb?'.
58 Frey, 'Baptism', 107.
59 Cf. von Wahlde, *The Gospel and Letters of John*, 2.83.
60 Note the similarities with the little parable of the wine and wineskins, usually held to be largely authentic, in Mark 2:22 pars. Cf. also Deines, *Jüdische Steingefasse*.
61 Von Wahlde, *The Gospel and Letters of John*, 2.97–98; McGrath, '"Destroy This Temple"', 40.
62 E.g., Borchert, *John 1–11*, 160, calls it 'a historiographical monstrosity that has no basis in the texts of the Gospels'.
63 Robinson, *Priority of John*, 185.

Jesus' meaning here suggests, however, that it didn't clarify matters entirely! There is a *Sitz im Leben Jesu*, nevertheless, that makes good sense of Jesus' words at a historical level that he might have expected Nicodemus to grasp. Ezekiel 36:25–27 offers an important Old Testament precedent for combining water and the Spirit in a context of the cleansing of Israel from its impurities and idolatries in order to follow God's laws better.[64] Torah-obedience is not a dominant Johannine concept, so this kind of purification (v. 25) is not likely to be something that either tradition or redaction invented but solid core Jesus material, even if he reapplies the imagery.

The narrative about the Samaritan woman at the well (John 4:4–42) is one of the few unique passages in John that reads as if it might have belonged in the Synoptics, especially Luke, instead (except that it probably would have been much shorter). The chapter links Jesus with a paradigmatically dispossessed woman who ends up being an evangelist to her own people. It discusses key issues of holy space or geography, and it reflects on the already-but-not-yet presence of the Messiah. None of this, however, required the metaphorical references to 'living water' in verses 10–15. Are there, as in chapter 3, implications here for the importance of cleanliness and purification, which cut somewhat against the grain of Jesus welcoming an outcast tainted with the stigma, whether or not deserved, of being highly impure?[65] We will see something similar to the 'spring of water welling up to eternal life' (4:14) again in John 7:37–39, but it will not be the major theological emphasis in that context either.

By this time, we are sensing that there are a cluster of concepts, not all naturally linked with one another into a consistent motif, involving water, cleansing, purity, newness, the Spirit, and eternal life. We will not see them recur in every pericope; indeed, the closer we get to the end and climax of the Gospel, the fewer and further between they will appear. There is nothing explicit in the next passage, the healing of the nobleman's son (John 4:46–54), apart from the fairly obvious fact that all of Jesus' healing miracles promoted a return to physical wholeness. It is intriguing that verse 46 not only brings Jesus back to Cana for the only other time narrated in the Gospels, but that we read again that this is where he had turned water into wine. It is hard to imagine that the book's audiences would have so quickly forgotten this detail; the repetition of the gist of the miracle may be preparing the reader for Jesus' 'second sign' (v. 12). But it has the added effect of confronting the reader with something about water with a possible double meaning.[66]

Similar to the first miracle in Cana, the healing by the pool of Bethesda in John 5 involves water only to the extent that it does *not* provide the solution to the desperate individual's plight. The role of the pool has been magnified by the Byzantine textual addition of the superstition about its healing powers, though some such belief has to be presupposed to make sense of the shorter, older version of the account (i.e., without vv. 3b–4).[67] The dominant redactional interest is clearly Jesus' healing on the Sabbath and the debate it engenders, made all the more striking by the delay in introducing the day of the week in the narrative until verse 9, But also like the miraculous provision of wine from water, here what Jesus can provide is contrasted with what purification is

---

64 See esp. Belleville, '"Born of Water and Spirit"'.
65 Miller, 'The Woman', 73, thinks so, noting the regular requirement of 'living' (i.e., flowing) water in the Levitical laws on ritual purification.
66 Carson, *John*, 238, suspects so, commenting that 'the one who transformed water into wine, eclipsing the old rites of purification and announcing the dawning joy of the messianic banquet, is the one who continues his messianic work, whether he is rightly trusted or not, by bringing healing and snatching life back from the brink of death (cf. Is. 35:5–6; 53:4a [cf. Mt. 8:16–17]; 61:1)'.
67 Bryan, 'Power in the Pool' esp. 8–9.

hoped for from traditional sources.[68] Recent research suggests that at least one of the twin pools at Bethesda was often used as a major *mikvah* for people entering the Temple precincts from the north, making the links with purification that much clearer.[69] But John makes nothing of it at all in the rest of the chapter in the debate over the authority of the Son, so it is all the more likely historical rather than redactional.

Chapter 6 proceeds to the multiplication of the loaves. There is no water here, no discussion of cleansing, no debate about purity. But then again, like the Hound of the Baskervilles that should have barked, those absences may be significant. With a gathering of five thousand men (v. 19; plus their families, according to Matt. 14:21), there would have been at least some who would have wondered about the appropriate ritual handwashing before meals.[70] In the wilderness, there would scarcely have been water for so many to wash. But that is not an issue for Jesus, at least not as the account is narrated here. This is the replication of manna provided in the wilderness around which some Messianic expectations were centered, most likely why we learn of the crowd's reaction, as they call Jesus the Prophet who was to come into the world (Deut. 18:15–18).[71] But here there is no accompanying miraculous provision of water from any rock, either to slake their thirst or wash their hands.

The next part of the chapter narrates Jesus' walking on the water on the Sea of Galilee. No purification appears here either, but the narrator, in keeping with the emphases in Matthew and Mark, highlights Jesus' divine power over the wind and the waves (cf. Job 9:8; Psalm 77:19). The multiple attestation of this focal point of the narrative, its meaningful Jewish backgrounds, and the minor amount of Johannine redaction all support its historicity.[72] Unlike the Synoptics, however, the Fourth Gospel uses the feeding of the 5000 and the water-walking miracles to introduce the Bread of Life discourse in Capernaum. Discussion will turn from consuming bread and fish to eating Jesus' flesh and drinking his blood. A majority of commentators finds this a foreshadowing (or even a displacement) of the Last Supper, at least for John. At the historical level, however, it would be anachronistic to imagine anyone understanding it this way yet.[73] Despite claims that this would be unthinkable imagery in a Jewish context, because of its cannibalistic appearance, it is better to take the imagery to refer to the strikingly intimate relationship Jesus is predicting people must have with him, even to the point of suffering and dying for him if necessary, in order to receive eternal life, the ultimate cleansing from corruption and death.[74]

One of the festive portions of the Feast of Tabernacles, which unifies the setting of the material in chapters 7–9, was the daily water-drawing ceremony in which priests would fill flagons from the pool of Siloam and process to the Temple joyously citing Isaiah 12:3, 'with joy you will draw water from the wells of salvation'.[75] At the climax of this festival week, Jesus proclaimed to the crowds that those who are thirsty should come to him and drink (v. 37). While there is debate over whether Jesus claimed that the rivers of living water would flow just from him or also from those who

---

68　Thompson, 'Healing at the Pool of Bethesda'. This point stands whether or not the challenge to the superstitious beliefs was directly attached to Asclepius. See further Bruce, 'John 5:1–18'.
69　Von Wahlde, 'The Pool(s) of Bethesda'.
70　Poon, 'Superabundant Table Fellowship'.
71　An expectation that largely persisted only into very early Jewish-Christian preaching (see Acts 3:23, 7:37), so most likely historical. See Longenecker, *Christology*, 32–38.
72　Latourelle, *Miracles*, 144–47.
73　Heilmann, 'A Meal in the Background of John 6:52–58?', esp. 485–86. It also does not make as good literary sense as is often believed. See Warren, *My Flesh Is Meat Indeed*.
74　Cf. Barrett, *John*, 284.
75　Beasley-Murray, *John*, 113–15.

drink from him (cf. NIV with NIV mg),[76] another link between water and the Spirit (v. 39; recall John 3:5) appears. Because of the interruption in the later canonical forms of the Gospel with the story of the woman caught in adultery, it is easy to lose sight of the unity of chapters 7–8. The main theological emphases are the divisions that Jesus' presence and claims cause among the people and among their leaders. Even among some who at first appear to believe, a heart of diabolical disbelief soon emerges.[77] Chapter 8 climaxes with Jesus' striking claim that 'before Abraham was born, I am' (v. 58), so that an attempted stoning results. We have come a long way from rivers of living water. Whatever Christological heightening may be present here, at least the cleansing power of Jesus' living water seems securely embedded in the foundation of the narrative.[78]

The account of the healing of the man born blind, which dominates John 9, follows from a metaphor that is well known from the Synoptics also: Jesus and therefore derivatively his followers are the light of the world. Unlike other healings of blind people in the Gospels, however, only this one involves a body of water. Here the blind man is sent to wash in the pool of Siloam. Different from the account of the healing of the crippled man *by* the pool of Bethesda, here the water *in* the pool *is* involved with the healing of the blind man. Siloam, too, appears to have been used as a giant *mikvah*, probably the largest in Jerusalem, only at the south rather than the north end of the Temple precincts.[79] But it is clear that the story is not saying that this water had special healing powers. Jesus has already worked the miracle with the mudpack he places over the man's eyes; the purpose of washing in Siloam is simply to remove the mud, which could have been done more simply elsewhere. The associations of Siloam with purification, therefore, must be intentional. Again, they would appear to be at the core of the episode, since the more dominant theological emphases lie elsewhere: the accusation once again of working on the Sabbath, the blindness of the Pharisees who were disputing with the formerly blind man and his family, and the identity of Jesus.

Chapter 10 is unified by the theme of Jesus as the Good Shepherd. Yet there seems to be a chronological break at verse 22 as the narrative jumps from Tabernacles to Hanukkah ('the Feast of Dedication'—Gk. ἐγκαίνια).[80] Commemorating the Maccabean revolt, in which bad shepherds in Israel were replaced with good ones, at least at first, is a perfect opportunity for Jesus to talk about himself as the Good Shepherd, but if this were an unhistorical insertion, one would have expected it at the beginning of the chapter where the theme emerges. Some later manuscripts sensed the aptness of that fit and changed τότε in verse 22 to δέ; even if not original the δέ represents an ancient interpretation.[81] Yet, if John were gratuitously adding the reference to the festival, one would also have expected him to make something more of the fact that the re-dedication of the Temple in 164 B.C. also involved its purification. That verse 36 has Jesus speaking also of his consecration or sanctification (ὃν ὁ πατὴρ ἡγίασεν; elsewhere in John of Jesus only in 17:19), of which very few commentaries make much of anything.[82] This is a link that Jesus' original audience in Jerusalem on this occasion would have made more readily than a mixed congregation of Jews

---

76 English Translations tend to favor the non-Christological reading; commentaries, the Christological one.
77 For the best exposition of this passage, see Motyer, *Your Father the Devil*, 141–59. This must be supplemented with Hunn, 'Who Are "They"?'. Motyer deals well with those who turned out not to be genuine adherents; Hunn, with the probable partial change(s) of audience throughout chap. 8.
78 Cf. Johnson, 'The Jewish Feasts', 127.
79 Von Wahlde, 'The Pool of Siloam'.
80 For this reason, Poirier, 'Hanukkah', argues that all of chap. 10 took place at Hanukkah. Yet the beginning of chapter 10 is tied closely to chap. 9, which seems to follow directly from chap. 8. So Poirier, fairly unconvincingly, has to argue for all of 8:12–10:39 occurring at the Feast of Dedication.
81 But see Metzger, *Textual Commentary*, 231, for complicating factors.
82 But see Brown, *John I–XII*, 411.

and (perhaps a majority of) Gentiles at the end of the first century in and around Ephesus (if that is the initial audience of the Fourth Gospel). As a result, Jesus' teaching in the second half of chapter 10 seems as historically secure a part of the chapter as any.[83]

Chapter 11 has even less explicitly about purity. Showcasing the claim of Jesus to be 'the resurrection and the life' is the obvious theological highlight. A perceived rivalry between Martha and Mary has likewise elicited significant analysis, without any consensus on the characterization, particularly of Martha.[84] How the raising of Lazarus ironically led to Caiaphas and his cronies plotting to put him to death (as if that would work!) forms the chapter's climax. At the same time, raising someone from the dead is as dramatic a form of purification in this life as one might imagine, and the narrative lingers just long enough over the imagined putrefaction of Lazarus' corpse after four days (v. 39) to make us suspect that something more lay just below the surface at the historical level (if one be permitted to postulate one) of the passage.[85] That Lazarus emerges from the tomb still bound by the graveclothes fits the fact that he is returning to merely earthly life but also has an evidentiary value to it. No one can dispute that this was Lazarus who had died who is emerging. Human help is still needed to bring him back to wholeness, even the normal wholeness of earthly life. And soon his life will be in danger once more. Invention out of whole cloth seems unlikely to have included all these built-in limitations.[86]

As much as a week in advance of Passover, festival pilgrims came to Jerusalem, seeking ceremonial purification for entering the Temple precincts (John 11:55).[87] But why were they looking for Jesus already at that point and surprised not to see him? Apparently, they assumed, even at this late date in his ministry, that he still practiced the purity laws of his Scripture.[88] He *does* come early, if not seven then six days ahead of time, but nothing is said about whether he takes a *mikvah* bath. Instead, 12:1–8 narrates a different kind of cleansing—anointing with perfume—by Mary of Bethany. The quantity is enough for the cleansing and preservation of a royal corpse, which may be John's reason for including the story.[89] Interestingly, Judas' objections are said to be disingenuous (v. 6); presumably he didn't regularly object every time a king or nobleman was given an elaborate burial. How much more appropriate, then, for Jesus to be treated this way. Most of church history would come to misunderstand Jesus' teaching about always having the poor with you (v 8; as if it were an excuse for *not* helping the poor!), but at least it identified the theologically climactic moment of the text. The very next passage, typically dubbed the triumphal entry, builds on the understood claims of Jesus to be a king, while the debate over the anointing recedes from view. Historically, though, more than first meets the eye seems to be at work with the question of purity.[90]

In chapter 13, there is no difficulty in seeing cleansing or purity as pervasive in the theme of

---

83 See further Ensor, *Jesus and His Works*, 245–46.
84 Particularly helpful is Moloney, 'The Faith of Martha and Mary'.
85 Cf. Tovey, 'On Not Unbinding the Lazarus Story'.
86 On the historicity of a core event here, see further Blomberg, *The Historical Reliability of John's Gospel*, 171–72.
87 Esp. if they had experienced corpse impurity, as many would have, in a culture where death was very public. See von Wahlde, *The Gospel and Letters of John*, 2.520.
88 Bruce, *John*, 253, notes that the need for such purification was laid down in Num. 9:6ff., and that Josephus (War 6.290) tells us pilgrims came about a week early for Passover and 1.229 tells us it was for purification. Cf. also Haber, *'They Shall Purify Themselves'*, 181–206.
89 Bruce, *John*, 257.
90 Cf. already Westcott, *John*, 177, who explains that 'the act of anointing was symbolic of consecration to a divine work. This Mary felt to be imminent'.

footwashing and in finding it historically plausible.[91] Peter's overly literal interpretation of Jesus' words, coupled with Jesus' response (vv. 9–10), shows that Jesus is speaking primarily at the spiritual or symbolic level. People need to be spiritually clean and, since this is not about baptism specifically,[92] questions about immersion need not come into play (v. 10). When he commands his disciples to wash one another's feet and explains that he has set them an example, he is first of all thinking of an application to menial service as a demonstration of intense love and devotion.[93] Yet baptism and the Last Supper (neither of which John explicitly mentions anywhere)[94] are also rich with symbolism, and almost every branch of the Christian church throughout history has understood them as ordinances or sacraments, to be literally imitated, because of their symbolic significance. Might the handful of denominations and churches that have added footwashing as a further sacrament or ordinance have recognized the power of the literal action to demonstrate outwardly the spiritual cleansing at work?[95] Might the importance of purity of all kinds in Jesus' ministry have been unwittingly minimized down through the ages?

Chapters 14–21 do not disclose the same frequency of the purity motif. Crucifixion, after all, is a very impure activity, supposedly limited to very corrupt individuals and creating very unclean corpses. Were the issue of cleansing one of the major theological emphases John wanted to highlight in the Fourth Gospel, one would have expected a heightened rather than a diminished focus on it as the climax of the Gospel with Jesus' death loomed ever nearer. If it was a historical reality that the final redaction of the Gospel was not concerned to stress, then we could understand why it took a back seat. Still, the references that do appear prove intriguing.

The Farewell Discourse can be outlined in chiastic fashion.[96] John 15:1–17 is then the climactic center, itself dividing into parallel parts in verses 1–8 and 9–17. On the other hand, not all the alleged parallels between the supposedly matching halves of this inversely parallel structure are as clear or as close as others. Perhaps it represents the rhetorical skeleton of Jesus' original address, which almost certainly was much longer, and which John has not labored to preserve as much as if it were his central focus.[97] With or without such parallelism, however, 15:1–17, with its metaphor of the vine and the branches and its call for self-giving love, is widely recognized as the theological heart of these three chapters.[98] Tucked into this heart or central section is a key reference to purification. Those who remain in Jesus are the branches which καθαίρει. In the metaphor at hand, it is natural to translate this as 'he prunes', but the most common meaning of the verb is to clean or cleanse.[99] Nothing is made of this, but it is just one more indication that when one looks below the surface of the main themes John stresses, cleansing and purification language proves more frequent than a superficial glance discloses.

The so-called 'high-priestly' prayer in chapter 17 likewise has exactly one reference, but an important one, to cleansing. Verses 17–19 contain Jesus' prayer to the Father for him to 'sanctify' his disciples by the truth of God's word (v. 17). This is no separatist retreat, however, because he

---

91   Clark-Soles, 'Of Footwashing and History', 261.
92   Despite the occasional claim to the contrary. Dunn, 'The Washing', 252, concludes that sacraments and ritual purity are far from John's mind here.
93   Van der Watt, 'Meaning'.
94   The significance of which is debated. For a good taxonomy of approaches, see Paschal, 'Sacramental Symbolism'.
95   Cf. Clark-Soles, 'Of Footwashing and History', 268; Kanagaraj, *John*, 136.
96   Brouwer, *Literary Development*.
97   Cf. my argument for a chiastically arranged parables source in Luke's travel narrative, which has influenced but not entirely determined his redactional arrangement of pericopae, in Blomberg, 'Midrash'.
98   See esp. Kunene, *Communal Holiness*.
99   Lee, *Flesh and Glory*, 93, states explicitly that the pruning of the branches is purification.

immediately adds that he has sent them into world as the Father sent him (v. 18). But then he returns to the previous topic, concluding, 'For them I sanctify myself, that they too may be truly sanctified' (v. 19). A more formally equivalent translation would be 'so that they also might be sanctified in truth' (NRSV, ESV) or 'by the truth' (NKJV, CSB). As he has just explained, 'your word is truth' (v. 17). It becomes too easy to read 'sanctify' through Pauline lenses and forget that the root meaning is to consecrate or set apart, which could even be by anointing. There are certainly overtones of purification here,[100] but the major Johannine themes of the prayer are the relationships between the Father and the Son and the need for unity among the disciples.

Chapter 18:28 contains a passing reference to the reason the Jewish leaders who brought Jesus to Pilate remained outside the Praetorium: 'to avoid ceremonial uncleanness' (NIV) or 'ritual defilement' (NRSV). The Greek reads simply, 'in order that they not be defiled' or 'stained' (ἵνα μὴ μιανθῶσιν). In other words, they do not want to become impure. But why do we even need to be told all this? John is going to develop an artistic sequence of Pilate alternating between being inside the palace with Jesus and outside the palace with his opponents in 18:28–19:16a.[101] But is this so odd? Would readers have expected the whole group of Jewish leaders to be inside clamoring for Jesus' execution? Perhaps the purpose clause is merely to help identify the sequence and chronology of events; despite many claims to the contrary, this actually helps to show that John does not contradict the Synoptics on the date of the crucifixion.[102] But the most we can say with any confidence is that it is another passing reference to matters of purity that seems to be deeply embedded at the core of the account, since little or nothing is made of it among the overall theological emphases of the Passion Narrative.

The final pre-resurrection reference to anything at all related to our topic appears in 19:34 when the piercing of Jesus' side led to a sudden flow of blood and water. In context, it appears merely to demonstrate the genuineness of Jesus' death, since an affirmation of the truth of the testimony of the man who saw this, presumably the Beloved Disciple, follows immediately.[103] But it is intriguing how often Patristic commentary found cleansing symbolism here, not only of Christ's death but even of subsequent martyrs.[104] Jesus' blood, like the water he offers, has been associated with eternal life. We do not have to read Pauline theology into the text to wonder if there is a relic of something quite old and quite traditional here. Still, it is hard to tell, and nothing more is made of it.

Of course, as we have seen with Lazarus, resurrection itself, especially when it is to full and eternal life as with Jesus' resurrection, is the ultimate form of cleansing. Apart from that fact, the only possible hint of purity issues appears when Peter jumps into the water after seeing Jesus on shore (21:7). But surely that is just because he's been in the fishing boat and is now, with his characteristic impulsiveness, eager to see Jesus. Perhaps. We are told also that he wrapped his outer garment around him because he had taken it off. The literature here typically assumes this is for modesty's sake as he comes closer to his Lord.[105] Are these two assumptions in tension with each other? He could have easily left his outer garment in the boat and gotten to shore more quickly. His inner garment would have prevented him from being too immodest in the presence

---

100 Esp. with the verbal allusion to the pruning of 15:2. See Whitacre, *John*, 414.
101 See, e.g., Moloney, *John*, 493–97.
102 For details, see Blomberg, *Historical Reliability of John's Gospel*, 221–25; cf. Pitre, *Jesus and the Last Supper*, 352–60.
103 Lincoln, *John*, 480, after a thoughtful consideration of one other candidate, the soldier responsible for the piercing of Jesus' side.
104 Klawiter, "'Living Water'".
105 E.g., Stube, *Graeco-Roman Rhetorical Reading*, 211; Heil, *Blood and Water*, 156, n. 8; though both of these scholars hint at issues of shame and cleansing as well.

of just one additional man. Granted, when the heavily laden boat got close enough to the shore it had to be dragged, but that is not likely to have been the case for the full hundred yards. Are we to imagine Peter swimming faster than the boat could be paddled? Is it too farfetched to suggest that Peter might have actually wanted to immerse himself in the water as a kind of ad hoc cleansing before returning to see the one he denied? The sequel in verses 15–23 will make it clear that he has not yet been 'reinstated' by Jesus, and he likely feels very unworthy if not also unclean.[106] But it is very hard to know with any confidence.

If all one countenances is literary criticism or a study of the final form of a Gospel, it becomes easy at this point to say that one has simply found another important motif for the final editor of the Fourth Gospel; entire books have been written about the water-motif in John.[107] It does not rise to the level of a major theme, but it remains an important subordinate motif. If one allows all the decades of source, form, tradition and redaction criticism to have had any validity, utilizing them even in a very cautious and chastened fashion, it seems much more likely that we have identified a pre-Johannine motif that did not sufficiently interest the final editor for him to make more of it than he did, but was nevertheless deeply embedded enough in the tradition that he preserved and thereby affirmed it at numerous points.[108] How much more might he have omitted since it wasn't a main emphasis?

6. Purity in John and the Synoptics

Of course, the emerging fourth quest does not intend to stop at such a point. It is not merely parity of the Fourth Gospel that is desired but integration of the historically probable material of the Fourth Gospel with what can be most securely affirmed about the historical Jesus from the Synoptics. If such integration proves too difficult, the Johannine material will most likely remain suspect. In this case, however, it is not that hard. It is widely agreed today that the historical Jesus would have kept the Mosaic purity laws, just as he would have obeyed the rest of the Law. Whatever one decides about the teaching attributed to him that appears to foresee a change in part of the Law with the arrival of the new covenant and therefore with the behavior of those who outlive him, while the Mosaic covenant remains in force unchanged, he would have been an exemplary follower of it. Because ritual purity has no close counterpart in the Western world, it may be the least studied aspect of the Law today, and especially in *New* Testament studies. The likelihood seems great that matters of purity played a much larger role for Jesus than most of us have realized.[109] In an essay on a number of the passages we have surveyed, Gary Burge concludes that 'in a word, *wherever the Johannine water motif appears, we should wonder if ritual purification is its most natural referent*' (italics his), and that 'Jesus's use of "water" does not need to be found in Hellenistic religious symbols, nor is it merely a literary device of the Gospel's author. It is a primitive echo of Jesus-traditions taking us back to the earliest moments of Christian memory'.[110]

At the same time, few aspects of the Law escaped Jesus' countercultural interpretations.

---

106 See esp. George, *Reading the Tapestry*, 123–24.
107 Jones, *The Symbol of Water*; Ng, *Water Symbolism*; Crutcher, *That He Might Be Revealed*; Song, *Water*.
108 Cf. Kazen, *Jesus and Purity*, esp. 197–98. Miller, *At the Intersection of Texts and Material Finds*, 141, adds that 'it is remarkable just how much of the water imagery used in the Gospel of John is already prevalent in late Second Temple Judaism'.
109 Cf. Jensen, 'Purity and Politics'; Magness, '"They Shall See the Glory of the Lord"'.
110 Burge, 'Siloam', 266, 268.

One may debate in numerous instances whether Jesus was merely quibbling with certain Pharisaic interpretation of the law (the so-called 'traditions of the ancestors') or pointing to a more fundamental issue, but the overall impression we get from the Synoptics is a much greater concern for moral than for ritual purity, most likely to redress an imbalance he perceived among at least some of the religious leadership of his day.[111] Even that is probably too simplistic a way of putting it, but it has the heuristic value of suggesting a trajectory of emphasis.

Particularly striking in this light, as one of the twelve core historical segments of the Jesus of the Synoptics, are Jesus' meals with sinners. As I have developed in book-length detail, much of Jesus' ministry can be encapsulated with the concept that holiness or purity is more contagious than impurity, a direct reversal of certain strands of Jewish thinking that had been growing in recent Second Temple Jewish thought.[112] That the Fourth Gospel, too, preserves references, many of them brief and in passing, to matters of purity meshes well with these observations. In John, it is the spiritual water that Jesus provides that matters. If one is to be literally immersed in water, it must be through the ministry of Jesus or the forerunner, John the Baptist, who heralded him. The jars for the old water rites of purification give way to the new wine that Jesus offers. He alone has the living water that bubbles up to eternal life or flows from him in rivers of life. If ritual handwashing is not possible in a particular setting, don't worry about it. If the water of a pool is believed to have healing power, come to Jesus who really does have it. If he nevertheless tells you to go wash in a certain pool, you should do it not because that water is special, but because he has commanded it. He is the one who can provide true consecration, dedication, sanctification. As one remains in him, as branches of a vine, he will prune (i.e., clean) one for additional service. Washing one another's particularly filthy feet is great preparation for and an object lesson about even the most disliked forms of service to others. Jesus also merits regal anointing. The holiest building in the world may be destroyed, but Jesus will be the new Temple. Resurrection for Jesus' disciples will one day outdo even what Lazarus experienced, though both are amazing acts of restoration to wholeness.

7. Conclusion

Simply put, a mining of both the Synoptics and the Fourth Gospel suggests issues of purity and impurity were more central to the ministry of the historical Jesus than has usually been acknowledged. Purity was closely related to holiness in ancient religious thought, especially in Judaism.[113] Superficial, visible actions could give impressions of holiness that did not match internal or underlying realities. True holiness may involve close association with that which is unholy in hopes of transforming it into something holier. As Hannah Harrington has shown, the Jesus movement formed a bridge between Pharisaic and then rabbinic Judaism on the one hand and paganism on the other.[114] Preserving the balance between adopting godly behavior that matters and is attractive, while avoiding unnecessary rules and restrictions that repel many, has been the perennial challenge for Jesus' followers and one not often achieved.

Indeed, just as in certain strands of the Judaism of Jesus' day, too often in the history of

---

111 Ottenheijm, 'Impurity', 146–47.
112 Blomberg, *Contagious Holiness*, esp. 65–95. Cf. Lockshin, 'Is Holiness Contagious?'.
113 Cf. Stare, 'Die Reinheitsthematik'; Busse, 'Reinigung und Heiligung'.
114 Harrington, *Holiness*, 206.

Christianity the church has reversed Jesus' thinking about what is most 'catching'. Impurity, it is widely believed, corrupts so quickly and so completely, that well-intentioned people must do their best to avoid it and to avoid the particularly impure or corrupt people who embody it. Jesus holds out the vision and the hope that, buttressed by a community of like-minded godly people, holiness can overflow to those who need to catch it and understand it in its most wholesome and winsome forms. Churches that grow and remain healthy over time usually recognize this, even if intuitively more than exegetically. In the increasingly post-Christian West, it may be this authentic Christianity that is the primary hope for reversing, in positive ways, trends of the church's diminishing influence in the world.

Bibliography

Allison, Dale C. Jr.	*Constructing Jesus: Memory, Imagination, and History* (Grand Rapids: Baker, 2010).
Allison, Dale C. Jr.	'The Secularizing of the Historical Jesus', *PRS* 27.2 (2000), 135–51.
Anderson, Paul N.	'Why the Gospel of John is Fundamental to Jesus Research', in James H. Charlesworth with Jolyon G. R. Pruszinski (eds.), *Jesus Research: The Gospel of John in Historical Inquiry* (London and New York: T&T Clark, 2019), 7–46.
Anderson, Paul N.	'Incidents Dispersed in the Synoptics and Cohering in John: Dodd, Brown and Johannine Historicity', in Tom Thatcher & Catrin Williams (eds.), *Engaging with C. H. Dodd on the Gospel of John. Sixty Years of Tradition and Interpretation* (Cambridge: Cambridge University Press, 2013), 176–202.
Anderson, Paul N.	*Riddles of the Fourth Gospel* (Minneapolis: Fortress, 2011).
Anderson, Paul N.	*The Fourth Gospel and the Quest for Jesus: Modern Foundations Reconsidered* (London and New York: T&T Clark, 2008).
Anderson, Paul N., Felix Just, & Tom Thatcher (eds.)	*John, Jesus, and History* (3 vols.; Atlanta: SBL, 2007–16). Vol, 1: *Critical Appraisals of Critical Views* (2007); Vol. 2: *Aspects of Historicity in the Fourth Gospel* (2015); Vol. 3: *Glimpses of Jesus through the Johannine Lens* (2016).
Askwith, Edward H.	*The Historical Value of the Fourth Gospel* (London: Hodder & Stoughton, 1910).
Barrett, C. K.	*The Gospel according to St. John* (London: SPCK; Philadelphia: Westminster, 1978 [2nd ed.]).
Barton, Stephen	'The Believer, the Historian and the Fourth Gospel', *Theology* 96 (1993), 289–302.
Bauckham, Richard	*The Testimony of the Beloved Disciple: Narrative, History, and Theology in the Gospel of John* (Grand Rapids: Baker, 2007).

Bauckham, Richard (ed.)   *The Gospels for All Christians: Rethinking the Gospel Audiences* (Grand Rapids: Eerdmans, 1998).

Beasley-Murray, George R.   *John* (Nashville: Thomas Nelson, 1999, rev. ed.).

Belleville, Linda L.   '"Born of Water and Spirit": John 3:5', *TrinJ* 1 (1980), 125–41.

Berger, Klaus   *Im Anfang war Johannes: Datierung und Theologie des vierten Evangeliums* (Stuttgart: Quell, 1997).

Blanton, Ward   *Displacing Christian Origins: Philosophy, Secularity, and the New Testament* (Chicago and London: University of Chicago Press, 2007).

Blomberg, Craig L.   'The Sayings of Jesus in Mark: Does Mark Ever Rely on a Pre-Johannine Tradition', in Stanley E. Porter & Hughson T. Ong (eds.), *The Origins of John's Gospel* (Leiden and Boston: Brill, 2016), 81–98.

Blomberg, Craig L.   'The Authenticity and Significance of Jesus' Table Fellowship with Sinners', in D.L. Bock & R.L. Webb (eds.), *Key Events in the Life of the Historical Jesus: A Collaborative Exploration of Context and Coherence* (Tübingen: Mohr Siebeck, 2009; Grand Rapids: Eerdmans, 2010), 215–50.

Blomberg, Craig L.   'Jesus, Sinners and Table Fellowship', *BBR* 19 (2009), 35–62.

Blomberg, Craig L.   *Contagious Holiness: Jesus' Meals with Sinners* (Leicester and Downers Grove: IVP, 2005).

Blomberg, Craig L.   *The Historical Reliability of John's Gospel: Issues and Commentary* (Leicester and Downers Grove: IVP, 2001).

Blomberg, Craig L.   'Midrash, Chiasmus, and the Outline of Luke's Central Section', in R. T. France & David Wenham (eds.), *Gospel Perspectives*, vol. 3 (Sheffield: JSOT Press, 1983; Eugene, OR: Wipf & Stock, 2003), 217–61.

Bock, Darrell L., & Benjamin I. Simpson   *Jesus according to Scripture* (Grand Rapids: Baker, 2017 [2nd ed.]).

Bock, Darrell L., & Robert L. Webb (eds.)   *Key Events in the Life of the Historical Jesus: A Collaborative Exploration of Context and Coherence* (Tübingen: Mohr Siebeck, 2009; Grand Rapids: Eerdmans, 2010).

Borchert, Gerald   *John 1–11* (Nashville: B & H, 1996).

Borg, Marcus   *Meeting Jesus Again for the First Time* (San Francisco: Harper San Francisco, 1994).

Bornkamm, Günther   *Jesus of Nazareth* (London: Hodder & Stoughton; New York: Harper & Bros., 1960).

Brouwer, Wayne   *The Literary Development of John 13–17: A Chiastic Reading* (Atlanta: SBL, 2000).

Brown, Raymond E.   *The Gospel according to John I–XII* (Garden City, NY: Doubleday, 1966).

Bruce, F. F.	*The Gospel of John* (Basingstoke: Pickering & Inglis; Grand Rapids: Eerdmans, 1983).
Bruce, Patricia	'John 5:1–18 The Healing at the Pool: Some Narrative, Socio-Historical and Ethical Issues', *Neot* 39 (2005), 39–56.
Bryan, Steven M.	'Power in the Pool: The Healing of the Man at Bethesda and Jesus' Violation of the Sabbath (Jn. 5:1–18)', *TynB* 54 (2003), 7–22.
Bultmann, Rudolf	*Jesus and the Word* (London: Fontana; New York: Scribner's, 1958 [German: 1926]).
Bultmann, Rudolf	*The History of the Synoptic Tradition* (Oxford: Blackwell; New York: Harper & Row, 1963 [German: 1921]).
Burge, Gary	'Siloam, Bethesda, and the Johannine Water Motif', in Paul N. Anderson, Felix Just, and Tom Thatcher (eds.), *John, Jesus, and History. Vol. 3: Glimpses of Jesus through the Johannine Lens* (Atlanta: SBL, 2016), 259–70.
Busse, Ulrich	'Reinigung und Heiligung im Johannesevangelium', in Bart J. Koet, Steve Moyise, & Joseph Verheyden (eds.), The *Scriptures of Israel in Jewish and Christian Tradition: Essays in Honour of Maarten J. J. Menken* (London and Boston: Brill, 2013), 141–58.
Calvert, D. G. A.	'An Examination of the Criteria for Distinguishing the Authentic Words of Jesus', *NTS* 18 (1972), 209–19.
Carson, D. A.	*The Gospel according to John* (Leicester: Apollos; Grand Rapids: Eerdmans, 1991).
Charlesworth, James H.	'The Historical Jesus in the Fourth Gospel: A Paradigm Shift?', *JSHJ* 8 (2010), 3–46.
Charlesworth, James H.	*Jesus as Mirrored in John: The Genius in the New Testament* (London: Bloomsbury T&T Clark, 2019; New York: Bloomsbury T&T Clark, 2020).
Clark-Soles, Jaime	'Of Footwashing and History', in Paul N. Anderson, Felix Just, and Tom Thatcher (eds.), *John, Jesus and History. Vol. 2: Aspects of Historicity in the Fourth Gospel* (Atlanta: SBL, 2015), 255–69.
Crossan, John Dominic	*The Historical Jesus: The Life of a Mediterranean Jewish Peasant* (San Francisco: HarperSanFrancisco, 1991).
Crutcher, Rhonda G.	*That He Might Be Revealed: Water Imagery and the Identity of Jesus in the Gospel of John* (Eugene: Pickwick, 2015).
Deines, Roland	*Jüdische Steingefässe und pharisäische Frömmigkeit: Ein archäologisch-historischer Beitrag zum Verständnis von Joh 2.6 und der jüdischen Reinheitshalacha zur Zeit Jesu* (Tübingen: J. C. B. Mohr, 1993).
Dodd, C.H.	*The Founder of Christianity* (London: Collins, 1971).
Dodd, C. H.	*Historical Tradition in the Fourth Gospel* (Cambridge: Cambridge University Press, 1963).

Dunn, James D. G.	*Jesus Remembered* (Grand Rapids: Eerdmans, 2003).
Dunn, James D. G.	'The Washing of the Disciples' Feet in John 13 1–20', *ZNW* 61 (1970), 247–52.
Ehrman, Bart D.	*Jesus: Apocalyptic Prophet of the New Millennium* (Oxford: Oxford University Press, 1999).
Ensor, Peter W.	*Jesus and His Works: Johannine Sayings in Historical Perspective* (Tübingen: Mohr Siebeck, 1996).
Evans, Craig A.	'Assessing Progress in the Third Quest for the Historical Jesus', *JSHJ* 4 (2006), 35–54.
Farmer, William R.	*The Gospel of Jesus: The Pastoral Relevance of the Synoptic Problem* (Louisville: Westminster John Knox, 1994).
Farmer, William R. (ed.)	*New Synoptic Studies: The Cambridge Gospel Conference and Beyond* (Macon: Mercer University Press, 1983).
Farmer, William R.	*The Synoptic Problem: A Critical Analysis* (London and New York: Macmillan, 1964).
Farrer, Austin M.	'On Dispensing with Q', in Dennis E. Nineham (ed.), *Studies in the Gospels: Essays in Memory of R. H. Lightfoot* (Oxford: Blackwell, 1955), 55–88.
Fortna, Robert T.	*The Fourth Gospel and Its Predecessor* (Philadelphia: Fortress, 1988).
Fortna, Robert T.	*The Gospel of Signs* (Cambridge: Cambridge University Press, 1970).
Fredriksen, Paula	*Jesus of Nazareth, King of the Jews: A Jewish Life and the Emergence of Christianity* (New York: Alfred Knopf, 1999).
Frey, Jörg	'Baptism in the Fourth Gospel, and Jesus and John as Baptizers', in R. Alan Culpepper & Jörg Frey (eds.), *Expressions of the Johannine Kerygma in John 2:23–5:18: Historical, Literary, and Theological Readings from the Colloquium Ioanneum 2017 in Jerusalem* (Tübingen: Mohr Siebeck, 2019), 87–115.
Gathercole, Simon J.	'The Critical and Dogmatic Agenda of Albert Schweitzer's *The Quest of the Historical Jesus*', *TynB* 51 (2000), 261–83.
George, Larry D.	*Reading the Tapestry: A Literary-Rhetorical Analysis of the Johannine Resurrection Narrative (John 20–21)* (New York: Peter Lang, 2000).
Goodacre, Mark S.	*The Case against Q: Studies in Markan Priority and the Synoptic Problem* (Harrisburg, PA: Trinity Press International, 2002).
Goulder, Michael D.	*Luke: A New Paradigm* (Sheffield: JSOT, 1989).
Haber, Susan	*'They Shall Purify Themselves', Essays on Purity in Early Judaism* (Adele Reinhartz, ed.; Atlanta: SBL, 2008).
Hägerland, Tobias	'The Future of Criteria in Historical Jesus Research', *JSHJ* 13 (2015), 43–65.

Harrington, Hannah	*Holiness: Rabbinic Judaism and the Graeco-Roman World* (London and New York: Routledge, 2001).
Headlam, A. C.	*The Fourth Gospel as History* (Oxford: Blackwell, 1948).
Heil, John P.	*Blood and Water: The Death and Resurrection of Jesus in John 18–21* (Washington, DC: Catholic Biblical Association of America, 1995).
Heilmann, Jan	'A Meal in the Background of John 6:52–58?', *JBL* 137 (2018), 481–500.
Hengel, Martin	*The Johannine Question* (London: SCM; Philadelphia: Trinity Press International, 1989).
Hengel, Martin, & Anna Maria Schwemer, *Jesus and Judaism* (Waco: Baylor University Press, 2019 [German: 2007]).	
Higgins, A. J B.	*The Historicity of the Fourth Gospel* (London: Lutterworth, 1960).
Holland, H. Scott	*The Fourth Gospel* (London: John Murray, 1923).
Holmén, Tom (ed.)	*Jesus from Judaism to Christianity: Continuum Approaches to the Historical Jesus* (London and New York: T&T Clark, 2007).
Hooker, Morna D.	'On Using the Wrong Tool', *Theology* 75 (1972), 570–81.
Hooker, Morna D.	'Christology and Methodology', *NTS* 17 (1971), 480–87.
Hunn, Debbie	'Who Are "They" in John 8:33?', *CBQ* 66 (2004), 387–99.
Jensen, Morten H.	'Purity and Politics in Herod Antipas's Galilee: The Case for Religious Motivation', *JSHJ* 11 (2013), 3–34.
Jeremias, Joachim	*New Testament Theology. Vol. 1: The Proclamation of Jesus* (London: SCM; New York: Scribner's, 1971).
Johnson, Brian D.	'The Jewish Feasts and Questions of Historicity in John 5–12', in Paul N. Anderson, Felix Just, and Tom Thatcher (eds.), *John, Jesus, and History. Vol. 2: Aspects of Historicity in the Fourth Gospel* (Atlanta: SBL, 2015), 117–29.
Jones, Larry P.	*The Symbol of Water in the Gospel of John* (Sheffield: Sheffield Academic Press, 1997).
Kanagaraj, Jey	*John* (Eugene: Cascade, 2013).
Käsemann, Ernst	'The Problem of the Historical Jesus', in *Essays on New Testament Themes* (London: SCM; Naperville, IL: Allenson, 1964 [German: 1954]), 15–47.
Kazen, Thomas	*Jesus and Purity Halakhah: Was Jesus Indifferent to Impurity?* (Stockholm: Almqvist & Wiksell, 2002; Winona Lake: Eisenbrauns, 2010).
Keener, Craig S.	*The Historical Jesus of the Gospels* (Grand Rapids: Eerdmans, 2009).
Keith, Chris, & Anthony LeDonne *Jesus, Criteria and the Demise of Authenticity* (London and New York: T&T Clark, 2012).	

Klawiter, Frederick C.	'"Living Water" and Sanguinary Witness: John 19:34 and Martyrs of the Second and Early Third Century', *JTS* 66 (2015), 553–73.
Kunene, Musa V. M.	*Communal Holiness in the Gospel of John: The Vine Metaphor as a Test Case with Lessons from African Hospitality and Trinitarian Theology* (Carlisle: Langham, 2012).
Latourelle, René	*The Miracles of Jesus and the Theology of Miracle* (New York: Paulist, 1988 [French: 1986]).
Lee, Dorothy A.	*Flesh and Glory: Symbolism, Gender and Theology in the Gospel of John* (New York: Crossroad, 2002).
Licona, Michael	'Is the Sky Falling in Contemporary Historical Jesus Research', *BBR* 26 (2016), 353–68.
Lierman, John (ed.)	*Challenging Perspectives on the Gospel of John* (Tübingen: Mohr Siebeck, 2006).
Lincoln, A. T.	*The Gospel according to Saint John* (London and New York: Continuum; Peabody: Hendrickson, 2005).
Lockshin, Martin I.	'Is Holiness Contagious?', in Carl S. Ehrlich, Anders Runesson, & Eileen Schuller (eds.), *Purity, Holiness, and Identity in Judaism and Christianity: Essays in Memory of Susan Haber* (Tübingen: Mohr Siebeck, 2013), 253–62.
Longenecker, Richard N.	*The Christology of Early Jewish Christianity* (London: SCM; Naperville, IL: Allenson, 1970).
Magness, Jodi	'"They Shall See the Glory of the Lord" (Isa 35:2), Eschatological Perfection and Purity at Qumran and in Jesus' Movement', *JSHJ* 14 (2016), 99–119.
McGrath, James F.	'"Destroy This Temple": Issues of History in John 2:13–22', in Paul N. Anderson, Felix Just, and Tom Thatcher (eds.), *John, Jesus and History. Vol. 2: Aspects of Historicity in the Fourth Gospel* (Atlanta: SBL, 2015), 35–43.
Meier, John P.	*A Marginal Jew: Rethinking the Historical Jesus* (5 vols. [to date]; New York: Doubleday; New Haven: Yale University Press, 1991–).
Metzger, Bruce M.	*A Textual Commentary on the Greek New Testament* (New York & London: UBS, 1975 [2nd corr. ed.]).
Miller, Stuart S.	*At the Intersection of Texts and Material Finds: Stepped Pools, Stone Vessels, and Ritual Purity among the Jews or Roman Galilee* (Göttingen and Bristol, CT: Vandenhoeck & Ruprecht, 2015).
Miller, Susan	'The Woman at the Well: John's Portrayal of the Samaritan Mission', in Paul N. Anderson, Felix Just, and Tom Thatcher (eds.), *John, Jesus and History. Vol. 2: Aspects of Historicity in the Fourth Gospel* (Atlanta: SBL, 2015), 73–81.
Moloney, Francis J.	'The Fourth Gospel and the Jesus of History', *NTS* 46 (2000), 42–58.

Moloney, Francis J.	*The Gospel of John* (Collegeville, MN: Liturgical, 1998).
Moloney, Francis J.	'The Faith of Martha and Mary: A Narrative Approach to John 11:17–40', *Bib* 75 (1994), 471–93.
Motyer, Stephen	*Your Father the Devil: A New Approach to John and the Jews* (Carlisle: Paternoster, 1997).
Murphy, Catherine M.	*John the Baptist: Prophet of Purity for a New Age* (Collegeville: Liturgical, 2003).
Neill, Stephen, & N. T. Wright	*The Interpretation of the New Testament 1861–1986* (Oxford: Oxford University Press, 1988 [2nd ed.]).
Ng, Wai-Yee	*Water Symbolism in John: An Eschatological Interpretation* (NY: Peter Lang, 2001).
Ottenheijm, Eric	'Impurity between Intention and Deed: Purity Disputes in First Century Judaism and in the New Testament', in Marcel J. H. M. Poorthuis & Joshua Schwartz (eds.), *Purity and Holiness: The Heritage of Leviticus* (Leiden and Boston: Brill, 2000), 129–47.
Painter, John	'The Fourth Gospel and the Founder of Christianity: The Place of Historical Tradition in the Work of C. H. Dodd', in Tom Thatcher & Catrin Williams (eds.), *Engaging with C. H. Dodd on the Gospel of John. Sixty Years of Tradition and Interpretation* (Cambridge: Cambridge University Press, 2013), 257–84.
Paschal, R. Wade Jr.	'Sacramental Symbolism and Physical Imagery in the Gospel of John', *TynB* 32 (1981), 151–76.
Pitre, Brent	*Jesus and the Last Supper* (Grand Rapids: Eerdmans, 2015).
Poirier, J. C.	'Hanukkah in the Narrative Chronology of the Fourth Gospel', *NTS* 54 (2008), 465–78.
Poon, Wilson C. K.	'Superabundant Table Fellowship in the Kingdom: The Feeding of the Five Thousand and the Meal Motif in Luke', *ExpT* 114 (2003), 224–30.
Porter, Stanley E.	*John, His Gospel, and Jesus: In Pursuit of the Johannine Voice* (Grand Rapids: Eerdmans, 2015).
Porter, Stanley E.	*The Criteria of Authenticity in Historical-Jesus Research: Previous Discussion and New Proposals* (Sheffield: Sheffield Academic Press, 2000).
Robinson, J. Armitage	*The Historical Character of St. John's Gospel* (London: Longmans Green, 1908).
Robinson, James M.	*A New Quest of the Historical Jesus* (London: SCM; Naperville, IL: Allenson, 1959).
Robinson, John A. T.	*The Priority of John* (J. F. Coakley, ed.; London: SCM, 1985; Oak Park, IL: Meyer-Stone, 1987).

Robinson, John A. T.	'The New Look on the Fourth Gospel', in *Studia Evangelica*, V. 18 = *Texte und Untersuchungen* 73 (1959), 338–50. Republished in *Twelve New Testament Studies* (London: SCM, 1962), 94–106.
Rubio, Fernando B.	'The Fiction of the "Three Quests": An Argument for Dismantling a Dubious Historiographical Paradigm', *JSHJ* 7 (2009), 211–53.
Sanday, William	*The Authorship and Historical Character of the Fourth Gospel* (London: Macmillan, 1872).
Sanders, E. P.	*Jesus and Judaism* (London: SCM; Philadelphia: Fortress, 1985).
Sanders, E. P.	*Paul and Palestinian Judaism* (London: SCM; Philadelphia: Fortress, 1977).
Schröter, Jens	*Jesus of Nazareth: Jew from Galilee, Savior of the World* (Waco: Baylor University Press, 2014 [German: 2006]).
Schweitzer, Albert	*The Quest of the Historical Jesus: A Critical Study of Its Progress from Reimarus to Wrede* (Minneapolis: Fortress, 2001 [German: 1906], expd. ed.).
Song, Seung-In	*Water as an Image of the Spirit in the Johannine Literature* (New York: Peter Lang, 2019).
Stare, Mira	'Die Reinheitsthematik im Johannesevangelium', *SNTSU* 40 (2015), 79–95.
Stein, Robert H.	'The "Criteria for Authenticity"', in R. T. France and David Wenham (eds.), *Gospel Perspectives*. Vol. 1: *Studies of History and Tradition in the Four Gospels* (Sheffield: JSOT, 1980; Eugene: Wipf & Stock, 2003), 225–53.
Stube, John C.	*A Graeco-Roman Rhetorical Reading of the Farewell Discourse* (London & NY: T&T Clark, 2006).
Theissen, Gerd, & Dagmar Winter	*The Quest for the Plausible Jesus* (M.E. Boring, trans.; Louisville: Westminster John Knox, 2002 [German: 1997]).
Theissen, Gerd, & Annette Merz	*The Historical Jesus: A Comprehensive Guide* (London: SCM; Minneapolis: Fortress, 1998 [German: 1996]).
Thompson, Marianne Meye	'The Historical Jesus and the Johannine Christ', in R. Alan Culpepper & C. Clifton Black (eds.), *Exploring the Gospel of John* (Louisville: Westminster John Knox, 1996), 21–42.
Thompson, Robin	'Healing at the Pool of Bethesda: A Challenge to Asclepius?', *BBR* 27 (2017), 65–84.
Tovey, Derek M. H.	'On Not Unbinding the Lazarus Story: The Nexus of History and Theology in John 11:1–44', in P.N. Anderson, F. Just, & T. Thatcher (eds.), *John, Jesus and History*. Vol. 2: *Aspects of Historicity in the Fourth Gospel* (Atlanta: SBL, 2015), 213–23.
Tuckett, Christopher M.	*The Revival of the Griesbach Hypothesis: An Analysis and Appraisal* (Cambridge: Cambridge University Press, 1983).

Twelftree, Graham H.	'Jesus the Baptist', *JSHJ* 7 (2009), 103–25.
van Belle, Gilbert	'The Return of John to Jesus Research', *LS* 32 (2007), 23–48.
van der Watt, Jan	'The Meaning of Jesus Washing the Feet of His Disciples (John 13)', *Neot* 51 (2017), 25–39.
Vermes, Geza	*The Authentic Gospel of Jesus* (London: Allen Lane, 2003; New York: Penguin, 2004).
von Wahlde, Urban C.	'The Pool of Siloam: The Importance of the New Discoveries for our Understanding of Ritual Immersion in Late Second Temple Judaism and the Gospel of John', in P.N. Anderson, F. Just, & T. Thatcher (eds.), *John, Jesus, and History*. Vol. 2: *Aspects of Historicity in the Fourth Gospel* (Atlanta: SBL, 2015), 155–73.
von Wahlde, Urban C.	'The Pool(s) of Bethesda and the Healing in John 5: A Reappraisal of Research and of the Johannine Text', *RB* 116 (2009), 111–36.
von Wahlde, Urban C.	*The Gospel and Letters of John*. Vol. 2: *Commentary on the Gospel of John* (Grand Rapids: Eerdmans, 2010).
Warren, Meredith J. C.	*My Flesh Is Meat Indeed: A Nonsacramental Reading of John 6:51–58* (Minneapolis: Fortress, 2015).
Wassen, Cecilia	'Jesus' Table Fellowship with "Toll Collectors and Sinners": Questioning the Alleged Purity Implications', *JSHJ* 14 (2016), 137–57.
Weaver, Walter P.	*The Historical Jesus in the Twentieth Century 1900–1950* (Harrisburg, PA: Trinity Press international, 1999).
Wenham, David	'A Historical View of John's Gospel', *Themelios* 23 (1998), 5–21.
Wenham, David	'The Enigma of the Fourth Gospel: Another Look', *TynBul* 48 (1997), 149–78.
Westcott, B. F.	*The Gospel according to St. John* (London: James Clarke, 1958 [rev. ed.]).
Westerholm, Stephen, & Martin Westerholm	*Reading Sacred Scripture: Voices from the History of Biblical Interpretation* (Grand Rapids: Eerdmans, 2016).
Whitacre, Rodney A.	*John* (Downers Grove and Leicester: IVP, 1999).
Winter, Dagmar	'Saving the Quest for Authenticity from the Criterion of Dissimilarity: History and Plausibility', in C. Keith & A. Le Donne (eds.), *Jesus, Criteria and the Demise of Authenticity* (London and New York: T&T Clark, 2012), 115–31.
Winter, Dagmar	'The Dissimilar Jesus: Anti-Semitism, Protestantism, Hero Worship and Dialectical Theology', in Bruce Chilton, Anthony Le Donne, & Jacob Neusner (eds.), *Soundings in the Religion of Jesus: Perspectives and Methods in Jewish and Christian Scholarship* (Minneapolis: Fortress, 2012), 129–42.

Witetschek, Stephan	'The Hour of the Lamb? Some Remarks on John 19:14 and the Hour of Jesus's Condemnation and/or Crucifixion?', in P.N. Anderson, F. Just, & T. Thatcher (eds.), *John, Jesus and History. Vol. 3: Glimpses of Jesus through the Johannine Lens* (Atlanta: SBL, 2016), 95–107.
Witherington, Ben III	*The Jesus Quest: The Third Search for the Jew of Nazareth* (Downers Grove: IVP, 1997).
Wright, N.T.	*Jesus and the Victory of God* (London: SPCK; Minneapolis: Fortress, 1996).
Wright, N.T.	*The Challenge of Jesus: Rediscovering Who Jesus Was and Is* (Downers Grove: IVP, 1999).

Craig L. Blomberg
Denver Seminary, Littleton, CO, USA.
craig.blomberg@denverseminary.edu

The Two Ways of the Lord in Luke and Acts
Distinguishing Two Metaphorical Uses of One Term

ARCO DEN HEIJER

Abstract

The expression 'the way (of the Lord/of God)' is often understood as a self-designation of the early Christians and interpreted against the background of Isaiah 40:3–5. This article argues that the expression is used metaphorically in Luke and Acts in two distinct ways. In the quotation from Isaiah 40 in Luke 3:4–5, the way denotes the way on which the Lord comes to Jerusalem. This way is to be distinguished from the way on which the Lord wants his disciples to walk, as a metaphor for what he teaches them through his apostles. The extensive usage of way-metaphors serves the Lukan presentation of the teaching of Jesus and his disciples as instruction in the way of life that has been taught by the God of Israel since ancient times. It emphasises the continuity between the ancient people of Israel and the Jewish and non-Jewish disciples of Jesus.

1. Introduction

One of the problems scholars face in speaking about early Christianity is how to name it.[1] The name 'Christians' is relatively rarely attested in the first and second centuries and remains for a long time a name used only by outsiders.[2] Hence the scholarly convention of speaking about the Jesus-movement or the Christ-movement, Christ-followers or Christ-believers, cumbersome compounds to describe those gathered around the memory and worship of Jesus.

In the context of discussions about self-designations of early Christians, it is often remarked that they called themselves 'the Way'.[3] Sometimes, this term is interpreted as 'movement', and considered an attractive alternative to 'Christianity' because of the flexibility and openness that a movement suggests.[4] The basis for speaking about early Christians as 'the Way' is provided in

---

1 I would like to thank Rob van Houwelingen and Taylor Wilton-Morgan for their comments on content and language of this article.
2 Cf. the recent overview in Van der Lans and Bremmer, 'Tacitus', 317–22.
3 Cf. e.g. Van der Lans and Bremmer, 'Tacitus', 318; Haenchen, *Apostelgeschichte*, 308.
4 Especially in Pathrapankal, 'Christianity', 533–39.

a few passages of Acts. Scholarship on these passages has noted parallels to the use of 'the Way' as self-designation in Qumran[5] or in philosophical literature,[6] and/or has connected it to Isaiah 40:3–5 (and its interpretation in Second Temple Judaism), where the term 'the way of the Lord' appears in a passage also quoted in Luke 3:4–5.[7]

Through an analysis of the use of metaphorical usages of 'the way' in Luke and Acts, this article argues against two popular views: that 'the way' is a self-designation of the Christians as group, and that it is to be interpreted primarily in the light of Isaiah 40.[8]

First, I will argue that the term 'the way (of the Lord/of God)' is used metaphorically in two distinct ways in the two books to Theophilus. In the quotation of Isaiah 40 in Luke 3:4–5, it is used to refer to the way on which the Lord comes to Jerusalem, whereas in most other passages, the term refers to the way on which the Lord wants his disciples to walk, as a metaphor for the conduct that he has taught his apostles, who pass it on to other disciples. This usage also has a background in the Old Testament, but not primarily in Isaiah 40. In both cases, 'the Lord' refers to the God of Israel and also to Jesus in deliberate ambiguity, as Kavin Rowe has shown.[9] That Luke[10] uses the metaphor in two different ways will be argued by exegesis of Luke 3:4–5 on the one hand, and key texts on 'the way (of the Lord / of God)' in Acts on the other hand. Second, the wider use of way-metaphors in Luke and Acts will be explored. The focus will be on the use of these metaphors, rather than on understanding the narrative as a whole as a 'journey narrative'.[11] In the conclusion, I will address the question why Luke employs these metaphors with regard to the disciples of Jesus.

My understanding of metaphor is informed by Conceptual Metaphor Theory and *Bildfeld* theory.[12] Both theories do not interpret metaphors in isolation, but as part of a larger domain or *Bildfeld*. Thus, although this article concentrates on instances of ὁδός in Acts, it also includes, for instance, metaphorical references to 'walking'. Moreover, in line with conceptual metaphor theory, it does not only look at instances where the metaphor is clearly intended as a style figure, but also instances where it has become part of normal Greek language.

---

5 Especially 1QS 9.17, 10.21. Cf. Repo, *Der 'Weg'*, with Gnilka, Review, and Hengel, Review. Cf. also Fitzmyer, *Essays*, 282–83; Barrett, *Acts*, 1:448; Keener, *Acts*, 2:1626–27.
6 See especially Urcioli, 'Quella ὁδός', who refers to Lucian, *Hermot.* 46. There, Lucian speaks about the 'ways' of philosophy in reference to the various schools of thought (αἱρέσεις). This differs from the usage in Acts which speaks in absolute terms about 'the way'.
7 Cf. e.g. the interpretation of Bauckham, 'The Early Jerusalem Church', 76: 'For the earliest Christian community the task of *preparing* the way [...], proclaimed by John the Baptist, might well have been considered already complete. They were now travelling the way' (italics original). Cf. further McCasland, 'The Way'; Pathrapankal, 'Christianity'; Olsson, 'De som hörde till Vägen', 270; Trebilco, *Self-Designations*, 254; Hengel and Schwemer, *Die Urgemeinde*, 24–25, 237; Pao, *Acts*; Mallen, *The Reading*.
8 Older literature arguing against 'the way' as designation of a 'movement' or group of people, includes especially Zahn, *Apostelgeschichte*, 321; Michaelis, 'ὁδός', 93; Lyonnet, 'La voie', 149–64. Martin Hengel endorses Repo's term 'Richtungsbenennung' ('Term for a school of thought') in Hengel, Review, 362. In the recent book of Anna Maria Schwemer, which builds on notes by Martin Hengel, ἡ ὁδός is considered a designation of both the Christians and their teaching, Hengel and Schwemer, *Urgemeinde*, 237. Similarly Völkel, 'ὁδός'. According to Silva, 'ὁδός', 459, 'both the community and the proclamation—which also comprises a partic. walk of life or way—are involved in the term and both belong together'.
9 Cf. Rowe, *Early Narrative Christology*.
10 I follow tradition in calling the author of the Third Gospel and Acts 'Luke', without implying a particular view on the authorship of these books, except that both books *ad Theophilum* were written by the same author. For a different view, cf. Walters, *The Assumed Authorial Unity*.
11 On this, cf. e.g. Germiquet, 'Luke's Journey Narrative'.
12 On conceptual metaphor theory, cf. e.g. Lakoff and Johnson, *Metaphors*; Kövecses, *Metaphor*. On *Bildfeld* theory, cf. Weinrich, 'Münze'; Peil, 'Überlegungen'.

2. The Way Metaphor in the Quotation of Isaiah in Luke 3:4–6

The central argument for interpreting the ὁδός-metaphors in Luke and Acts in the light of Isaiah 40:3–5 is the quotation of this text in Luke 3:4–5. How does the term ὁδός κυρίου function there?

The quotation comments on the activity of John the Baptist, who 'went into the entire region around the Jordan, where he proclaimed an immersion that signals a change of mind[13] in order to receive forgiveness of sins' (βάπτισμα μετανοίας εἰς ἄφεσιν ἁμαρτιῶν, Luke 3:3).[14] To proclaim (κηρύσσειν) is the act of a herald (κήρυξ), which explains the link with the quotation from Isaiah. John's voice is the 'voice of someone calling in the desert' (Luke 3:4). The words of this voice apply to his practice of calling people to change their mind in repentance. This is the Lucan version:

> Prepare the way of the Lord,
> make straight his paths.
> Every ravine will be filled up,
> and every mountain and hill will be reduced,
> and the winding roads will be made into a straight [way],
> and the rough ones into smooth ways,
> and all flesh will see the salvation (τό σωτήριον) of God. (Luke 3:4–6)

The passive forms in Luke 3:5 obscure the agent of this action, but since they follow the imperatives of verse 4, it is most natural to assume that it is the result of human action. The metaphor of 'preparing the way' is taken from the image of a king who comes to his city and expects to be welcomed and to enter the city on well-paved roads. In poetic hyperbole, Isaiah speaks of 'ravines', 'mountains' and 'hills', to indicate the huge effort required in preparing the way of the Lord. This 'way of the Lord' is the way on which God will come through the desert to his people to bring salvation, rather than the way on which the people will travel from Babylon back to Jerusalem—indeed, it is hardly conceivable that the exiles would have to prepare the road to their homeland in order to enable God to bring them back. What is in view is the reverent welcoming of God as he comes to his people to save them.[15]

Luke understands this preparation of the way as a metaphor for a change of mind (μετάνοια) that results in righteous conduct. To the multitudes who want to be baptised, John says: 'Bring forth valuable fruits of your change of mind' (Luke 3:8). Thus, the preparation of the way of the Lord consists in preparing God's people to live righteously (Luke 1:17). This usage of the metaphor resembles that in the Community Rule of Qumran, where 'preparing the way of ••••' (Isaiah 40:3) consists of 'study of the law'.[16]

---

13 Cf. BDAG, s.v. μετάνοια.

14 All translations of biblical texts in this article are my own, based on the critical text of NA-28.

15 *Pace* Trebilco, *Self-Designations*, 250. Borgman, *The Way*, 30, glosses over the difference when he speaks of repentance as 'the daily texture of preparing and going God's Way'. Pao, *Acts*, 66, notes that the use of the term 'Way' 'evokes the Exodus tradition in an attempt to (re)define the people of God', but is not clear about precisely to what this way refers in Isaiah 40:3–5 and in Luke 3:4–6. In contrast, Rotman, *The Call*, 70–75, 147–48, rightly emphasizes that the way in view here is the way of God who comes to his people to save them. Indeed, this is the most likely interpretation of Isaiah 40:3–5 itself, as argued by Lund, *Way Metaphors*, 87. Cf. also Barstad, *A Way*. Differently Lim, *The 'Way of the Lord'*, but see Tiemeyer, *Review*. For a general critique of the use of 'New Exodus'-motifs in New Testament scholarship, cf. Smith, 'Uses'.

16 1 QS 8:12–15, cf. 9:19 (The scroll uses four dots to replace the tetragrammaton). Many scholars assert that 'the way of the Lord' is interpreted as 'study of the Law' here, e.g. Fitzmyer, *Essays*, 282; Hengel and Schwemer, *Die Urgemeinde*, 237. However, more accurately, it is the preparation of the way (1 QS 8:12–15) or the levelling of the way (9:19) that is interpreted as such.

3. The Coming of the Lord on the Way to Jerusalem

In the Gospel of Luke, the metaphor of God's inspection or visitation (ἐπισκοπή) is taken from the same *Bildfeld*, as Brent Kinman has argued persuasively.[17] God comes as a king to inspect his people and he will punish the inhabitants if he does not receive a proper welcome or if they will be found to be disobedient. Indeed, the Lucan Jesus predicts in Luke 19:44 that Jerusalem will be destroyed because the city has not recognised the moment of her visitation. In Jesus, the Lord himself has come to visit Jerusalem. Jesus came on a donkey, in accordance with the prophecy of Zechariah about the coming of the king of Zion,[18] hailed by a multitude of disciples (Luke 19:29–40), but he was crucified at the instigation of Jerusalem's Jewish authorities—and for this, Peter indicts his audience in his Pentecost speech (see Acts 2:36).

Thus, John had come to prepare the way for Jesus. This is evident in Luke 7:27, where Jesus says about John, 'this is the one about whom it is written: "Look, I send my messenger ahead of you, who will prepare your way before you."' The 'I' is God, the 'messenger' is John, the 'you' is Jesus. Also Paul, looking back at Jesus' ministry, speaks in Pisidian Antioch explicitly of Jesus' (royal) entry when he looks back on John's proclamation: 'From his seed [i.e. of David], according to the promise, God raised a saviour (σωτῆρα) for Israel, Jesus, after John had gone as herald in front of him at his entry (προκηρύξαντος Ἰωάννου πρὸ προσώπου τῆς εἰσόδου αὐτοῦ), proclaiming an immersion as signal of a change of mind for the whole people of Israel' (Acts 13:23–24).

To conclude: the way of the Lord referred to in the quotation of Isaiah 40:3–5 in Luke 3:4–6 is the way on which the Lord comes to his people as king to save them, and the preparation of this way is a metaphor for the change of mind and conduct to which John the Baptist exhorted his audience. Jesus' journey to Jerusalem in the so-called Lukan travel narrative (Luke 9:51–19:44) can be understood as the way of the Lord prepared by John. However, this 'way of the Lord' should be distinguished from the other usage of the expression 'the way of the Lord', to which we now turn.

4. Observations on 'the Way' as Metaphor in Acts

In Acts, the expression 'the way of the Lord' refers not to the way on which the Lord comes to his people, but to the way on which the Lord directs his disciples to walk, as a metaphor for their conduct, as will be argued below. The relevant passages in Acts are well-known: in Acts 9:2, 'those who are of the way' refers to the 'disciples of the Lord' (9:1) whom Saul sought to take captive in the synagogues of Damascus. In Acts 18:25–26, Apollos is described as 'informed/instructed concerning the way of the Lord', but since he knew only the baptism of John, Priscilla and Aquila explained 'the way of God' more accurately to him. The manuscripts show a lot of variation here, alternating between 'way' and 'word' and 'the Lord' and 'God'. In Acts 19:9, some Jews in Ephesus who refuse to be persuaded by Paul about the things concerning the kingdom of God, 'spoke badly about the way before the multitude'. Shortly afterwards, 'no small tumult arose about the way' (Acts 19:23), the occasion being Paul's teaching that gods made by hands are no gods (19:26). In Acts 22:4, Paul looks back at his persecution of the disciples and says that he 'persecuted this way unto death'. Finally, in Acts 24:14, Paul claims in his defence speech before Felix ('who knew the things about the way quite accurately', 24:22) that he serves the God of his ancestors according to 'the way which they call a αἵρεσις'. What is meant by this way?

---

17   Kinman, *Jesus' Entry*.
18   Zech 9:9, an allusion made explicit in the Matthean version, Matt 21:5.

Acts 18:25–26 provides a good starting point. Here, 'the way of the Lord/of God' occurs explicitly as an object of instruction. It denotes that which the 'disciples of the Lord' (Acts 9:1) learn and teach. Thus, it is in a paradigmatic relation with a number of other terms that function as object of the apostolic teaching activity, most prominently 'the word of God/the Lord' and 'the teaching (διδαχή) of the Lord'. These parallel constructs suggest that 'the way of the Lord/of God' in these passages denotes 'the way taught by the Lord'[19] rather than 'the way on which the Lord comes as saviour and king'. The metaphor in view here is a different one from the metaphor in Luke 3:1. Here, the image is that the Lord teaches his disciples a way on which to walk, and 'walking the way of God' is a metaphor for having the right views on Jesus (based on Scripture) and on the Spirit, and for living accordingly. After the supplementary instruction by Priscilla and Aquila (about baptism), Apollos is able to demonstrate through the Scriptures that Jesus is the Anointed one: the way of the Lord which they teach is based on the Scriptures of Israel (Acts 18:28).

Acts 19:9 and 23 and 24:14 confirm this interpretation and further clarify the content of this teaching. In Acts 19:9 it relates to 'the things about the kingdom' concerning which Paul speaks in the synagogue. In Acts 19:23 the tumult regarding the way relates to Paul's teaching to the Gentiles: that 'gods made by hands are no gods', an argument presented more extensively and eloquently in Paul's speech at the Athenian Areopagus (see especially Acts 17:29). And when Paul states before Felix that he serves God according to 'the way which they call a αἵρεσις' (Acts 24:14), his defence is that this involves nothing else than 'believing all things which are according to the Law and written in the prophets' and 'having a hope on God which they themselves also expect, that there will be a resurrection of righteous and wicked' (Acts 24:14–15). As a result, Paul trains to keep his conscience free from stumbling (Acts 24:16). Thus, the 'way' taught by Priscilla and Aquila, Paul, and others, comprises both belief and conduct.

Further insight in the meaning of 'the way of the Lord' is given through the comparison with a αἵρεσις in Acts 24:14. Paul is said to be a leading figure (πρωτοστάτην) of the αἵρεσις of the Ναζωραῖοι, the disciples of Jesus of Nazareth (Acts 24:5). This outsider designation of the disciples aligns them with the αἵρεσις of the Pharisees and that of the Sadducees. David Runia has argued that αἵρεσις refers to a 'school of thought', rather than a 'sect' or 'heresy', in Greek philosophical texts as well as in Philo and Josephus.[20] In Acts 5:17 he finds the first use of αἵρεσις for a group ('all those with the high priest' are described as 'this being the αἵρεσις of the Sadducees').[21] This meaning may also be in view in Acts 24:5, but still, this group is defined by its thought, its teaching. In Acts 28:22, the Jews in Rome express their desire to 'hear what your thoughts are (ἀκοῦσαι ἃ φρονεῖς), because it is known to us that this αἵρεσις is spoken against everywhere'. The rumours about the controversies concerning the αἵρεσις which Paul adheres to contrast with the lack of anything bad they have heard about Paul's person (Acts 28:21). Hence, they want to question him about his viewpoints. The αἵρεσις denotes a set of convictions about Jesus and the kingdom of God, based on interpretation of the Law of Moses and the Prophets (Acts 28:23): the convictions which the disciples, also known as the Christians (Acts 11:26), believe and according to which they live. In the mouth of the Roman Jews, the pronoun in 'this αἵρεσις' has a pejorative function, but the term αἵρεσις as such is not pejorative. Like the Greek philosophical αἱρέσεις, the

---

19 Cf. Martin Hengel: 'Die Christen lebten nach dem von Jesus gebotenen דרך ('The Christians lived according to the way commanded by Jesus'). Hengel, Review, 363.
20 Cf. especially Josephus, B.J. 2.118–119, where αἵρεσις is used alongside the remark that 'philosophy is practiced among the Judeans in three forms' (Τρία γὰρ παρὰ Ἰουδαίοις εἴδη φιλοσοφεῖται). See also Saldarini, Pharisees, 123–27. Saldarini defines αἵρεσις as 'a coherent and principled choice of a way of life, that is, of a particular school of thought' (p. 123).
21 Runia, 'Philo of Alexandria'. See also Cadbury, 'Names', 390.

Jewish αἵρεσεις constitute—at least from the perspective of Jews like Josephus, whose cultural milieu the author of Acts seems to share to a large extent[22]—various schools of thought from which people choose one by which to study and live.[23] Ancient philosophy constitutes a 'way of life',[24] and so do the Jewish philosophies. If the 'way of the Lord' is similar to a αἵρεσις, it refers primarily to a body of teaching, not to a group.

However, if the term αἵρεσις as such is not pejorative, this raises the question why does Paul himself not adopt the term αἵρεσις, speaking instead of 'the way *which they call* a αἵρεσις' (24:14)? The answer must be sought in his insistence on serving the God of the ancestors according to the Scriptures. Unlike the αἵρεσεις of Pharisees, Essenes and Sadducees, which had become established and respectable schools of thought by the first century c.e., the αἵρεσις of the Nazarenes was a new one, named after Jesus of Nazareth, crucified under Pontius Pilate along with two criminals (κακοῦργοι, Luke 23:32). The writings of Josephus illustrate the reputation of such a novel αἵρεσις, a 'fourth philosophy', among the Roman élite. Indeed, Tacitus, Pliny, and Suetonius express their contempt about the *Christiani* as adherents of a novel and pernicious *superstitio*.[25] Hence, Luke's Paul neither affirms being a 'leading figure of the school of thought of the Nazarenes' (Acts 24:5) nor affirms that he tries to persuade king Agrippa in order to make him a Christian (Acts 26:28). Rather, he expresses his wish that Agrippa be like him: someone who serves God according to the Law and the Prophets. The 'way' to which the disciples adhere is not a new school of thought established by Jesus of Nazareth, it is the way that has been taught in Israel from ancient times onwards, the *mos maiorum* ('traditional custom') of Israel.[26]

What is the background of this usage of 'the way of the Lord' as 'the way which the Lord teaches his disciples to walk', as metaphor for human belief and conduct that closely parallels the expression 'the word of the Lord'? The metaphor of the way, road, or path that the Lord teaches people to go is widely attested in the Old Testament, especially in the Psalms and the Prophets— but not in Isaiah 40:3–5.[27] It resembles the motif of the Two Ways, widespread in Jewish and early Christian literature.[28] However, it differs slightly from this motif in that 'the way' is contrasted to 'deviating from the way' in Acts (as well as in some passages in Qumran literature)[29] rather than 'the right way' being contrasted to 'the wrong way'.

Can the interpretation of 'the way of the Lord' as a body of teaching be applied to all references to 'the way' in Acts? It faces a challenge in explaining Acts 22:4, where Paul claims to have persecuted 'this way' unto death. Here, indeed, 'this way' refers to the men and women whom Paul chained and handed over into prisons (Acts 22:4b). Although the pronoun 'this' does not have a clear antecedent in the text, it is clear from the surrounding narrative that Paul is referring to the way of which he is considered to be a leader, whom Jews from Asia Minor accused of teaching against the nation, the law, and the temple (Acts 21:28). In his defence, Paul begins to emphasise his meticulous instruction in the ancestral law under Gamaliel and his zeal for God. Driven by this zeal, he persecuted 'this way' until Jesus appeared to him and appointed him as witness for all men. Here, 'this way' functions as shorthand for 'those who are of the way' (Acts 9:2), the 'disciples of the

---

22   Cf. Böttrich, 'Das lukanische Doppelwerk'.
23   The primary meaning of αρεσις is 'choice', and hence also 'object of choice'.
24   Hadot, *Qu'est-ce que la philosophie antique?*
25   Cf. Barclay, 'Jews'.
26   Cf. Backhaus, 'Mose'.
27   E.g. Ps 24:8 LXX, Mic 4:2; Isa 2:3; 59:8; Jer 5:4-5; 39:39 LXX (=32:39 MT).
28   Johnson, *The Acts*, 162.
29   E.g. 1QS 10.21.

Lord' (Acts 9:1). Indeed, it is the close paradigmatic relationship with the phrase 'the word of the Lord' that provides the best explanation for this metonymic usage of the term 'the way of the Lord'. Just like the expression 'the way' occurs both independently and followed by a genitive of κύριος or θέος, we find occurrences of 'the word', 'the word of the Lord', and 'the word of God'.[30] And, notably, the term 'the word' also functions as a metonym for those who believe the word, in the recurrent statements concerning the 'growth of the word'. In 6:7, the growth of the word and the increase of the number of disciples are juxtaposed, whereas in 12:24, the word is said to have 'grown and increased': the growth and increase can only refer to the number of those who believe the word.[31]

To conclude: the term 'the way (of the Lord/of God)' in these texts from Acts denotes the way on which the Lord, or God, teaches his disciples to go, as a metaphor for how they interpret the Scriptures, acknowledge Jesus as the Anointed One, and serve God by living righteously. While 'those of the way' can be considered a self-designation of the early Christians, and although Paul is once said to have used the term metonymically to express how he sought to eradicate the way by persecuting its adherents, it is inaccurate to claim that Acts depicts the disciples as calling themselves the Way. Moreover, 'the way of the Lord' in these passages has a different referent than the 'way of the Lord' in Isaiah 40 and Luke 3.

5. Wider Usages of Way-Metaphors in Luke and Acts

Having arrived at this point, we can search Luke and Acts for wider usages of the two 'way of the Lord'-metaphors.

5.1 Ways of the Lord in the Song of Zechariah (Luke 1:68–79)

In the Song of Zechariah, we encounter both metaphorical usages of ὁδός—as the way on which the Lord comes and as way on which the Lord directs his disciples to walk—in close proximity.[32] Zechariah engages in prophecy (ἐπροφήτευσεν) as he praises God for having raised up a horn of salvation in the house of David, in remembrance of his covenant with the patriarchs (Luke 1:67–73). This is a prophecy concerning Jesus, the saviour from the seed of David (cf. Acts 13:23). Then, Zechariah addresses his child, John, who will 'go before the Lord to prepare his ways', a preparation that consists in 'giving knowledge of salvation to his people'. Indeed, 'the sunrise will visit us from on high (ἐπισκέψεται ἡμᾶς ἀνατολὴ ἐξ ὕψους) to appear to those sitting in darkness and shadow of death, to direct our feet on the way of peace' (Luke 1:78–79). Thus, the Lord comes to his people on 'his ways', which need to be prepared, in order to bring salvation and to direct their feet on 'the way of peace': once he has come, he will show them the way and enable them to 'serve him (λατρεύειν αὐτῷ) in holiness and righteousness all the days of their lives'. The link of the 'way of peace' with 'serving God' recurs in Paul's words in Acts 24:14, discussed above.

Zechariah and Elizabeth themselves already walk on this way. This is suggested by the use of the verb πορεύω when they are introduced immediately after the Prologue (Luke 1:1–4) as righteous before God, 'walking (πορευόμενοι) in all commandments and regulations of the Lord, blamelessly' (Luke 1:6). The narrative about the old barren couple evokes the narratives about

---

30 Absolute: Acts 4:4; 11:19; 'the word of God': 6:7; 12:24; 17:13; 'the word of the Lord': 13:49; 19:20; 'the word of salvation': 13:26.
31 Acts 6:7; 12:24; 19:20.
32 They also appear in close proximity in 1QS 9:18–21.

Israel's patriarchs, especially Abraham and Sarah, although it is this now the man, rather than the woman, who is unable to trust God's promise, and the woman who acts in obedience by calling her son John rather than Zechariah. They walk the way of the Lord on which God has directed Israel through his commandments. Their son is to bring the people back on this way in preparation of the Lord, and the teaching of Jesus and his apostles intends to direct people on this same way, the way of righteousness.

5.2 Philip Showing the Way to the Eunuch (Acts 8:26–40)

The narrative about Philip and the eunuch from Ethiopia interweaves the actual journey of the eunuch masterfully with his progress in understanding Scripture.[33] An angel of the Lord commands Philip to go to the 'way' (ὁδόν) from Jerusalem to Gaza (Acts 8:26), where he encounters the eunuch reading Isaiah on his return journey from Jerusalem. He asks whether he understands what he reads, and the eunuch replies: 'How could I, if no one shows me the way (ὁδηγήσει με)' (Acts 8:31). In response, Philip brings the good message about Jesus from this Scripture (Acts 8:35). As they go along the way (κατὰ τὴν ὁδόν), they encounter water for baptism. After his baptism, the eunuch goes his way (τὴν ὁδὸν αὐτοῦ) rejoicing. The literal way from Jerusalem to Gaza is thus connected to a metaphorical way—a way of interpreting Scripture. What Priscilla and Aquila will do for Apollos, who is already powerful in Scripture and informed about the way of the Lord, but needs a more accurate exposition of the way of God, is done by Philip for the eunuch, showing him the way by proclaiming Jesus from Isaiah.

Indeed, the interweaving of the actual journey with instruction in the metaphorical 'way of the Lord' is what we encounter in the narrative about Saul's journey to Damascus as well. Jesus meets him 'on the way on which he was going' (Acts 9:17) and after his vision of Jesus, he is found 'on the path called the right one' (Acts 9:11). Many ancient cities have a 'Straight Way', but Luke hardly mentions the street name here to inform his readers about Saul's exact location in Damascus.[34] Saul is back on track, ready to be baptised, and will from now on live in obedience to God (cf. Acts 26:19).

5.3 Bar-Jesus Makes the Straight Ways of the Lord Crooked (Acts 13:4–12)

'The ways of the Lord are straight', concludes the book of Hosea, 'the righteous will walk in them, but the wicked will stumble on them'.[35] In Paphos on Cyprus, Paul unmasks Bar-Jesus as an 'enemy of all righteousness', who bends 'the straight ways of the Lord' (διαστρέφων τὰς ὁδοὺς [τοῦ] κυρίου τὰς εὐθείας, Acts 13:10). Paul reproaches him for this after his attempt to 'turn the governor away from the faith', where the same verb is used (διαστρέψαι τὸν ἀνθύπατον ἀπὸ τῆς πίστεως, Acts 13:8). The implication is that Paul, who is speaking the 'word of God' (13:9), is teaching the straight ways of the Lord, on which to walk means to believe and live righteously. Again, the usage of the metaphor is very much in line with what we encountered in other passages. It has its background in the Old Testament, but not in Isaiah 40:3–5.[36]

---

33 On this passage, cf. the insightful discussion in Baban, *On the Road*, 207–71, who highlights Hellenistic models for these 'on the road encounters', as a dramatic literary depiction of moments of revelation and recognition.
34 Cf. Keener, *Acts*, 3:1652–53.
35 Hos 14:10 LXX: εὐθεῖαι αἱ ὁδοὶ τοῦ κυρίου, καὶ δίκαιοι πορεύσονται ἐν αὐταῖς, οἱ δὲ ἀσεβεῖς ἀσθενήσουσιν ἐν αὐταῖς.
36 According to Pao, *Acts*, 68, Acts 13:10 contains an allusion to Isa 40:3, but Hos 14:10 resembles the wording of Acts 13:10 more closely and, moreover, understands the ways of the Lord as ways on which the righteous walk, rather than ways that need to be prepared for the Lord to come.

5.4 Announcing a Way of Salvation (Acts 16:17)

We encounter another use of the way-metaphor in Acts 16:17, where a slave follows Paul and his companions, shouting 'these men are servants of the Most High God, who announce to you a way of salvation'. Her words stand in marked contrast to those of her masters, who bring Paul and Silas before the *duumviri* (στρατηγοί)[37] and say: 'these men are agitating our city, being Jews, and they announce customs which it is not permitted for us to admit or practice, since we are Romans' (Acts 16:20–21). The verbal agreement between these two sentences suggests a parallel between 'way of salvation' (ὁδὸν σωτηρίας) and 'customs' (ἔθη).[38] Although the expression 'way of salvation' is in itself not remarkable, a dead metaphor that indicates a 'manner of being saved', as part of a narrative where way-metaphors are so pervasive, it encourages further reflection.

The narrative addresses the ancient view that each people has its own customs and traditions according to which it should live. Jews live by Jewish ἔθη, Romans by Roman ones. In the narrative of Acts, Jews repeatedly show concern that Jesus and Paul change or abandon the Jewish ἔθη.[39] Paul is charged particularly with 'teaching all Jews among the nations not to circumcise their children and not to walk (περιπατεῖν) according to the customs' (Acts 21:21). In those contexts, Paul insists on being a Jew who says nothing else than what Moses and the Prophets say (Acts 26:22). Here in Philippi, where Paul is charged with challenging Roman customs, he insists on being a Roman and effectively accuses the governors of acting contrary to Roman customs by punishing them without a proper hearing (Acts 16:37–38).

The motif of ἔθη can be traced through the narrative of Acts, culminating in Acts 25–26, where Festus takes pride in acting according to Roman custom (Acts 25:16), Agrippa is introduced as familiar with the customs and disagreements of the Jews (Acts 26:3), and both conclude that Paul is innocent (Acts 26:31–32). The narrative of Acts refutes both the accusation that the teaching of the apostles is incompatible with Roman customs and that it threatens Jewish customs. The way of the Lord, which is also a 'way of salvation' emerges as a way viable both for Romans and for Jews, a claim embodied in the dual identity of Paul as Jew and Roman. The term 'way of salvation', used in Acts 16:17, parallels the expression 'word of salvation' that is used in Acts 13:26. It refers to the salvation through Jesus that has been sent both to Jews (13:26) and to Gentiles (28:28).

5. Why is Luke so Fond of These Metaphors?

We have found in Luke and Acts extensive usage of way-metaphors. On the one hand, this is not surprising, since making a journey is in general one of the most common metaphorical domains that humans use to express more abstract concepts.[40] Still, the specific ways in which the author of Luke and Acts uses the metaphor, interweaving narratives about physical roads and ways and about going along the metaphorical way of the Lord, suggests a very conscious use of these metaphors. What purpose does this serve? Below, I will focus on the function of Luke's second way-metaphor, that of the 'way of the Lord' as metaphor for the belief and conduct taught to the disciples.

---

37 Cf. Brélaz, 'Outside the City Gate', 126; Mason, *Greek Terms*, 161–62.
38 Acts 16:17 and 16:20–21 share the words οὗτοι οἱ ἄνθρωποι […] καταγγέλλουσιν.
39 Acts 6:14; 15:1; 21:21; cf. 28:17.
40 Cf. Kövecses, *Metaphor*, 34–35, who lists 'life is a journey' among the 'highly conventionalized' conceptual and linguistic metaphors.

Birger Olsson has observed that the absolute and unexplained usage of the term ἡ ὁδός suggests that it was familiar to the intended audience of Acts and functions as language used among insiders.[41] Indeed, in a sense, 'the way' is understood as 'our way', just like 'the brothers' are 'our brothers' and 'the assemblies' are 'our assemblies'. However, it is 'our way' in the sense of 'the way we adhere to, the way we walk', which is the way taught by God. While this may thus have been a more widespread term among early Christians, this is not born out by evidence.[42] The closest parallel is found in the Qumran writings, which can be taken to indicate the extent to which Luke and Acts are Jewish literature.[43] However, we may still ask which reasons the author of Acts had to employ this designation so frequently and creatively. To understand these reasons, it is crucial to see, on the one hand, the connection with the interpretation of the Scriptures, and on the other hand, the relationship with the outsider designation αἵρεσις τῶν Ναζωραίων ('school of thought of the Nazarenes').

According to many recent exegetes of Acts, the book was written to provide its readers a narrative account of their identity, through the story about the early days of the church and about the ministry of Paul.[44] It is a story that, among other things, explains the origin of the name Χριστιανοί in Antioch (Acts 11:26), but it also makes clear that this was not how the disciples were originally called, nor a name of which Paul was particularly fond (cf. Acts 26:28–29). This is relevant at a time when the term *Christiani* has a negative connotation among Roman authors and a Roman governor like Pliny the Younger displays his piety and loyalty by highlighting his efforts to eradicate this superstition.[45] Luke emphasises the ancient roots of this movement by writing its history as a part and continuation of the history of Israel (cf. especially the speeches of Stephen in Acts 7:2–53 and of Paul in Acts 13:16–41). Christians are not adherents of a new *superstitio*, but groups of people who live in piety and virtue as they serve the God of Israel according to the ancient Jewish Scriptures.

The term 'the way' is useful in bringing this message across, by emphasizing that this teaching is grounded in thorough knowledge of the Law and the Prophets. However, it goes beyond a mere claim of antiquity. It is not just an ancient way according to which Paul serves God, it is the way of God. The centre of Paul's defence in Acts 22–26 is that he, just like Socrates, has acted out of obedience to a heavenly vision (Acts 26:19). In this respect, Paul is an identity figure for the (Christian) readers of Acts: they are people who follow the way of God, and to fight against them is to fight against God (Acts 5:39; 26:14)—and the fate of God-fighters is well-known in the ancient world.[46] This provides assurance both in the context of the experience of persecution by Romans and in the context of conflicts and conversations with those Jews with whom they have their disagreements (ζητήματα).[47]

---

41 E.g. Olsson, 'De som hörde till Vägen', 271.
42 A close parallel is found in 2 Peter 2:2,15,21, where 'the way of the truth', 'the straight way', and 'the way of the righteousness' are used. The metaphor of walking on the way (or leaving it to wander on wrong ways) is in view here, used in verse 21 in parallel to 'the holy commandment handed over to them' (τῆς παραδοθείσης αὐτοῖς ἁγίας ἐντολῆς). However, the absolute use of 'the way' is unique for Luke among early Christian literature, cf. Urcioli, 'ὁδός', 130. Eusebius, *H.E.* 5.1.48, could well be dependent on the usage in Acts.
43 Böttrich, 'Das lukanische Doppelwerk'; Oliver, *Torah Praxis*.
44 Schröter, 'Kirche'; Backhaus, 'Lukas'; Wolter, 'Das lukanische Doppelwerk', 261–89; Butticaz, *L'identité*; Marguerat, 'The Image', 22–47; Baker, 'Peter'.
45 The statements of Pliny the Younger, *Ep.* 10.96, regarding his urge to persecute all Christians should be taken with a grain of salt. They are an effective display of piety, just like Trajan's reply is a conscious display of *clementia*, but the reality may well be that groups of Christians who did not create trouble were left undisturbed.
46 Cf. Moles, 'Jesus'; van Houwelingen, 'A Godfighter', 83–100; Kochenash, 'Better Call Paul "Saul"'.
47 Cf. further my dissertation: den Heijer, *Portraits*.

Thus, it is not its openness that makes the term 'the way' attractive to Luke. Rather, it is the bold assertion of divine legitimation and ancient Scriptural authority that goes with the term that explains his extensive use of this metaphor in Acts. Early Christians did not call themselves 'the Way', they walked it, serving the God of Israel as the Lord had taught them. And they could do so only because the Lord had come to them on his way, a way prepared by John the Baptist, as he came to inspect his city. The narrative of Luke and Acts is better understood if these two 'ways of the Lord' are clearly distinguished.

Bibliography

Baban, O.D. — *On the Road Encounters in Luke-Acts. Hellenistic Mimesis and Luke's Theology of the Way* (Exeter; Milton Keynes: Paternoster, 2006).

Backhaus, K. — 'Lukas der Maler. Die Apostelgeschichte als intentionale Geschichte der christlichen Erstepoche', in Gerd Häfner and Knut Backhaus (eds.), *Historiographie und fiktionales Erzählen: zur Konstruktivität in Geschichtstheorie und Exegese* (Biblisch-theologische Studien 93; Neukirchen-Vluyn: Neukirchener Verlag, 2009), 30–66.

Backhaus, K. — 'Mose und der Mos Maiorum: Das Alter des Judentums als Argument für die Attraktivität des Christentums in der Apostelgeschichte', in Christfried Böttrich, Jens Herzer, and Torsten Reiprich (eds.), *Josephus und das Neue Testament: Wechselseitige Wahrnehmungen. II. Internationales Symposium zum Corpus Judaeo-Hellenisticum 25.–28. Mai 2006, Greifswald* (WUNT 209; Tübingen: Mohr Siebeck, 2007), 401–28.

Baker, C.A. — 'Peter and Paul in Acts and the Construction of Early Christian Identity: A Review of Historical and Literary Approaches', *Currents in Biblical Research* 11,3 (2013), 349–65.

Barclay, J.M.G. — '"Jews" and "Christians" in the Eyes of Roman Authors c. 100 C.E.', in Peter J. Tomson and Joshua Schwartz (eds.), *Jews and Christians in the First and Second Centuries: How to Write Their History* (CRINT 13; Leiden: Brill, 2014), 313–26.

Barrett, C.K. — *A Critical and Exegetical Commentary on the Acts of the Apostles* (ICC, 2 vols; Edinburgh: T&T Clark, 1994)

Barstad, H.M. — *A Way in the Wilderness: The 'Second Exodus' in the Message of Second Isaiah* (JSS.M 12; University of Manchester, 1989).

Bauckham, R. — 'The Early Jerusalem Church, Qumran, and the Essenes', in James Davila (ed.), *The Dead Sea Scrolls as Background to Postbiblical Judaism and Early Christianity* (STDJ 46; Leiden: Brill, 2003), 63–89.

Borgman, P. — *The Way according to Luke: Hearing the Whole Story of Luke-Acts* (Grand Rapids: Eerdmans, 2006).

Böttrich, Chr.	'Das lukanische Doppelwerk im Kontext frühjüdischer Literatur', *Zeitschrift für die neutestamentliche Wissenschaft und die Kunde der älteren Kirche* 106.2 (2015), 151–83.
Brélaz, C.	'"Outside the City Gate". Center and Periphery in Paul's Preaching in Philippi', in Steve Walton, Paul R. Trebilco, and David W.J. Gill (eds.), *The Urban World and the First Christians* (Grand Rapids: Eerdmans, 2017), 123–40.
Butticaz, S.D.	*L'identité de l'Eglise dans les Actes des apôtres: De la restauration d'Israël à la conquête universelle* (BZNW 174; Berlin: De Gruyter, 2011).
Cadbury, H.J.	'Names for Christians and Christianity in Acts', in Kirsopp Lake, Henry J. Cadbury, and Frederick J. Foakes-Jackson (eds.), *The Acts of the Apostles* (vol. 5; The Beginnings of Christianity 1; London: Macmillan, 1933), 390.
Danker, F.W.	*A Greek-English Lexicon of the New Testament and Other Early Christian Literature (BDAG)* (3rd edn; Chicago; London: University of Chicago Press, 2000).
Fitzmyer, J.A.	*Essays on the Semitic Background of the New Testament* (London: Chapman, 1971).
Germiquet, E.	'Luke's Journey Narrative: A Literary Gateway of the Missionary Church in Acts', *Scriptura* 103 (2010), 16–29.
Gnilka, J.	Review of Eero Repo, *Der 'Weg' als Selbstbezeichnung des Urchristentums: eine traditions-geschichtliche und semasiologische Untersuchung* (1967), in *Revue de Qumran* 6,1 (1967), 157–59.
Hadot, P.	*Qu'est-ce que la philosophie antique?* (Collection folio 280; Paris: Gallimard, 1996).
Haenchen, E.	*Die Apostelgeschichte* (16th edn; KEK; Göttingen: Vandenhoeck & Ruprecht, 1977).
Heijer, A.J. den	*Portraits of Paul's Performance in the Book of Acts: Luke's Apologetic Strategy in the Depiction of Paul as Messenger of God* (WUNT 2nd series; Tübingen: Mohr Siebeck, forthcoming).
Hengel, M. and A.-M. Schwemer	*Die Urgemeinde und das Judenchristentum* (Geschichte des frühen Christentums 2; Tübingen: Mohr Siebeck, 2019).
Hengel, M.	Review of Eero Repo, *Der 'Weg' als Selbstbezeichnung des Urchristentums: eine traditionsgeschichtliche und semasiologische Untersuchung* (1967), in *Theologische Literaturzeitung* 92.5 (1967), 361.
Houwelingen, P.H.R. van	'A Godfighter Becomes a Fighter for God', in Pieter G.R. de Villiers and Jan Willem van Henten (eds.), *Coping with Violence in the New Testament* (STAR 16; Leiden: Brill, 2012), 83–100.
Johnson, L.T.	*The Acts of the Apostles* (Sacra Pagina 5; Collegeville, MN: Liturgical Press, 1992).

Keener, C.S. *Acts. An Exegetical Commentary* (4 vols; Grand Rapids: Baker Academic, 2012–2015).

Kinman, B. *Jesus' Entry into Jerusalem: In the Context of Lukan Theology and the Politics of His Day* (AGJU 28; Leiden: Brill, 1995).

Kochenash, M. 'Better Call Paul "Saul": Literary Models and a Lukan Innovation', *Journal of Biblical Literature* 138,2 (2019), 433–49.

Kövecses, Z. *Metaphor: A Practical Introduction* (2nd edn; New York: Oxford University Press, 2010).

Lans, B. van der, and J. Bremmer 'Tacitus and the Persecution of the Christians: An Invention of Tradition?', *Eirene* 53 (2017), 299–331.

Lakoff, G., and M. Johnson *Metaphors We Live By* (Chicago: University of Chicago Press, 1980).

Lim, B.H. *The 'Way of the Lord' in the Book of Isaiah* (LHBOTS 522; New York: T&T Clark, 2010).

Lund, Ø. *Way Metaphors and Way Topics in Isaiah 40-55* (FAT 28; Tübingen: Mohr Siebeck, 2007).

Lyonnet, S. '"La voie" dans les Actes des Apôtres', *Recherches de science religieuse* 69.1 (1981), 149–64.

Mallen, P. *The Reading and Transformation of Isaiah in Luke-Acts* (LNTS 367; London; New York: T&T Clark, 2008).

Marguerat, D. 'The Image of Paul in Acts', in *Paul in Acts and Paul in His Letters* (WUNT 310; Tübingen: Mohr Siebeck, 2013), 22–47.

Mason, H.J. *Greek Terms for Roman Institutions: a Lexicon and Analysis* (Toronto: Hakkert, 1974).

McCasland, S.V. 'The Way', *Journal of Biblical Literature* 77.3 (1958), 222–30.

Michaelis, W. 'ὁδός', in G. Friedrich (ed.) *Theologisches Wörterbuch zum Neuen Testament* (vol. 5; Stuttgart: Kohlhammer, 1954) 40–118.

Moles, J. 'Jesus and Dionysus in "The Acts of the Apostles" and Early Christianity', *Hermathena* 180 (2006), 65–104.

Oliver, I.W. *Torah Praxis after 70 c.e.: Reading Matthew and Luke-Acts as Jewish Texts* (WUNT 2.355; Mohr Siebeck, 2013).

Olsson, B. 'De som hörde till Vägen (Apg 9:2)', in Reidar Hvalvik and Hans Kvalbein (eds.), *Ad Acta: Studier til Apostlenes gjerninger og urkristendommens historie; Tilegnet professor Edvin Larsson på 70-årsdagen* (Oslo: Verbum, 1994), 267–87.

Pao, D.W. *Acts and the Isaianic New Exodus* (WUNT 2.130; Tübingen: Mohr Siebeck, 2000).

Pathrapankal, J.	'Christianity as a "Way" According to the Acts of the Apostles', in Jacob Kremer (ed.), *Les Actes des Apôtres. Traditions, rédaction, théologie* (BETL 48; Leuven: Ducelot; Leuven University Press, 1979), 533–39.
Peil, D.	'Überlegungen zur Bildfeldtheorie', *Beiträge zur Geschichte der deutschen Sprache und Literatur* 112 (1990), 209–41.
Repo, E.	*Der 'Weg' als Selbstbezeichnung des Urchristentums: eine traditionsgeschichtliche und semasiologische Untersuchung* (AASF.B 132.2; Helsinki: Suomalainen Tiedeakatemia, 1964).
Rotman, M.	*The Call of the Wilderness: The Narrative Significance of John the Baptist's Whereabouts* (CBET 96; Leuven: Peeters, 2019).
Rowe, C.K.	*Early Narrative Christology: The Lord in the Gospel of Luke* (BZNW 139; Berlin: De Gruyter, 2006).
Runia, D.T.	'Philo of Alexandria and the Greek Hairesis-Model', *Vigiliae Christianae* 53.2 (1999), 117–47.
Saldarini, A.J.	*Pharisees, Scribes and Sadducees in Palestinian Society* (Edinburgh: T&T Clark, 1989).
Schröter, J.	'Kirche im Anschluss an Paulus: Aspekte der Paulusrezeption in der Apostelgeschichte und in den Pastoralbriefen', *Zeitschrift für die neutestamentliche Wissenschaft und die Kunde der älteren Kirche* 98.1 (2007), 77–104.
Silva, M.	'ὁδός', in *New International Dictionary of New Testament Theology and Exegesis* (2nd edn; 5 vols; Grand Rapids: Zondervan, 2014), 3:459.
Smith, D.L.	'The Uses of "New Exodus" in New Testament Scholarship: Preparing a Way through the Wilderness', *Currents in Biblical Research* 14.2 (2016), 207–43.
Tiemeyer, L.-S.	Review of Bo H. Lim, *The 'Way of the Lord' in the Book of Isaiah* (2010), in *Journal of Theological Studies* 62.1 (2011), 275–77.
Trebilco, P.R.	*Self-Designations and Group Identity in the New Testament* (Cambridge: Cambridge University Press, 2012).
Urcioli, E.R.	'«Quella ὁδός che essi chiamano αἵρεσις». Alle origini dell'autocomprensione filosofica dei seguaci di Gesù', *Annali di storia dell'esegesi* 28.1 (2011), 117–36.
Völkel, M.	'ὁδός', in Horst Balz and Gerhard Schneider (eds.), *Exegetisches Wörterbuch zum Neuen Testament* (3rd edn; 3 vols; Stuttgart: Kohlhammer, 2011), 2:1200–03.
Walters, P.	*The Assumed Authorial Unity of Luke and Acts: A Reassessment of the Evidence* (SNTSMS 145; Cambridge: Cambridge University Press, 2009).

Weinrich, H.	'Münze und Wort. Untersuchungen an einem Bildfeld', in Heinrich Lausberg and Harald Weinrich (eds), *Romanica. Festschrift für Gerhard Rohlfs* (Halle: Niemeyer, 1958), 508–21.
Wolter, M.	'Das lukanische Doppelwerk als Epochengeschichte', in *Theologie und Ethos im frühen Christentum: Studien zu Jesus, Paulus und Lukas* (WUNT 236; Tübingen: Mohr Siebeck, 2009), 261–89.
Zahn, Th.	*Die Apostelgeschichte des Lucas* (Leipzig: Deichert, 1919).

Arco den Heijer
Theological University Kampen, the Netherlands
ajdenheijer@tukampen.nl

Decentralization in Luke-Acts

NICKOLAS A. FOX

Abstract

Within the landscape of Luke-Acts scholarship, many have noticed the programmatic nature of Acts 1:8, where Jesus promises that the Holy Spirit will come and the disciples will be witnesses in Jerusalem, Judea, Samaria, and the ends of the earth. However, the 'decentralization' phenomenon has been under-appreciated in that it is not new with Acts 1:8 nor is it restricted to geographical dimensions. Rather, decentralization is a narrative motif that runs throughout Luke-Acts. It is not restricted to geography, but involves personal decentralization as well. This personal decentralization is shown in Acts through an outward movement of mission that seeks to include outsiders and is punctuated by the Holy Spirit driving new missionary initiatives, even to the degree that the Twelve, like Jerusalem, are left on the periphery. This article traces the elements of geographical and personal decentralization through Luke's birth narratives, Galilean ministry, travel and passion narratives, as well as their continuation into the key scenes in Acts, such as the ministry in Jerusalem and in Samaria, Saul's conversion, the story of Cornelius, and Paul's missionary Journeys. It argues that geographical and personal decentralization are key to Luke's narrative purposes.

Within the landscape of Luke-Acts scholarship, many have noticed the programmatic nature of Acts 1:8, where Jesus promises that the Holy Spirit will come and the disciples will be witnesses in Jerusalem, Judea, Samaria, and to the ends of the earth.[1] These four spheres become like concentric circles of outward motion, tracking the move of the gospel and the Spirit in an outward trajectory throughout the rest of Acts. A word for this phenomenon is 'decentralization'.[2] When we think about the motif of decentralization, we do right to remember this obvious feature of outward geographic movement, but we cannot stop there. We must pay attention to two other elements: first, the concept of decentralization in the famous quote by Jesus in Acts 1:8 is not new but had seeds planted long before, running throughout the Gospel of Luke; and second, there are personal and cultural dimensions to this decentralization as well. More specifically, the Holy Spirit moves both outward in a geographical sense, with Jerusalem no longer the focus of Christian ministry, and outward with regard to people. The Holy Spirit empowers new

---

1 I am indebted to Nikki Bloom, who served as an editor on this project.
2 As best I can tell, this term was coined by my PhD supervisor, Thorsten Moritz.

people as converts, disciples, and ministers, leaving the Twelve to the periphery, like Jerusalem. We see from the text that this geographical and personal decentralization is key to Luke's two-volume narrative, and more, that it is actually all driven by the Spirit.

For the purpose of this article, the working definition of decentralization will refer to the early Christian movement's directionality away from established Jewish norms, symbols of centralization, and power structures (food laws, power of a few, Sanhedrin, temple, Jerusalem-centric faith, etc.) toward a more inclusive, open faith that welcomes outsiders as participants and owners of the faith.[3] This decentralization in Luke-Acts has geographic, personal, and cultural elements. Each will be examined in turn.

Luke-Acts is geographically aligned. After early involvement in Jerusalem, obvious symbols of centralized religion (i.e. Zechariah ministering in the temple), and early ministry of Jesus in Galilee (Luke 4:14–9:50), Jesus resolutely sets out for Jerusalem in Luke 9:51, thus beginning the travel narrative portion of Luke. This journey to Jerusalem in Luke is balanced by the inverse in Acts, which shows a clear move away from Jerusalem (cf. Acts 1:8). Interestingly, in Second Temple Judaism, there was a geographical understanding of God's presence seen as concentric circles of holiness (m. Kel. 1.6–9) where the Holy of Holies is the center, with the other areas of the temple, the temple mount, and Jerusalem representing subsequent circles of holiness.[4] Thus, the movement away from Jerusalem in Acts is in direct opposition to the holiness economy of the Jewish temple and Jerusalem in Second Temple Judaism. Even in this movement away from Jerusalem, it never fully disappears from the picture in Acts, as there are frequent references to it throughout the book (Act 15; 16:4; 19:21; 20:16, 22; 21; 22). While some would see this as Jerusalem remaining in the center of holiness and importance in Acts, the reality is that Jerusalem becomes more and more the center of persecution and opposition of the Christian movement (as evidenced by the numerous hints of danger for Paul and his eventual arrest (i.e. Acts 20:22–24; 21:10–11, 30–32). Support for the changing role of Jerusalem is found in seeds of decentralization that are already present in Luke. While Jesus does go to Jerusalem, specifically the temple (Luke 2:22–52; 19:28–44; 19:47–20:8), there are numerous examples where Jesus opposes the temple and Jerusalem-centric orientation. For example, Jesus goes to the 'other side' and does ministry in Gentile lands (Luke 8:26–39). Additionally, when he and the disciples experience Samaritan opposition, Jesus rejects the way of Elijah from the Old Testament (Luke 9:51–56; 2 Kings 1:10–14) and presents woes against Jewish cities, Chorazin, Bethsaida, Capernaum, suggesting they are worse than the famous pagan cities, Tyre and Sidon (Luke 10:13–15). Finally, Jesus cleanses the temple in Luke 19:45–46, calling it 'a den of robbers'.

This geographic decentralization necessarily includes personal and cultural dimensions; for example, travel for Jesus outside the land of Israel led to ministering to Gentiles (Luke 8:26–39). One might be tempted to see concentric circles of perceived holiness within the people of the first century as it was seen geographically with God's presence. For example, there are important, well-connected Jews who are living a holy life with respect to the Jewish system of the first century. This would include the Pharisees,[5] priests, and even named characters in Luke like Zechariah and Simeon. A second circle would include respectable Jews who were Greek-speaking instead

---

3   Fox, *Hermeneutics*, 63–64.
4   The Mishnah suggests there are 10 circles of holiness in all. See m. Kel 1.6–9.
5   Despite Jesus' challenge of the Pharisees' hypocrisy, they at least have the perception among the people, and likely the readers, as being right with God.

of Hebrew-speaking, seen in places like Acts 6.[6] The third circle may be thought of as Jews who are marginalized in some way, such as women, people of ignoble professions like fishermen and shepherds, and the sick. The fourth might include outsiders of a respectable nature, that is, those who are not Jewish but who maintain respectable relationships with the Jews. The centurion in Luke 7 and Cornelius in Acts 10 are obvious examples of this, and Lydia (Acts 16:14) could be included here as well. Lastly, the outermost ring features outsiders who were wicked or perceived as such, including most Roman soldiers, idol worshipers, and other pagan Gentiles. Also considered in this least holy group might be certain Jews perceived in particularly heinous ways, such as tax collectors and prostitutes. Some characters in Luke-Acts that fall in this category are Levi, Zacchaeus, the jailer from Acts 16, the centurion at the foot of the cross, and the owners of the slave girl in Acts 16. It is noteworthy that Luke strategically includes characters from all of these spheres as receivers of the message in his two volumes. There is decentralization among the sharers of the message as well, with the duty of preaching and communicating the message shifting from the Twelve to others. While the narrative starts in the temple with Zechariah, a priest, there is a movement outward away from important Jewish people. Over the course of two volumes, a mission unfolds that increasingly includes all people, even those that are off the holiness grid.

This geographical and personal decentralization naturally results in the decentralization of cultural norms. Some of these have already been mentioned, such as the temple and Jerusalem. Indeed, it is hard to overstate the importance and centrality of these locations to Jewish life and culture in Second Temple Judaism. But what is more, many of the systems that first-century Judaism had in place to protect God's holiness also naturally served to exclude outsiders. First-century Judaism was fairly closed to Gentile outsiders; even though conversion may have been an option for some, it required so much from the proselyte (i.e. food laws, purity codes, circumcision, no longer entering the homes of Gentile friends and family, etc.) that few took this option.[7] Thus, for the kingdom of God to be open to non-Jewish outsiders, these restrictive cultural practices needed to be decentralized, and, in some cases, abandoned altogether. This is exactly what unfolds with the food laws, purity codes, and the special place of the temple over the course of Luke-Acts. On this point, Green suggests that, 'far from serving as a sacred place for the worship of God by Gentiles (and Samaritans), the temple functions as a segregating force, symbolizing socio-religious demarcations between insider and outsider. The time of the temple is not over. It will serve as a place of prayer and teaching. But it is no longer the center around which life is oriented'.[8] For Luke, likely a Gentile and interested in welcoming God-fearers and Gentiles into the move of God,[9] any such segregating force needs to be decentralized.

While decentralization is an underdeveloped feature in Luke-Acts studies, a few scholars do notice this trend. Beers, for example, finds that:

> my project suggests the need for future research in Acts scholarship regarding the decentralization motif. A common scholarly argument is that Luke reserves a distinctive role for the twelve apostles; however, my research, with its focus on those outside the twelve embodying the servant task, suggests exactly the opposite. The lack of activity on the part of

---

6   The Greek-speaking Jews specifically mentioned in this text are widows, rather than those who might be considered respectable; however, this reference shows us that Greek-speaking Jews did exist in this context.
7   This problem also led to the existence of a group called the God-fearers, who seem to be of considerable interest for Luke; see my *Hermeneutics of Social Identity in Luke-Acts*, 53–88.
8   Green, 'Demise', 512.
9   For a review of the scholarly discussion regarding the identity, background, and purposes of Luke in his two volumes, see my *Hermeneutics of Social Identity in Luke-Acts*, 7–11.

the apostles (with the possible exception of Peter and perhaps John) thus implicitly critiques them, though the positive side to their apparent sedentary life is the extension of the Isaianic mission to the larger group of Jesus' followers. It is this latter group in Acts who is truly faithful to Jesus' commission and continues to preach the good news "with all boldness and without hindrance" (Acts 28:31).[10]

Furthermore, Beers employs this term with regard to Luke 10 and the decentralization of the Twelve into a larger group. She also uses it to describe the shift that takes place at Pentecost, the Spirit empowering all who are present and not only the Twelve, seeing this as similar to Numbers 11:29 where Moses wishes everyone would prophesy.[11] Similarly, Johnson writes, 'Luke has shown his reader how the good news spread both geographically and demographically, reaching in the evangelization of the detested Samaritans and the sexually mutilated Ethiopian those who would be considered at best marginally Jewish by the strict standards of the Pharisees'.[12]

Others have acknowledged parts of this as well, such as Keener, who writes that 'those who feel most secure with power, including among God's people, are most susceptible to the blindness power brings. The marginalized, by contrast, are most ready to depend on Christ the healer, liberator, and savior'.[13] As some scholars have noticed this motif and, in Beers' case, the need for it to be developed more fully, this is the task of this article. This theme will be traced throughout Luke-Acts, showing that decentralization is a key narrative purpose in these two volumes. To that end, a few things are worth keeping in mind.

Firstly, decentralization should not be confused with the theme of universalism, or the shift from a particular focus on Jews to a wider focus on all peoples (i.e. Gentiles). The move to a universal scope as a thematic element is widely attested in Luke-Acts scholarship. Moore, for example, sees the programmatic text of Acts 1:8 as '[denoting] both geographical and ethnic universalism'.[14] Keener suggests that most scholars recognize the universal mission as 'one of the central themes (if not *the* central theme) in the book of Acts'.[15] Suffice it to say, this is an observable and present feature in the book and one that gets ample attention in Luke-Acts scholarship. That said, it is different than decentralization. The particularism-to-universalism shift may be thought of as a 'two dimensional' widening of the missional scope. Decentralization, on the other hand, involves an elaborate, 'three dimensional' narrative expansion that encompasses both volumes, with expectations, or 'seeds', planted in volume one and then brought to germination and full bloom in volume two. Rather than widening a scope that is already present, it instead inverts the directionality of the entire narrative through the use of strategic narrative presentations and a reconfiguration of the primary signs and symbols around which the people of God were oriented and within the system as it stood. Each of these elements will be discussed further below.

Secondly, the pattern in Acts demonstrates the Holy Spirit is the one to initiate new missionary endeavors, not the church. Rather, the church, primarily in Jerusalem, will show reluctance in

---

10   Beers, *Followers*, 179.
11   Beers, *Followers*, 108, who also notes the text-critical issue regarding Jesus' sending of the 70/72 in Luke 10:1–23.
12   Johnson, *Acts*, 186.
13   Keener, *Acts*, 508.
14   Moore, '"To the End of the Earth"', 24, who suggests Acts is written 'to indicate how a new movement emerging out of Judaism came to incorporate Gentiles'.
15   Keener, *Acts*, 505. Also, see Cadbury, *Making*, 316; Dupont, *Salvation*, 11–33; Wilson, *Gentiles*; Maddox, *Purpose*, 56; Senior and Stuhlmueller, *Biblical Foundation*, 255–79; Matson, *Household Conversion Narratives*, 184; Richard, 'Pluralistic Experiences', 24–31; Peterson, *Acts*, 79–83.

welcoming and engaging with outsiders at various times, while the Spirit will use others outside of the church leadership to accomplish new missionary initiatives. This can be seen when, despite the charge by Jesus to be witnesses beyond Jerusalem, they have yet to move beyond the Holy City in Acts 7. Massive persecution is required to move the gospel outward, and then it is Phillip, one elected to help distribute food, who first ministers to Samaritans and other outsiders (i.e. the Ethiopian Eunuch) in Acts 8, albeit with miraculous spiritual activity. Peter, by contrast, is a centralized leader and one of the Twelve, but his experience with Cornelius is unquestionably mediated by the Holy Spirit, to his own reluctance of breaking long held Jewish norms. Thus, we see the Spirit is the primary driver of decentralization in the book of Acts.[16]

Thirdly, Luke uses minor characters throughout his two volumes. Minor characters are those who come from humble, unlikely means, or who are seen as outsiders and who surprisingly play a part in the narrative at all (i.e. fishermen, shepherds, Gentiles, women, the poor, an Ethiopian eunuch, etc.).[17] While the apostles represent the centralized church in the early part of Acts, they entered the narrative as minor characters themselves, as fishermen, tax collectors, zealots, and in Peter's case, someone who asked Jesus to leave him because he was a sinful man (Luke 5:8). Yet the Twelve are some of the most central characters in Luke's Gospel. This pattern of the ones who are unexpected—minor characters—being the ones to play significant roles in the narrative will continue through two volumes and is centrally related to the decentralization we will see.

Fourthly, this research is at odds with a particular stream of Acts scholarship, represented by Jacob Jervell and others.[18] Jervell argues that Luke is a Christian Jew writing to other Christian Jews, and thus sees the disciples, Jerusalem, and the symbols of Jewish identity as remaining the center of the story.[19] While this perspective is needed to balance out the over-focus on Gentiles and overlooking Jews in the early church, both of which sometimes occur in Luke-Acts scholarship, the evidence points to somewhere in the middle. I argue elsewhere, after John Nolland, that Luke-Acts is best understood if we read it as written to God-fearers.[20] This approach best explains the Jewish nature of Luke's argument while still paying attention to the diversity and outward movement of the two-volume work. Here I will attempt to be faithful to the Jewish nature of Luke's writings, not missing the profound Jewish roots present in the text, while at the same time following the narrative where it goes, which is away from the temple, Jerusalem, and the restrictive religious practices of first-century Judaism to a more open and inclusive faith that does not replace Jews as participants in God's kingdom, but does make room for others, even to the ends of the earth.[21]

---

16 I am not suggesting that the Judaism of the First Century was narrowminded, power hungry, and inflexible. In fact, Judaism in the First Century is incredibly diverse, with myriad groups and factions. Rather than one Judaism, we may do well to talk about multiple different Judaisms to better reflect this diversity. The focus of this article is the literary presentation in Luke-Acts, which represents Christianity as overwhelmingly Jewish early on, but also with some considerable persecution from the Jewish establishment as well.

17 This is not to suggest that these minor characters have no social standing. The Ethiopian Eunuch, for example, is a person of great importance in his context in Ethiopia. However, from the perspective of Jerusalem-centric Judaism and early Christianity, he is an outsider. Tannehill, *Narrative Unity*, 2.109, suggests that Isaiah 56:3–8 may be in the background of the scene in Acts 8, for it focuses on eunuchs and foreigners; 'the Ethiopian Eunuch is both'.

18 See Jervell, *Luke and the People of God;* and *Theology*, Brawley, *Luke-Acts*.

19 Jervell, *Theology*, 5, 7, 12, 13, 20. Despite declaring that Luke was a Christian Jew, Jervell acknowledges that he could be a God-fearer (p.5). I argue, *Hermeneutics*, 8–9, that Luke was likely a Gentile, but possibly a God-fearer.

20 Fox, *Hermeneutics*, 62; Nolland, *Luke 1:1–9:20*, xxxii.

21 My argument in *Hermeneutics* is one of social identity, suggesting that in order for two separate groups to merge, a larger, superordinate identity must be created, a larger banner under which both groups can exist.

Lukan Backgrounds

The Gospel of Luke opens with a faithful and righteous elderly couple who are unable to have children, reminding the reader of Abram and Sarai in Genesis (ch. 12).[22] As with the couple in Genesis, this is an unlikely pair to start a redemption narrative, and yet the perfect start to the story of outward mobility. The man, Zechariah, is a priest and encounters an angel in the temple (εἰς τὸν ναόν)—the definition of centralized religious space—and is told he and his wife, Elizabeth, will have a son. The last time the reader will encounter this term (ναός) in Luke,[23] the curtain separating it from outside space tears, symbolically representing the outward (rather than centralized) move of God's Spirit and presence.[24]

Meanwhile, a young unmarried couple enters the narrative as Mary, too, is visited by an angel, told she is highly favored and will have a son. In response, she sings a song, the Magnificat, which is rife with themes of reversal: exalting the humble (1:48, 52), scattering the proud (1:51), bringing down rulers (1:52), and feeding the poor while sending the rich away empty (1:53). These elements of reversal are the seeds of decentralization early in the narrative that hint at future and fuller germination in volume two. In addition, God choosing the lowly to participate in his story as opposed to the wealthy, the important, the royal, etc. is the personal side of decentralization, a reconfiguration of who is important in God's story. About ten verses later, Zechariah is said to be filled with the Holy Spirit and offers his own song of prophecy. The name 'Zechariah' means 'God remembers', which is a good working title of his song focusing on God's promises to Abraham and Israel. It ends with pointing to his son, John, as the one going before the Lord (1:76).

The theme of reversal and decentralization continues in the birth of Jesus, whose birth is anything but regal by human standards. One may expect the coming of the Messiah to be a much more centralized affair. For example, one may expect him to be born in a rich person's home in Jerusalem, lauded with wealth, worshipped by important religious people, heralded far and wide as the coming Messiah along with the news that this new baby will further establish the priesthood, temple, and Jewish structure as it stands.[25] Instead, Luke presents exactly the opposite. He is laid in a feeding trough (i.e. manger) because there is no room in the inn and he is visited by lowly shepherds. The shepherds had their own experience with angels as well, making Luke's emphasis on angelic activity unmissable (2:8–20).[26] As heaven declares the arrival of the Messiah, most of the establishment is unaware of it because God instead chose the marginalized to be given a front row seat.[27] Jesus is presented at the temple to Simeon's excitement and Anna's prophetic rejoicing. Simeon declares Jesus as 'a light of revelation for the Gentiles' (2:32), perhaps the most overt hint

---

22 Green, 'Problem', 68–71, traces the similarities between the story of Abraham in Genesis 11–21 and the birth narratives in Acts, finding no fewer than 24 points of allusion.

23 It is not entirely clear where Zechariah's encounter happens. Bock, *Luke: 1:1–9:50*, 79, suggests it is the Holy Place (or Holy of Holies). However, since it is clear that the burning of incense spread far beyond the Day of Atonement and the Holy of Holies both from scripture (Exod. 30:8; Lev. 10:1; Num. 7:14–86; 16:12–13) and the Mishnah (see *Yoma* 2:4 and *Eduyot* 8:1), and that the Holy of Holies was only entered once per year by the high priest (Lev. 16), this seems unlikely. The better understanding may be placing Zechariah and the angel in the Court of Priests offering the Tamid offering, which would be at daybreak with few if anyone around, allowing for what appears to be a private encounter.

24 There is some discussion about which curtain tears in Luke 23:45. I will discuss those options more later on.

25 Some of these elements, such as kings worshipping Jesus with wealth, are present in Matthew's birth narrative. However, these are absent from Luke.

26 For a full treatment of Luke's use of angels and visions in his narrative, see Fox, *Hermeneutics*, 165–68.

27 Zechariah and Simeon may be thought to be part of the establishment, as a priest in the former case and an elderly temple dweller in the latter. However, each of them speaks a decentralizing message, thus contributing to the overall decentralizing agenda. What is more, if they are seen as members of the establishment, they are the exceptions that prove the rule, as every other participant in Jesus' birth is marginalized in some way.

at decentralization early in the book and a teaser for what will transpire in Acts. Even in these first two chapters through the songs of Mary and Zechariah and angelic visitations for a virgin girl, an elderly, childless couple, and lowly shepherds, Luke begins to establish the remarkable nature of God's decentralizing activity among the common and unremarkable.[28]

John, whose ministry begins in chapter three, is a subversive figure in mainstream Judaism in the first century.[29] He fits with the trajectory of decentralization as he challenges and calls into question the mainstream Jewish establishment. He emerges from the wilderness like Elijah,[30] undermines Abrahamic ancestry (Luke 3:7–9), urges people to give away wealth (Luke 3:10–11), and includes tax collectors and soldiers in his movement (Luke 3:12–14). Furthermore, John is calling the Jewish people to repentance and baptism, a radical step usually reserved for pagans and converts.[31] All of these are decentralizing acts that challenge the status quo of Judaism as it stands. John also demonstrates the cost of decentralization as he is arrested for challenging Herod, thrown into prison, and eventually killed.[32] Here we see an early example of what will become the norm for radical followers of the way of Jesus, namely persecution, prison, and in some cases, death.[33]

Shortly after the arrest of John, Jesus begins his own public ministry. After a summary statement about Jesus teaching in the synagogues around Galilee and everyone praising him, Jesus goes to his home town in Nazareth on the Sabbath and reads from the prophet Isaiah. The quotation from Isaiah 61 pronounces the year of the Lord's favor and has been called a paradigm for Jesus' ministry throughout the rest of Luke.[34] However, while these elements of inclusion and grace for the captive and poor are certainly key to Jesus' ministry, they are not new in chapter 4, but have been common through the first several chapters of Luke: the Magnificat, the birth of Jesus, the song of Simeon, and John the Baptist. It is noteworthy that Jesus omits the rest of Isaiah 61:2, leaving off 'and the day of vengeance of our God'. Jesus' ministry, to the chagrin of much of Israel, will not include revenge on Israel's enemies, but rather will invite those same enemies to become part of the movement centered around the Messiah! To emphasize this point, Jesus' commentary after the scripture reading includes two stories of outsiders being healed in place of Israelites. At this, the people become furious, drive him out of town, and try to throw him off a cliff (Luke 4:28–29). The seeds of decentralization here are clear. Jesus is challenging the preferential treatment of Israel against Gentiles and other outsiders, as well as foreshadowing the inclusive mission that will be more fully realized in Acts.

The next few chapters focus on Jesus' ministry in Galilee (4:31–9:50). In this section there are

---

28 The exception to this may be Zechariah and Elizabeth, who Luke suggests are remarkable in their piety. They remind the reader of Abram and Sarai.
29 Webb, *John the Baptizer* is a thorough introduction to John, particularly the conclusions at pp. 214-215 and pp.381-383, which offer good summaries of John's baptism and his prophetic ministry. Webb suggests (p.381) that John expected 'a radical reorientation of the concrete, socio-historical situation in which the Jewish people in Palestine found themselves'.
30 Although, unlike Matthew and Mark, Luke does not mention John wearing camel's hair and a leather belt, a clear reference to Elijah in 2 Kings 1:7-8, so it may be that Luke is playing down the connection between John the Baptist and Elijah.
31 Webb, *John the Baptizer*, 214-15, offers a good summary of John's baptism and what it was designed to do.
32 This narrative is not spelled out as clearly in Luke as it is in Matthew and Mark. Rather, Luke 3:19-20 records John's arrest, and Luke 9:7 suggests that Herod thinks Jesus is John having come back from the dead. No narrative of John's death is recorded in Luke, but there is the scene of John sending messenger to Jesus asking if he is the one to come in Luke 7:20-22.
33 Peter, Paul and Silas, James, Stephen, and Jesus himself all experience some version of this pattern in Acts.
34 See Fitzmyer, *Luke I–X*, 529 and Bock, *Luke*, 1.394 for examples of seeing this scene as setting a course for the rest of Jesus' ministry.

some key scenes that show the decentralizing effect of Jesus. Luke 5 has two scenes that would be shocking to ancient readers. First, he touches a man covered with leprosy (Luke 5:12–14), a stark contrast to the purity law of Leviticus 13:45–46: 'The person who has the leprous disease shall wear torn clothes and let the hair of his head be disheveled; and he shall cover his upper lip and cry out, "Unclean, unclean". He shall remain unclean as long as he has the disease; he is unclean. He shall live alone; his dwelling shall be outside the camp'.[35] In the holiness economy of the Levitical purity codes, isolating the diseased person makes sense to protect the camp, lest others become impure and unclean. With Jesus, however, the leprous man's impurity does not make Jesus impure; rather Jesus' own purity heals the man when he touches him. Jesus breaking the religious norms by touching the unclean man is a statement about the importance of people and the inclusion of God's good creation, even those outside the normal first-century Jewish standards. The established system of holiness moves in reverse as the system is reconfigured. This, too, is decentralization of a personal nature and it will continue throughout two volumes.

This motif carries forward immediately with the following story, the calling of Levi, the tax collector. Not only does Jesus invite a tax collector to follow him, but he goes to a banquet at Levi's house with many other tax collectors. This is enough to draw the critical eye of Pharisees and scribes, who say, 'Why do you eat and drink with tax collectors and sinners?' (Luke 5:30). This challenge gives Jesus the chance to clarify his mission, stating, 'Those who are well have no need of a physician, but those who are sick; I have come to call not the righteous but sinners to repentance' (Luke 5:27–32). This interchange is the first of several instances of a type-scene, which I call the 'Critic-Response Type-scene'.[36] Each of these scenes will see Jesus, or in the last instance, Peter, include outsiders, which draws criticism from religious leaders. Each time, the response is a clarification of mission and emphasis on the call to outsiders—a key element of decentralization. Once again, we see Jesus challenge the system of holiness as it stood in First Temple Judaism, in this case, choosing someone from the outermost circle of respectability and giving them a place of honor close to him and part of his ministry.

Also in the Galilean ministry is Jesus' encounter with the centurion (Luke 7:1–10). In Capernaum, a centurion has a sick servant for whom he cares and is about to die. Some of the Jewish elders come to ask Jesus to heal the servant and they 'appealed to him earnestly, saying, "He is worthy of having you do this for him, for he loves our people, and it is he who built our synagogue for us"' (Luke 7:4b–5). This picture of Jewish/Roman relationship is certainly noteworthy from the first-century perspective. However, something more is happening on a narrative level: namely, foreshadowing the Cornelius incident in Acts 10. Likewise, Luke 23:47 will show a centurion at the cross for Jesus' death as praising God and declaring Jesus as innocent (δίκαιος).[37] The narrative presentation of these centurions is strategic, as Luke is once again challenging the system as it stood, preparing the reader for a more radical change in volume two.

At the end of the Galilean ministry section is the transfiguration of Jesus, when he and three disciples are on a mountain to pray. The 'appearance of [Jesus'] face changed', his clothes turn white, and he is seen talking with Moses and Elijah about his exodus (τὴν ἔξοδον αὐτοῦ), perhaps the most overt reference to the New Exodus motif in the New Testament (Luke 9:28–31).[38] In

---

35 Leviticus 13 is largely about infectious diseases and the religious and communal implications of those diagnoses.
36 See more fully in Fox, *Hermeneutics*, 78–88, on Luke 15, Luke 19, and Acts 11.
37 In addition, Luke's account of Jesus and the centurion offers a more positive ethos of the centurion than does Matthew's account.
38 The New Exodus is a popular theme in Luke-Acts studies; cf. Fox, *Hermeneutics of Social Identity*. Also, see Pao, *Acts and the Isaianic New Exodus*.

addition, the divine voice speaks from heaven, saying 'This is my Son, my Chosen; listen to him!' Bock suggests there may be a reference to the Feast of Booths here in the disciples' desire to build tents, which Jesus rejects and shows his superiority over the other figures in the transfiguration.[39] If this illusion is legitimate, it lines up with other feasts that will be decentralized or repurposed in Luke-Acts, namely Passover and Pentecost. This experience seems to bring about a shift in the narrative and set the stage for the journey that will come just a few verses later.

The travel narrative to Jerusalem starts in 9:51, when Jesus 'set his face to go to Jerusalem', and ends with the entry to Jerusalem (19:28–40). The narrative structure of the journey to Jerusalem is key for several reasons.[40] First, it builds to the climax of the Jesus' arrest, crucifixion, and resurrection in Jerusalem. The narrative will continually remind the reader that Jesus is 'on the way' (Luke 9:52, 53, 56, 57; 10:1, 38; 13:22, 31, 33; 14:25; 17:11; 18:31, 35; 19:1, 11, 28). Second, the journey to Jerusalem in Luke will set the stage for the parallel reversal of the movement away from Jerusalem in Acts. Third, as Jesus approaches Jerusalem, his presentation as a prophet will increase as will his conflict with the Jewish leadership (Luke 5:33–6:11; 7:39; 11:14–20; 37–54). Jesus' embodying of the decentralization motif is regular in these chapters to the degree that there is not sufficient space to fully examine them here. However, mentioning a few of these key scenes is important.

The parable of the Good Samaritan in Luke 10 is a radical statement of outsiders becoming insiders. Despite the long history in the Talmud of Jewish Rabbis being the storied heroes in order to be faithful to the law and loving toward neighbor,[41] this story shows indifference by the priest and Levite coming down from Jerusalem and deep care and neighborly love by the Samaritan, the hated neighbor of the Jews. In fact, a chapter before, the Samaritans had not welcomed Jesus and the disciples because they were heading to Jerusalem and James and John wanted to call down fire to consume them, in the spirit of Elijah (2 Kings 1:10). Jesus' rebuke shows his break with the tradition that would perpetuate excluding outsiders, and instead, continues to challenge the symbols and system of first-century Judaism.

By chapter 13, Luke tells us that Herod is trying to kill Jesus. This initiates a scene where Jesus comments on his own ministry, but also the danger Jerusalem is to its prophets:

> Yet today, tomorrow, and the next day I must be on my way, because it is impossible for a prophet to be killed outside of Jerusalem. Jerusalem, Jerusalem, the city that kills the prophets and stones those who are sent to it! How often have I desired to gather your children together as a hen gathers her brood under her wings, and you were not willing! See, your house is left to you. And I tell you, you will not see me until the time comes when you say, "Blessed is the one who comes in the name of the Lord" (Luke 13:33–35).

Jesus foreshadows his entry into Jerusalem in Luke 19:38, but also the violence he will encounter in Jerusalem along with his own death. This is a key scene in the decentralizing nature of Luke-Acts because it does not see Jerusalem as the Holy City because of the location of Mt. Zion and the temple—the central locus of God's presence—but rather, as a place hostile to the work of God and his prophets, which certainly includes Jesus and his followers. In this prophetic statement by Jesus, the narrative groundwork is laid that will lead to Jerusalem becoming dangerous for the early Christians, who will be required to leave the city for fear of death. This is most notably true

---

39 Bock, *Luke* 1.869–71.
40 Johnson, *Luke*, 164.
41 This takes the form at times of amazing physical feats or of shrewd wisdom or knowledge of the law. For example, see Sanhedrin 101a; Taanit 19a; Kiddushin 81a; Jerusalem Talmud, Sotah 1:4.

for Paul, who will come to associate Jerusalem with his own arrest and death (Acts 2:22–24).

In Luke 14, Jesus goes to dinner at a Pharisee's house, which becomes the setting for a number of encounters with decentralizing elements. First, Jesus heals a man with dropsy on the Sabbath, which is the fifth time he has healed on the Sabbath in Luke, more than any of the other Gospels.[42] Along with circumcision and food laws, keeping the Sabbath was one of the primary symbols of Jewish identity in the first century.[43] Jesus' intentional breaking of the Sabbath and his ongoing challenge of the practice continues his trajectory of decentralization in his ministry. Next, he challenges their method for choosing seats at the table as they crave the places of honor, and instead urges them to take the lowly places (Luke 14:7–11). He then suggests that they should not invite their friends to a dinner party, but 'the poor, the crippled, the lame, and the blind' (Luke 14:13). The threefold challenge in this scene at the Pharisee's house—challenging Sabbath, seats of honor, and kindness to friends over the poor and infirmed—is a classic example of Jesus redefining what it means to be righteous in the first-century Jewish world. Rather than strict rules, seats of honor, and kindness reserved only for friends, the Jesus movement is to be marked by humility and doing good to the poor and the infirmed.

This theme is seen again in the contrast between The Rich Young Ruler and Zacchaeus in chapters 18 and 19. These two wealthy Jewish men both have encounters with Jesus. The Rich Young Ruler is seeking out Jesus to inquire how to inherit eternal life. Upon Jesus' response—keep the commandments, essentially—the man is confident that he has. However, when Jesus next instructs him to sell all he has and give it to the poor, he is unable to part with his great wealth and goes away sad. Zacchaeus, on the other hand, is also curious about Jesus; but as a chief tax collector and presumably infamous, he merely climbs a tree to see him pass. Jesus initiates contact, goes to his house, and Zacchaeus experiences a transformation that leads him to offer to pay back anyone he has cheated. This is also the third occurrence of the critic-response type-scene, where critics grumble and challenge Jesus for the company he keeps. The comparison of these two characters is significant because though they have similarities, their outcomes are quite different. The Ruler appears to be an insider by the standard of Jewish piety in the first century. (Although for Luke, wealth is a hazard to spiritual health and he instead establishes generosity as a norm through two volumes; see Luke 3:14; 7:41; 9:3; 12:13–21; 14:28; 15:13; 16:9–14; 18:18–23; 19:13–15; 21:4; 22:5. Acts 2:45; 3:1–8; 4:32–5; 4:36–5:11; 10:2). Zacchaeus is also wealthy, but as a Roman chief tax collector, he is very much an outsider to the norms of first-century Jewish piety. Thus, we again see a personal decentralization in the ministry of Jesus. The presumed insider goes away sad; the infamous villain has salvation—and the Messiah—come to his house. The scene ends as Jesus clarifies his mission to seek and save the lost.

As the travel narrative comes to a close, Jesus prepares to enter Jerusalem. In Luke's version of what has been termed the Triumphal Entry, the Pharisees rebuke Jesus' followers for quoting Psalm 118. Once again, those closest to the centralized Jewish establishment miss the movement of God in their midst. Jesus again speaks about Jerusalem, this time weeping over the city and the destruction that was coming upon it. He then enters the temple courts and drives out the sellers and moneychangers before he begins teaching every day in the temple courts. Thus, in rapid succession, Jesus enters the city, cleanses the temple, and takes occupation of the temple beginning the last week of his life. Here we see the city of Jerusalem, the holy city, represent

---

42 The others include Luke 4:31–7, 38–39; 6:6–11; 13:10–17.
43 Blomberg, *Jesus and the Gospels*, 49. For more on Jewish Identity in the first century, see Wright, *New Testament and the People of God*, 224–32.

violence and destruction, while the temple, the symbol of God's centralized presence, is called a den of robbers.

The upper room scene includes another central element of Jewish life and practice, namely the Passover Feast. The feast symbolizes God's salvation for his people and the end of bondage, themes that are present in Jesus' ministry as well. Jesus' script at the Passover shows again the meeting of traditional Jewish symbols with a Messiah who challenges and changes those symbols. Jesus changes the focus of Passover from the Exodus from Egypt, to the present New Exodus centered around himself. Moreover, he sets the stage for this new ritual to become central in the early church with his words, 'Do this in remembrance of me' (Luke 22:19).

Like Jesus' birth, his arrest and crucifixion involve numerous unnatural elements juxtaposed. Jesus, the prophetic figure and teacher of good,[44] is beaten and mocked by the guards (Luke 22:63–65), crucified alongside criminals (Luke 23:32–33), and forced to watch people gamble for his garments (Luke 23:34). Jesus prays for forgiveness of the ones killing him (Luke 23:34). As the religious leaders hurl insults at Jesus, the convicted thief crucified next to him finds assurance of being with Jesus in paradise (Luke 23:43), and a Roman centurion at the foot of the cross says, 'certainly this man was innocent' (Luke 23:47). In another surprising juxtaposition, Joseph of Arimathea (a respected yet dissenting member of the council, Luke 23:50–53) is the one who requests Jesus' body and arranges for it to be placed in a new grave, despite the council having been the decision-makers in finding Jesus guilty and handing him over to Pilate in the first place (Luke 23:50–53). Thus, we see that in perhaps every group—faithful Jews, tax collectors, thieves, and even the Sanhedrin—some respond to Jesus positively, even when most do not.

Finally, Jesus is crucified outside of the city of Jerusalem. A lasting image of decentralization is that of Jesus dragging his cross outside of the city.[45] The climax of Israel's covenantal relationship with God was expected to occur inside the city of Jerusalem, not outside.[46] These contrasts are befitting of a story that is full of decentralizing central symbols.

In standard Lukan fashion, minor characters—women—are the ones to witness and testify first to Jesus' resurrection. As with the birth narratives, which include angels in three different scenes, Jesus' resurrection includes angels as well.[47] The angels do not speak to kings and prophets, but to minor characters, like women and shepherds.[48]

Luke ends with the resurrected Jesus predicting the preaching of repentance to all nations, but starting in Jerusalem, promising 'power from on high', and blessing the disciples. The reader expects some of these elements from Luke to continue into Acts: angelic activity, minor characters, and challenging the Jewish establishment. These elements do indeed continue into Acts. But one might also expect for the Twelve to take central leadership roles throughout Acts, becoming the new main characters like Jesus was in Luke. This is the biggest surprise of Acts, namely that the Twelve are mostly absent, save for chapter one. The ones who do continue after that, Peter and John, are usually not initiators of ministry and spiritual activity, but rather, observers and verifiers. Indeed, the decentralizing nature of the Spirit, rooted in a desire to see the gospel go forward

---

44 Johnson, *Luke*, 70, offers a helpful proposition about the prophetic nature of Jesus and his ministry.
45 Indeed, Jesus needed help to do so, with the assistance of Simon of Cyrene. Simon was a diasporic Jew. Luke 23:26.
46 See McConville, 'Jerusalem in the Old Testament', and Wright, 'Jerusalem in the New Testament'.
47 For the occurrences of Angels in Luke-Acts, see Fox, *Hermeneutics*, 165-68.
48 The first occurrence of angels in the Lukan corpus is when the angel visits Zechariah in Luke 1:8–25. Although Zechariah is a priest, and we might expect him to be an insider, he is elderly and childless and while his access to the altar of incense certainly makes him a fortunate priest, this encounter starts the narrative of John and Jesus, both who will challenge the status quo.

regardless of who is available to facilitate that advancement, is so strong that even the disciples become decentralized in favor of outsiders and minor characters. Luke will take the reader on a journey that starts in Jerusalem with the Twelve and ends with ministry happening many hundreds of miles away with a whole new cast of characters.

After the preface to Acts, which mentions Theophilus again, the reader is taken back to the ascension scene from the end of Luke and a reminder of the promise of the Holy Spirit. Acts 1:8 is perhaps the most programmatic verse of decentralization in the Lukan corpus. In it, Jesus says, 'But you will receive power when the Holy Spirit has come upon you, and you will be my witnesses in Jerusalem and in all Judea and Samaria, and to the end of the earth'. This sets a geographical outline for at least the first half of the book.[49] Where Luke's Gospel was primarily a narrative journey to Jerusalem, particularly from Luke 9:51 onward, Acts will be a narrative journey away from Jerusalem.

Once again, the point is not the subjugation of Jerusalem or Judaism. Rather, in order to be a movement that emphasizes inclusion, decentralization is necessary. A movement that requires Jerusalem and the temple as a central feature of the faith is difficult to export. Likewise, a faith that can only be expanded by a handful of insiders (i.e. disciples, priests, etc.) is severely limited. However, a movement that is fueled by a Holy Spirit that empowers people for witness and whose presence is available anywhere is much more able to include outsiders and grow. The movement is not limited by the selectivity of human beings who tend to convert others like themselves. Indeed, the pattern in Acts is that the Holy Spirit, not the Twelve, initiates new missionary outposts and often among unlikely peoples, such as Samaritans, God-fearers,[50] Gentiles, and other outsiders.

Acts 2 opens in Jerusalem with a reminder that the time was the feast of Pentecost. Although originally a harvest festival, by the first century Pentecost was a celebration of the anniversary of the giving of the Law at Sinai.[51] A careful reader will notice similar symbols in both the Sinai event in Exodus 19 and in Acts 2: storm imagery (i.e. clouds, thunder, and lighting, vs. a violent wind; Exodus 19:16 and Acts 2:2), fire and smoke imagery (fire and smoke coming onto the mountain vs. tongues of fire coming to rest on those present; Exodus 19:18 and Acts 2:3), and response of the people (people tremble vs. people being amazed and astonished; Exodus 19:16 and Acts 2:7, 12). But a final symbol points to a stark difference: at Sinai, three thousand people are killed, while in the Pentecost scene, three thousand were converted and joined the movement (Exodus 32:28 and Acts 2:41). These similarities lead us to think that Luke is making a statement here regarding the reconstitution of God's people for mission.

After the description of the scene, Luke suggests there were Jews present from 'every nation under heaven' (Acts 2:5). Far from being a repudiation of Judaism or the Jewish people, this new movement is overwhelmingly Jewish in nature. However, it is also incredibly diverse, as Luke gives a detailed list of the nations represented (Acts 2:9–11). Despite the language diversity, the tongues the Spirit produces allow each person to hear the message in their own language. This diversity will continue through Acts, as nearly every chapter will introduce new challenges and new opportunities for advancement of the gospel.

---

49   The parameters for how thoroughly one sees this outline covering Acts has to do with how 'the ends of the earth' is understood, whether this met in chapter 8 or by the end of the book with Paul in Rome.
50   God-fearers refer to Gentiles who participate in the synagogue and worship the God of Israel, but have not taken the final step of conversion. For Cornelius as the prototypical God-fearer, see Fox, *Hermeneutics*, 75–78.
51   Dunn, *Baptism in the Holy Spirit*, 480–94; Turner, 'The Spirit in Luke-Acts', 79. See Exodus 23:16; Deuteronomy 16:9–12. See also the Book of Jubilees 6:17, which reads, 'Therefore, it is ordained and written in the heavenly tablets that they should observe the feast of Shebuot [i.e. 'Weeks' or 'Pentecost'] in this month, once per year in order to renew the covenant in all (respects), year by year' (Jubilees 6:17) in Charlesworth, *Old Testament Pseudepigrapha*, 2.67.

The tension in the next few chapters covering the apostles' ministry in Jerusalem can be summarized by Acts 4:3–4: 'And they arrested them and put them in custody until the next day, for it was already evening. But many of those who had heard the word believed, and the number of the men came to about five thousand'. Here we see both intense persecution and increased ministry success. This is an example of a primary theme that will develop in Acts: no matter what challenges the church faces, whether internal or external, the Spirit uses these challenges as opportunities for mission. Indeed, the story of Acts is one filled with challenges of all sorts. Imprisonment, flogging, a man offering to buy the Holy Spirit, and a dishonest couple who drop dead are all examples encountered by chapter 8. But at each turn, it only seems to help fuel the mission that the Spirit is empowering.

The Ananias and Sapphira incident, infamous in the New Testament for the shocking nature of immediate judgment, is actually a strong statement of decentralization. First, there is perhaps no more important feature in the life and identity of ancient Israel than 'The Land'. This central Jewish identity marker has a long textual and scholarly tradition.[52] However, the mission of Acts will not be limited to the land. Jesus' ministry, although mostly focused on the Jews and the land of Israel, also included interactions with Gentiles and those outside the land of Israel (Luke 7:9; 8:22–39; 10:13–15). Acts will see the mission make a radical departure from Jerusalem and the land of Israel proper to 'the ends of the earth', including Samaria, Ethiopia, and Rome. Secondly, a major prescriptive norm in Acts is generosity. We see the church being generous to those in need again and again, with exemplars of generous giving highlighted (as they were in Luke; see 3:14; 7:41; 9:3; 12:13–21; 14:28; 15:13; 16:9–14; 18:18–23; 19:13–15; 21:4; 22:5. Acts 2:45; 3:1–8; 4:32–5; 4:36–5:11; 10:2). Thus, Ananias and Sapphira selling a piece of land, refusing to part with the bounty and even lying about the amount in order to hold some back, shows their ongoing attempt to gain identity from the old system and symbols in traditional ways. In essence, they refused to embrace the new Christ-centered identity marked by generosity. Luke is not only making a strong statement against greed, but also to Jewish Christians who would desire to maintain traditional Jewish norms of land ownership while still following Christ. Ananias and Sapphira are contrasted with Barnabas, also known as Joseph the Levite from Cyprus, who first sold a field and laid the money at the disciples' feet, which immediately preceded the Ananias and Sapphira narrative (Acts 4:36–37). Thus, the stark contrast between this couple and Barnabas is key to understanding Luke's point.

Chapters 6 and 7 are undoubtedly the climax of tension between Jerusalem and the Christians in the first part of the book. A new character emerges—who is not part of the Twelve or even known in the narrative yet, but rather, a minor character selected to wait tables—named Stephen. Chapter 6 is dedicated to his remarkable character and capability as a newcomer on the scene. He is arrested on false accusations that he spoke against 'Moses and against God' (Acts 6:11). Chapter 7 is Stephen's speech defending himself against the charges, but also giving his recount of salvation history through a Christian lens. The speech ends with members of the Sanhedrin rushing forward in a rage to stone him while a young man named Saul gives approval to his death. While one may have thought in chapter 6 that Jerusalem was to remain the center of operations for the early Christians with Stephen as a key charismatic figure, those hopes are dashed by the end of chapter 7. Instead, the church is forced out of Jerusalem due to this intense persecution. We remember Jesus' charge at the beginning to take the message beyond Jerusalem, and it takes intense persecution for that charge to be realized.

---

52 For a full treatment of the history of the Land in Jewish and Christian history, see Fox, *Hermeneutics*, 208–16. See also Von Rad, 'Promised Land' and Wright, *God's People in God's Land*.

With the move out of Jerusalem comes a great deal of decentralizing missional activity. Philip is another of those selected to wait tables in Acts 6:1–5. Despite the fact that this group was selected to wait tables and free the Twelve up for ministry, they do a fair amount of ministry in their own right, as the Twelve continue to fade into the periphery.[53] Philip begins to minister in Samaria, which seems much easier than ministry in Jerusalem—no persecution but equally spectacular fruit.[54] Now with Philip following the Spirit's lead and being the instrument of a new missionary initiative, Peter and John are left to be verifiers of this new spiritual activity (Acts 8:14).

Immediately after this scene, an angel tells Philip to, 'rise and go toward the south to the road that goes down from Jerusalem to Gaza' (Acts 8:26). This intentional and specific direction by the angel is strategic, as Philip encounters an Ethiopian eunuch. Both descriptors of this character are quite important. First, he is from Ethiopia—from the Greek, Αἰθίοψ, meaning 'burnt face', a comment on complexion and skin color. In addition, some scholars suggest that Ethiopia was 'the ends of the earth' as prophesied by Jesus in Acts 1:8. Van Unnik, for example, argues that the phrase refers 'very definitely to the end, the extreme limit, of the world'.[55] However, not all agree.[56] Regardless of whether Ethiopia is seen as the ends of the earth or not, this man was seen as exotic, 'a strong representative of foreignness within a Jewish context'.[57] His conversion and inclusion as a clear step in moving away from traditional Jewish power structures which valued the children of Abraham above all others.

That the man is a eunuch is perhaps more significant. Eunuchs were specifically excluded from worship in Deuteronomy 23:1.[58] As with Jesus touching the leper in Luke 5:13, the intentional inclusion of this eunuch challenges and corrects a religious boundary of the old system for the purpose of a wider inclusion of God's people. The eunuch had been in Jerusalem to worship at the temple, but was presumably turned away. The Holy Spirit sends Philip to explain the gospel to this man—who is reading the suffering servant section of Isaiah—and he was baptized. The connection with Isaiah is important, as the prophet envisions the inclusion of eunuchs in the future age of redemption:

> For thus says the LORD:
> "To the eunuchs who keep my Sabbaths,
>   who choose the things that please me
>   and hold fast my covenant,
> I will give in my house and within my walls
>   a monument and a name
>   better than sons and daughters;
> I will give them an everlasting name
>   that shall not be cut off". (Isaiah 56:4–5).

---

53. Only Peter is mentioned in the narrative by name after chapter 8. John is only mentioned in Acts 12:2 when James is killed and the apostles as a group are mentioned at the Jerusalem council in 15:6, though only Peter is said to have spoken.
54. The ministry in Samaria is not without obstacles, however. This is where Simon the Sorcerer offers to buy the Holy Spirit, and Peter calls him to repentance because of his greed.
55. van Unnik, 'Der Ausdruck ἕως ἐσχάτου τῆς γῆς'.
56. Keener, *Acts*, 1.708, for example, suggests that Luke uses the phrase as the LXX does to talk of universality. Also, see Johnson, *Acts*, 26–27, who cites Deut 28:49; Ps 134:6–7; Isa 8:9; 48:20; 49:6; 62:11; Jer 10:12; 16:19; 1 Macc 3:9; Lake and Cadbury, *Translation and Commentary*, 9.
57. Tannehill, *Narrative Unity*, 2.108.
58. 'No one whose testicles are crushed or whose penis is cut off shall be admitted to the assembly of the Lord'. Also, see Wilson, *Unmanly Men*, 113–49, who argues that the eunuch is selected as a way to refigure masculinity in the Greco-Roman world, using other examples as well, such as Zechariah's inability to speak.

This text is concerned with the inclusion of the foreigner and the eunuch, both of which the figure in Acts 8 specifically reflects. In addition, the question about baptism seems to be phrased in such a way to challenge opponents of the inclusion of this Ethiopian eunuch: 'See, here is water! What prevents me from being baptized?' (Acts 8:36b). The answer implied in the narrative is a resounding, 'Nothing!' Again, we see the Holy Spirit initiating new missionary initiatives with 'whosoever will' obediently take the message forward with boldness. This scene is exemplary for its decentralizing themes, both in who it uses (i.e. Philip, not one of the Twelve) and who it converts (i.e. a foreign eunuch excluded from temple worship but welcomed into the family of God via the early church).

Following the conversion of the eunuch, the narrative turns again to Saul, the figure who approves of Stephen's death by the council. As mentioned, what appeared to be a dark day for the church—a charismatic minister is killed and persecution reached a level to scatter the disciples—actually helps the church by starting the outward movement of the gospel. However, in brilliant narrative form, Luke gives his audience a glimpse of Saul, who will become the main character in the second half of the book—an unlikely hero indeed! We now learn of his conversion, a story that will be told in Galatians and 1 Corinthians (1 Corinthians 15:3–8; Galatians 1:11–16), and retold twice more in Acts (22:6–21; 26:12–18). It is clearly a central story, for Paul will become the major figure of the second half of Acts as he continues the mode of decentralization, taking the gospel all over the Roman Empire. Despite Paul being a male Jewish Pharisee, his importance in Acts still reflects decentralization in that he is perhaps the least likely character to ascend to such a post, and certainly the opposite of what the reader expects. Nonetheless, the Spirit is relentless in pursuit of Paul.

Saul's conversion highlights more elements of decentralization. The Jewish leader is traveling to Damascus to arrest members of the Way and bring them back to Jerusalem, 'still breathing threats and murder against the disciples of the Lord' (Acts 9:1). The gospel has been spreading beyond what the narrative has even revealed, with active believers in Damascus appearing on the radar of the Jerusalem power structures. Saul's attempt to bring these Christians bound back to Jerusalem is in direct opposition of the decentralizing nature of the mission that is moving away from Jerusalem. Furthermore, Saul is perhaps the least likely character to be the primary missionary in the second half of Acts. Indeed it was powerful Jewish leaders in Jerusalem, of whom Saul is one, who gave the early church the most trouble (Acts 4:1–3, 15–18; 5:15–18, 26–40; 7:54–60). For the Spirit to use this figure as 'a chosen instrument' to accomplish the mission set out in Acts 1:8 and 'carry [Jesus'] name before the Gentiles and kings and the children of Israel' (Acts 9:15b), as opposed to one of the disciples who was present for that prophetic charge, is classic Lukan decentralization. The one who was sent to arrest members of the Way in the Damascus synagogue ends up preaching Jesus to this same audience. The one who was breathing out murderous threats quickly becomes the target of a murder plot for the same cause.

Despite the importance of these two conversion stories—the Ethiopian eunuch and Saul—for Luke's narrative, Cornelius' conversion in Acts 10 is the most important conversion story in the book and central to the decentralization trajectory. Much of the narrative so far—the themes of universality in the birth stories, the encounter with the centurion in Luke 7, the words of Jesus in Acts 1:8, the emphasis on diversity at Pentecost, the ever-widening mission as initiated and driven by the Holy Spirit—has been preparation for this moment. This story affects everything after it in the book of Acts, namely, the Jerusalem council and Paul's missionary journeys.

As with Stephen, we see Luke introduce a new character with strikingly positive language. Acts 10:2 reports that he was 'a devout man who feared God with all his household, gave alms generously to the people, and prayed continually to God'. Since previously in Acts had shown that generosity is central to the new way of life in the early church, Cornelius fits (Acts 2:45; 3:1–8; 4:32–5; 4:36–5:11). The centurion in Luke 7 was known as 'worthy', one who loves the nation of Israel, and who built the synagogue in Capernaum. The reader is reminded of this encounter with Jesus in the positive portrayal of Cornelius. In addition to the description, he sees an angel in a vision. Despite the relatively high number of angelic encounters and visions in Luke's corpus, this nonetheless puts him in elite company.[59] Zechariah, Mary, the shepherds, Jesus, the women at the tomb, Stephen, Ananias, Paul, and Peter are the others to see angels or visions.[60] This vision, though, is the strongest kind of evidence in the ancient world, as it is paired with Peter's vision.[61] Peter's vision of the sheet coming down from heaven with all sorts of non-kosher animals prepares him to have a positive encounter with Cornelius, a Gentile, and even enter his home, which breaks another longstanding Jewish tradition.[62] Shortly after Peter began speaking, the Spirit fell 'on all who heard the word' (Acts 10:44), which immediately recalls Pentecost, where many of the same elements were in place (people gathered, Peter speaking, speaking in tongues, and Holy Spirit activity). The Spirit falling on Gentiles is the proof to Peter and the reader that Gentiles are welcomed into the family of God, for the 'extreme opposite of the unclean is the holy'.[63]

After this remarkable series of events, Peter is left to defend his actions to the circumcision party in Jerusalem (Acts 11:2–3). Peter retells the events of the previous chapter and ends his defense with asking, 'If then God gave the same gift to them as he gave to us when we believed in the Lord Jesus Christ, who was I that I could stand in God's way?' (Acts 11:17). The reader is reminded when the Pharisees and teachers of the Law confronted Jesus previously in Luke for his community with sinners and tax collectors (5:30; 15:2; 19:7).[64] The result, however, is remarkably different. When Jesus defended himself and clarified his mission, there was never any indication that his critics were won over. Here, however, the text reports, remarkably, 'when they heard these things they fell silent. And they glorified God, saying, "Then to the Gentiles also God has granted repentance that leads to life"' (Acts 11:18).

It is difficult to overemphasize the importance this scene has for the theme of decentralization. The whole narrative has been building to this point where all of God's children—Jew and Gentile alike—are granted access to his family. This change does not happen in this scene alone, as we have seen it happen previously with diverse Jews in Jerusalem, ministry in Samaria, with the Ethiopian Eunuch, and even with Saul, the enemy of the church. But here we begin to glimpse the fully blooming flower of decentralization emerging from the seed God planted according to Luke's Gospel. Acts 15 will show the centralized church affirming what has already happened in the form of an official decision and a letter. The 'official church' in Acts is always behind the Spirit's

---

59   Zechariah: Luke 1:22, in the temple; The women at Jesus' tomb: Luke 24:23, being referenced on the road to Emmaus; Ananias: Acts 9:10,12, in the conversion of Paul; Cornelius: Acts 10:3, seeing a vision of an Angel giving him information about Peter; Peter: Acts 10:17, the vision of the animal and the sheet; 10:19, 11:5 Telling the story of his vision; 12:9 Peter's escape from prison; Paul: Acts 16:9–10, Man in Macedonia; 18:9, Jesus telling Paul not to be silent; 26:19, Paul referring back to his Damascus road experience.

60   I treat angels and visions together, as the language overlaps, as here with Cornelius, who is said to see a *vision* of an *angel*. Sometimes only one of those words is used.

61   Keener, *Acts*, 2.1644. Paul's conversion also involved paired visions, with Paul and Ananias both seeing visions independently.

62   Although the prohibition against entering the home of a Gentile and eating with him is not found in the Old Testament, it is found multiple other places in Jewish literature, such as Jubilees 22:16, Joseph and Aseneth 7:1, and 3 Maccabees 3:4, 6–7. For a fuller discussion of this issue and these texts, see Fox, *Hermeneutics*, 163–65.

63   Tannehill, *Narrative Unity*, 2.135.

64   For a full discussion of the reader response type-scene, see Fox, *Hermeneutics*, 78–88.

move and trying to play catchup. By the time the council in Acts takes place, not only have the conversions of Saul and Cornelius happened, but Paul and Barnabas have already completed the first missionary journey, preaching in the synagogues and public arenas in Asia.

The missionary journeys of Paul and his companions continue on the trajectory of decentralization as the Spirit empowers mission to various diverse spots around the Roman Empire. Paul does significant ministry work in Ephesus, Thessalonica, and Corinth, and he engages with the philosophers on the Aereopagus in Athens. Indeed, the Way is no longer a Jerusalem-bound sect, destined to clash with the local authorities. Instead, it has become a diverse, multinational movement that gets a hearing on one of the highest stages of philosophy. It is not always well received though, as Paul continually faces hardship and persecution. However difficult these hardships may be, the Holy Spirit is determined to use every opportunity to drive the mission, and they all serve to advance the gospel. Peter's and John's arrest in Acts 5 is thwarted by an angel who releases them from prison and instructs them to 'go and stand in the temple and speak to the people all the words of this Life' (Acts 5:20). Stephen's stoning forces the church to scatter but this leads to ministry in Samaria and conversion of the Ethiopian eunuch. Paul and Silas being sent to prison in Acts 16 leads to the conversion of the prison guard and his whole household (Acts 16:16–40). While there are certainly periods of persecution that Luke does not directly connect to the advancement of the gospel (i.e. Paul being stoned in Iconium and left for dead), it is common enough to clearly demonstrate Luke's aim to show the Holy Spirit's practical use of persecution for advancement of the gospel.

Persecution is also the reason for the final narrative arc in Acts, as Paul is arrested when he returns to Jerusalem. Rather than being the centralized location of God's presence, Jerusalem has become the centralized location of persecution for the messianic community. Paul's arrest in Acts 21 starts a series of trials and speeches before officials that carry the reader to the end of the book. Indeed, Paul will have an opportunity to speak before the angry mob at his arrest (Acts 22:1–21), the Sanhedrin (Acts 22:30–23:11), Felix (Acts 24), Festus (Acts 25), Agrippa and Bernice (Acts 25:23–26:32), and is finally sent to Rome to stand before Caesar (Acts 27–28). Even the journey to Rome as a prisoner on a boat results in both hardship and ministry opportunity, as the shipwreck results in Paul praying for healing for the father of the chief official of Malta (Acts 28:7–10).

By the end of Acts, we remember where it all started: with an old, childless couple, and a young virgin girl singing songs about the hope of redemption. This results in the powerful ministry of Jesus and his disciples followed by his unjust execution at the hands of the Romans and the Jewish leadership. His resurrection sparks hope in those closest to him. The early church starts humbly with the disciples and some others just figuring out what to do about the situation with Judas, but Pentecost brings new life. It is not primarily these disciples that take the mission forward, but instead we see the Holy Spirit use whomever is available over the course of the rest of the book. Luke ends his two-volume work with the greatest apostle, Paul, in Rome ready to appear before the most powerful ruler in the land, and we see the gospel go forth without hinderance. A movement that seemed to be centralized in Jerusalem-centric Judaism and restricted to Jews only becomes a decentralized movement that includes God-fearers, Gentiles, and churches all throughout Asia and Greece in addition to a diverse group of Jews. Indeed, Luke-Acts testifies to the decentralizing nature of the Holy Spirit to take God's message of loving inclusion into his kingdom to all people.

Thus, we have seen decentralization—geographic, personal, and cultural—happen in two volumes, with seeds planted in volume one that come to full bloom in volume two. Through strategic use of narrative, Luke presented Jesus as largely opposing the systems and symbols central to the holiness economy in Luke in order to welcome those on the outermost rings of the accepted understanding of respectability. Decentralization happened with regard to both hearers and sharers of the message. We have explored these themes suggested by Beers, Johnson, and Keener in depth and seen the radical nature of the decentralizing narrative through two volumes.

Bibliography

Beers, Holly — *The Followers of Jesus as the 'Servant': Luke's Model. From Isaiah for the Disciples in Luke-Acts* (New York: Bloomsbury T&T Clark, 2015).

Blomberg, Craig — *Jesus and the Gospels: An Introduction and Survey* (Nashville: B&H Publishing, 2009).

Bock, Darrell L. — *Acts* (Grand Rapids: Baker Academic, 2007).

Bock, Darrell L. — *Luke 1:1–9:50* (Grand Rapids: Baker Academic, 1994).

Brawley, Robert — *Luke-Acts and the Jews: Conflict, Apology, and Conciliation* (Atlanta: SBL, 1987).

Cadbury, Henry J. — *The Making of Luke-Acts* (London: SPCK, 1968).

Charlesworth, James H. (ed.) — *The Old Testament Pseudepigrapha*, Vol. 2 (Peabody, MA: Hendrickson Publishers, 2010).

Dunn, James D.G. — *Baptism in the Holy Spirit: A Re-examination of the New Testament on the Gift of the Spirit* (Louisville: Westminster John Knox, 1977).

Dupont, Jacques — *The Salvation of the Gentiles: Essays on the Acts of the Apostles* (John R. Keating, trans.; New York: Paulist, 1979).

Fitzmyer, Joseph — *Luke I–X* (Garden City: Doubleday, 1981).

Fox, Nickolas A. — *The Hermeneutics of Social Identity* (Eugene: Pickwick, 2021).

Green, Joel B. — 'The Demise of the Temple as "Culture Center" in Luke-Acts: An Exploration of the Rending of the Temple Veil (Luke 23.44–49)', *Revue Biblique* 101.4 (1994), 495–515.

Green, Joel B. — 'The Problem Of A Beginning: Israel's Scriptures In Luke 1–2', *BBR* 4.1 (1994), 61–85.

Jervell, Jacob — *Luke and the People of God* (Minneapolis: Augsburg, 1972).

Jervell, Jacob — *The Theology of the Acts of the Apostles* (Cambridge: Cambridge University Press, 1996, 2007).

Johnson, Luke Timothy — *The Acts of the Apostles* (Collegeville, MN: Liturgical Press, 1992).

Johnson, Luke Timothy — *Luke* (Collegeville, MN: Liturgical Press, 1991).

Keener, Craig S. — *Acts: An Exegetical Commentary*, Vol. 1 (Grand Rapids: Baker Academic, 2011).

Lake, Kirsopp, and Henry J. Cadbury, *The Beginnings of Christianity.* Part I: *The Acts of the Apostles* Vol. IV: *Translation and Commentary* (F.J. Foakes Jackson & Kirsopp Lake, eds.; Grand Rapids: Baker Book House, 1979).

Maddox, Robert *The Purpose of Luke-Acts* (Edinburgh: T&T Clark, 1982).

Matson, David Lertis *Household Conversion Narratives in Acts: Pattern and Interpretation* (Sheffield, UK: Sheffield Academic, 1996).

McConville, Gordon 'Jerusalem in the Old Testament', in P. W. L. Walker (ed.), *Jerusalem Past and Present in the Purposes of God* (Cambridge: Tyndale House, 1992), 21–51.

Moore, Thomas S. '"To the End of the Earth": The Geographical and Ethnic Universalism in Acts 1:8 in Light of Isaianic Influences on Luke', *JETS* 40.3 (1997), 389–99.

Nolland, John *Luke 1:1–9:20* (*Word Bible Commentary,* Vol. 35A; Grand Rapids: Zondervan, 2016).

Pao, David *Acts and the Isaianic New Exodus* (WUNT 2.130; Tübingen: Mohr Siebeck, 2000; republished: Eugene: Wipf & Stock, 2016).

Peterson, David G. *The Acts of the Apostles* (Grand Rapids: Eerdmans, 2009).

Richard, Pablo 'The Pluralistic Experiences of the First Christian Communities according to the Acts of the Apostles' *DVerb* 62–63 (2002), 24–31.

Senior, Donald P., and Carroll Stuhlmueller *The Biblical Foundation for Mission* (Maryknoll, NY: Orbis, 1983).

Tannehill, Robert *The Narrative Unity of Luke-Acts*, Vol. 2 (Minneapolis: Fortress. Press, 1994).

Turner, Max 'The Spirit in Luke-Acts: A Support or Challenge to Classical Pentecostal Paradigms', *Vox Evangelica* (1997), 75–101.

van Unnik, W. C. 'Der Ausdruck ἕως ἐσχάτου τῆς γῆς (Apostelgeschichte I 8) und sein alttestamenlicher Hintergrund', in *Sparsa Collecta: The Collected Essays of W.C. van Unnik* (Leiden: Brill, 1973), 386–401.

Von Rad, Gerhard 'The Promised Land and Yahweh's Land in the Hexateuch', in *The Problem of the Hexateuch and Other Essays* (Philadelphia: Fortress, 1966), 79–93; first published in German in *Zeitschrift des Deutschen Palastinavereins* 66 (1943), 191–204.

Webb, Robert L. *John the Baptizer and Prophet: A Sociohistorical Study* (Eugene: Wipf and Stock, 2006).

Wilson, Brittany E. *Unmanly Men: Refigurations of Masculinity in Luke-Acts* (Oxford: Oxford University Press, 2015).

Wilson, Stephen G. *The Gentiles and the Gentile Mission in Luke-Acts* (Cambridge: Cambridge University Press, 1973).

Wright, Christopher J. H.   *God's People in God's Land: Family, Land, and Property in the Old Testament* (Grand Rapids: Eerdmans, 1990).

Wright, N. T.   'Jerusalem in the New Testament', in P. W. L. Walker (ed.), *Jerusalem Past and Present in the Purposes of God* (Cambridge: Tyndale House, 1992), 53–77.

Wright, N. T.   *The New Testament and the People of God* (Minneapolis: Fortress Press, 1992).

Nickolas A. Fox
Crown College, St. Bonifacius, MN
nfox22@gmail.com

THESIS REPORT

Who Are the Righteous?
The Narrative Function of the Δίκαιοι in the Gospel of Luke

DENISE POWELL[1]

Who is righteous and how one becomes righteous are questions of considerable interest in Pauline scholarship. Little attention, however, has been paid to the same questions in Lukan studies. The parable of the Pharisee and the tax collector has sometimes been held up as an example of forensic justification in the Gospel of Luke, but this overlaying of a particular understanding of Pauline theology seems to jar against the broader story of Luke's narrative. Curiously, there are several places in the Gospel of Luke where Pharisees, tax collectors (or 'sinners') and 'righteous' (δίκαι*) terminology is found in close proximity (5:29–32; 7:29–30 (see also 34–35); 15:1–7; 18:9–14). In addition, as discussed below, several characters in Luke's Gospel are labelled or portrayed as 'righteous'. Even more intriguing is the climactic declaration of the Lukan centurion concerning the 'criminal' Jesus at the crucifixion scene: 'Truly this man was righteous' (23:47). The declaration appears to contain a Lukan redaction since the Markan and Matthean centurions declare Jesus to be the 'son of God'. It seems that, like Paul, Luke is also interested in the question of who is righteous and how one becomes righteous. Thus, my thesis sets out to examine the righteous characters in Luke's Gospel and determine what function they play in shaping the audience's understanding of what it means to be righteous.

To establish the validity of the study, an early chapter sets out the linguistic evidence to show that the δίκαι* word group functions as a *Leitwort* in the Lukan narrative. Not only are δίκαι* words used more frequently than in the other Synoptics, but they are used at important structural points. Δίκαι* language is used in a commissioning statement (5:32), in a prominent narrative aside (7:29) and at the climax of the narrative in the centurion's declaration (23:47). Furthermore, breaking the usual 'show, don't tell' rules of ancient narrative, several characters are introduced using explicit δίκαι* language: Zechariah and Elizabeth (1:6), Simeon (2:25), the lawyer who wanted to 'justify himself' (10:29), the unrighteous manager (16:8), the Pharisees who 'justify themselves'(15:16), the unrighteous judge (18:6), the audience of the 18:10–14 parable who were 'confident that they were righteous', the spies who 'pretended they were righteous' (20:20), and Joseph of Arimathea (23:50). All these occurrences are unique to Luke's narrative.[2]

---

[1] Supervisor: Dr Rick Strelan, University of Queensland. PhD awarded: 2018.

[2] In the case of Luke 5:32, the δίκαι* language is the same as in Mark's and Matthew's narratives but Luke appears to have significantly redacted the statement by adding 'to repentance'.

Having shown via the linguistic evidence that δίκαι* language and characters are significant in Luke's narrative, the rest of the thesis is devoted to tracing the δίκαι* theme through the Gospel of Luke, focusing particularly on characters who were either labelled or portrayed as δίκαι*. I moved through the narrative sequentially, taking into account the primacy effect, and audience anticipation and retrospection. This allowed me to ascertain the cumulative impact of the δίκαι* theme on the audience. I also utilised Yamasaki's work in point-of-view crafting to understand how a narrator can nudge the audience into seeing things from the perspective of particular characters. Attention to the narrator's subtle use of intertextuality with the LXX also yielded fruitful results.

I concluded that the characters in the birth narrative who are labelled or portrayed as δίκαι* establish the characteristics of the δίκαι*. They follow Torah diligently and are waiting with faithful anticipation for God to deliver his people. All the δίκαι* characters recognise Jesus as God's agent of deliverance. As reliable characters, their interpretation of events can be trusted by the narrative's audience who are influenced to take on the same interpretation. In addition, the primacy effect ensures that these characters become the standard against which the δίκαι* nature of subsequent characters are measured. When Peter, a self-confessed 'sinner' (5:8), falls down before Jesus, in a scene reminiscent of Isaiah's encounter with the divine, he becomes the first sinner to join the δίκαι* birth narrative characters in recognising Jesus as an agent of the divine. In contrast, the first words the audience hears from the lips of the Pharisees are 'who is this ...?' (5:21).

Uncertainty surrounding the question of who is righteous builds as several subsequent stories contrast an ostensibly righteous character with a sinner. In the story of Levi's banquet, the Pharisees identify Levi the tax collector as a 'sinner', a category from which they assume they are excluded. Jesus adopts their terminology to juxtapose the categories of 'righteous' and 'sinner' (5:32), categories that are familiar from the Psalms. It is Levi, however, who responds in the same way as Peter, 'leaving all' to follow Jesus, while the Pharisees 'murmur'—language which evokes the wilderness generation who murmured against God's agent, Moses. The story of the sinful woman and Simon the Pharisee, the obtrusive narrative aside in 7:29–30, and the parable trilogy of the 'lost' create more uncertainty as to which character belongs in which category. Finally, in the parable of the Pharisee and the tax collector, it is the 'sinner' who goes home righteous, while Luke's audience is led to conclude that the Pharisee does not.

The blurring of categories created by these stories serves as the backdrop for the interplay of categories regarding Jesus. Is he a sinner, as the crucifixion would suggest? Or is he 'righteous'? Luke's narrative implies that he is both. Jesus intentionally places himself in the category of 'sinner', but in doing so, paradoxically shows that he is the righteous servant of God. Throughout the narrative Jesus shows his solidarity with sinners, welcoming them, eating with them, and being labelled 'friend of sinners'(7:34). Jesus' identification as a 'sinner' gains momentum in the sword discourse of 22:35–38 and its aftermath in the arrest scene on Mount of Olives. In the upper room, Jesus instructs his disciples to arm themselves with swords. This instruction inevitably leads to an 'insurrection' at Mount of Olives when Jesus fails to stop his disciple using his sword to attack. It is, however, a parody of an insurrection in which two swords are considered 'enough' (22:38), and the only casualty is the ear of a servant, which is subsequently healed. The 'insurrection' is enough to allow Jesus to be 'counted among the lawless' in fulfillment of the divine plan (22:37), yet remain innocent of any wrongdoing, as announced numerous times by Pilate. Nonetheless, Jesus is led out to be crucified with two 'other' evil-doers (καὶ ἕτεροι κακοῦργοι δύο σὺν αὐτῷ, 23:32), a Lukan redaction that adds to the inference that Jesus is being identified as a sinner by the narrator. The crucifixion serves as Jesus' ultimate solidarity with sinners and it is at this climactic point that the centurion declares Jesus to be truly righteous. Since Jesus has placed himself in solidarity with sinners, and they with him, the centurion's declaration that Jesus is righteous has implications for all the sinners in the Lukan story. This is illustrated by the conversation between Jesus and the second criminal in which Jesus promises the criminal that he will find himself 'in paradise' (the abode of the righteous) with Jesus. The second criminal is presented as representative of all sinners who, by placing themselves in solidarity with Jesus, find themselves in the category of the righteous alongside him. Sinners have become righteous.

The thesis will be published as: *Who Are the Righteous?: The Narrative Function of the Δίκαιοι in the Gospel of Luke* (Maryland: Lexington Books/Fortress Academic, 2021).

Denise Powell
Australian College of Ministries
deniseapowell@gmail.com

THESIS REPORT

The Three Accounts of Paul's Conversion in Acts 9, 22 and 26
A Study of Consistency and Creativity in Narrative Retelling

ANDREW STEWART

The Damascus Road experience of Paul of Tarsus is probably the most famous example of religious conversion in history, and Luke's three accounts of the event in Acts have shaped its popular understanding. However, the differences between the three accounts have puzzled many readers, and led scholars either to seek ways of harmonising the accounts, or to question their reliability. The argument of this thesis is that these alternatives present a false dichotomy, and that the three accounts are consistent in their presentation of Paul's conversion and calling on road outside Damascus. Moreover, the divergences facilitate a deeper understanding of this immensely significant event.

The opening chapter addresses preliminary questions such as the significance of Luke's threefold account of Paul's conversion in the overall presentation of the event; the patterns of repetition in biblical narrative; and the elements in a narrative which make it either consistent or inconsistent. Five categories, ranging from exact repetition, through repetition with expansion, repetition with contraction, and the introduction of new elements, to tension arising from seeming contradiction, were defined as ways of describing consistency or inconsistency.

The tensions between the three accounts of Paul's call and conversion in Acts 9, 22 and 26 are briefly surveyed in chapter 2. Two approaches are taken to analyse the ways in which the variations between the three passages have been understood. First of all, the history of textual transmission is analysed to show when differences between the three accounts were thought to require harmonisation, and when they did not. It was noted that apparent discrepancies which have most troubled modern critics did not trouble ancient copyists. Then secondly, the critical study of the passages by six scholars of the nineteenth and twentieth centuries (Edward Zeller; Richard J. Knowling; Kirsopp Lake and Henry J. Cadbury; Ernst Haenchen; and Robert C. Tannehill) was surveyed. Their work helped to identify the tensions between the three passages and various ways of understanding them.

Before proceeding to a detailed exegesis of the three passages in Acts, chapter 3 surveyed the literary phenomenon of repetition and retelling in ancient literature, including ancient

Greek Epic, the Hellenistic Greek novel and Old Testament narrative. A fourfold taxonomy of redundancy, repetition, recalling, and retelling was defined. The final category of retelling was defined as multiple retelling, at length, of the same event. The only parallels for such multiple retelling were found in the Old Testament book of Chronicles. This led to a discussion of additional evidence that the author of Luke-Acts was influenced by the historiographical method of the Chronicler.

The main section of the thesis was an exegetical study of the three passages narrating Paul's conversion, apostolic calling, and the beginnings of his apostolic ministry: Acts 9:1–30; 22:1–21; and 26:1–23.

The specific challenges presented by the apparent tension between Acts 9:7 (where Luke tells us that, 'The men who were travelling with him [Paul] stood speechless, *hearing the voice*, but seeing no one') and Acts 22:9 (where Paul tells the crowd in Jerusalem that, 'those who were with me saw the light but did *not hear the voice* of the one who was speaking to me') have long presented a challenge to exegetes and grammarians. Since the 1959 study by Horst H. Moehring has been widely accepted as establishing that ἀκούω takes accusative and genitive direct objects interchangeably, so the rule of classical Greek grammar offers no way of resolving the tension between these statements. This question is addressed in a fresh study which surveys the syntax of ἀκούω in the LXX, the New Testament and other Koine literature. On the basis of the data surveyed, the thesis argues that accusative direct objects of ἀκούω refer to the *information* conveyed to the hearer, while genitive direct objects refer to the *quality* of what the hearer hears, including the manner in which it is heard. Thus Acts 9:7 describes the *heavenly quality* of the voice heard, while Acts 22:9 describes the non-hearing of *words spoken* by the risen Jesus.

In chapter 7 the exegetical data gathered in chapter 5, and supported by the argument of chapter 6, is synthesised using the five categories set out in chapter 1: exact repetition, expansion, contraction, new information, and seeming contradiction. Significant consistency was observed in Luke's accounts of Paul's pre-conversion life, the light from heaven, the initial words spoken to him by Jesus, and Paul's response. The disappearance of Ananias from the narrative and the telescoping of the narrative in Acts 26, so that Paul's apostolic commission appears to be given by Jesus on the road outside Damascus, are to be understood, not as contradictions, but the culmination of a narrative trajectory, implicit in the previous accounts, which present the risen Jesus as the source of Paul's apostolic commission.

Likewise, the tensions between Acts 9:7 and 22:9 are part of a larger narrative strategy which presents Paul's companions as representatives of the blind and deaf Israel, but which presents Paul as the servant of Isaiah 49:6, who participates in the ministry of the ultimate Servant of the Lord, the risen Jesus. Thus, in faithfulness to his commission to carry the name of Jesus 'before Gentiles and kings, *and the children of Israel*' (Acts 9:15), Paul preached boldly before the Jewish King, Herod Agrippa II. The tensions in the three accounts enable us to see a higher consistency, for the Lucan Paul is the apostle to the Gentiles who never ceased to seek the salvation of Israel.

This thesis was prepared under the supervision of Rev Dr Stephen Voorwinde, and submitted through the Melbourne School of Theology to the Australian College of Theology. The external examiners were Darrell Bock (Dallas Theological Seminary), Guy Waters (Reformed Theological Seminary, Jackson), and Alan Thompson (Sydney Missionary and Bible College). The award of Doctor of Theology was made in August 2020.

Andrew Stewart
Reformed Theological College
Melbourne, Victoria
astewart@rtc.edu.au

Book reviews

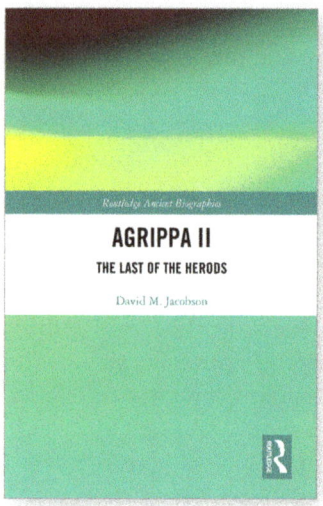

David M. Jacobson. *Agrippa II The Last of the Herods.* Routledge Ancient Biographies. London and New York: Routledge, 2019. xxxi + 231pp. ISBN 9780429447068 (e-book); ISBN 9781138331815 (hardback).

From the opening chapter of Luke's Gospel to Paul's climactic defence speech in Acts 26 the Herods play a significant role in the background of the Lucan narrative. Major figures alluded to include Herod the Great (Luke 1:5); his son and heir, Archelaus (alluded to in the parable of the wicked tenants in Luke 20:9–18); Herod Antipas (before whom Jesus appears in Luke 23:6–12); Herod Agrippa I (who had James executed and Peter arrested in Acts 12:1–5, and who came to a messy end in Acts 12:20–23); and Herod Agrippa II (who visited Governor Festus in Acts 25:13–22 and heard Paul defend his apostolic ministry in Acts 25:23–26:32). Ironically, while Agrippa II is allotted most space in the Lucan narrative, he is the least studied of the main Herodian rulers.

For this reason the publication of David M. Jacobson's biography, *Agrippa II The Last of the Herods*, is a welcome addition to the literature on the dynasty which had such a powerful influence on the culture and politics of Judea in the time of Jesus and early Christianity. While significant biographies have been written on Herod the Great, Herod Antipas and Herod Agrippa I, this is, according to the title page 'the first comprehensive biography of the last descendant of Herod the Great to rule as a client king of Rome.' Jacobson fleshes out his aims in an opening chapter which describes Agrippa II as something of a mystery. Could he have averted the ruinous events of 66–70? Why did he never marry or produce an heir? Apart from his encounter with Paul, documented in Acts 25–26, what else did he observe of early Christianity? How deeply attached was he to the Jewish faith? What did he do in the last decades of his life? When did he die? Why was he the last of the client kings who ruled as agents of Rome? Jacobson sets out to find what answers, if any, can be given to these questions by means of a detailed reconstruction of the social and political context in which Agrippa II lived.

One of the challenges facing Jacobson, and others who seek answers to these questions, is the abundance of information which comes from a single source—the writings of Josephus—and the paucity of evidence from other sources with which to compare Josephus. For that reason, chapter 2 discusses the reliability of Josephus as a historical source for the life of Agrippa II. The chapter contains a helpful discussion of Josephus' aims and biases as a writer, as well as his use of speeches in the Thucydidean tradition. Although there are divergences and even contradictions between Josephus' account of the *Jewish War* and later statements in the *Antiquities*, we are indebted to Josephus for 'a blow-by-blow account of the (Jewish) War which is of inestimable value, and not least because it was written by an important eyewitness' (p.14). Having said that, more could have been said at this stage about the information available from the book of Acts and Rabbinic sources, as these raise their own, very peculiar, methodological questions.

The main body of the biography is contained in chapters 3–7 which narrate Agrippa II's early years (chapter 3); Agrippa II in his Patrimony (chapter 4); Agrippa's address to the population of Jerusalem (chapter 5); Agrippa II in the opening phase of the Judean-Roman War (chapter 6); and the campaigns of Vespasian and Titus (chapter 7). Jacobson's narrative in these chapters is somewhat overwhelmed by the abundance of material available from Josephus. At times they read like a history rather than a biography. The focus on the political history of first-century Palestine, its client kings, high priests and Roman governors, allows Agrippa II to make only occasional appearances.

Students of the book of Acts might seek some illumination of the meeting between Agrippa II and Governor Festus in Acts 25 and the encounter between Agrippa II and the apostle Paul in Acts 26. However, this section of the biography is disappointing. Jacobson departs from the common dating of the Roman governors with whom Paul interacted (thus dating Antonius Felix 52/3–58, rather than 52/53–59/60; Porcius Festus 58–60, rather than 59/60–62; and Luccius Albinus 60–64, rather than 62–64). This makes it difficult to account for the lynching of James the Just in 62, at the instigation of Ananus son of Ananus the High Priest, following the sudden death of Festus and before the arrival of Albinus. It also leaves unaddressed the question of whether Agrippa II's encounter with Paul in 60 had any influence on his dismissal of Ananus from the High Priesthood. Had Agrippa's encounter with Paul led him to conclude that the Jerusalem Christians were not as dangerous as some imagined? Jacobson does not interact with this question.

More significantly, Jacobson's survey of Agrippa II's exchange with Paul in Acts 26 does not interact with the substantial body of New Testament scholarship on the passage, and in one place is inaccurate. He takes the phrase 'I know you do' in Acts 26:27 as an ironic riposte from Agrippa rather than an apologetic plea from Paul (p.43). There is, however, some discussion as to whether Agrippa's response in 26:28 was ironic or sincere. Although the question is not raised at this point, Jacobson later suggests that Paul's *captatio benevolentiae* in 26:2–3 might also be read as sarcasm (see p.140).

In the account of the Judean-Roman war and the campaigns of Vespasian and Titus in chapters 6 and 7 Jacobson rightly notes that Josephus has little to say about Agrippa II. The biography thus becomes a narrative of what Agrippa II failed to do. He failed to intercede with the Emperor on behalf of the people of Jerusalem. He failed to rein in the extremists on the Jewish side. He failed to intercede to protect the Temple from destruction and he failed to prevent the slaughter of Jewish captives after the fall of Jerusalem. The overall picture painted by Jacobson is one of impotence on the part of Agrippa II.

> **The overall picture is one of impotence on the part of Agrippa II.**

Jacobson's account of the last decades of Agrippa II's life in chapter 8 breaks free of the framework established by Josephus and draws on a range of epigraphical and numismatic evidence. Much valuable information is collated in two appendices. The first is a collection of inscriptions referring to Agrippa II and the second catalogues the coins known to have been issued by Agrippa II. This involves a discussion of the rather technical question of Agrippa II's regnal eras and how they enable coins to be dated. From this evidence Jacobson discusses the vexed question of the date of Agrippa II's death and comes down tentatively on the side of an early dating in 94/5.

In his concluding chapter, Jacobson draws together the data he has collated and describes

Agrippa the man. In spite of the generally favourable presentation of Agrippa by his contemporaries—Josephus and the author of Acts—Jacobson presents him as a pale shadow of his father, Herod Agrippa I. He was a man of 'middling intellect' (p.143) who lacked the ability to act decisively. In the aftermath of the destruction of Jerusalem he effectively washed his hands of his responsibilities to the Jewish people and failed to stand up for their interests when they needed him. Thus, he 'has been relegated to the margins of history' (p.144). In coming to this conclusion Jacobson is, perhaps, too reliant on the silences of the literary record. There are a number of plausible suggestions which might explain why Josephus has so little to say about Agrippa II in his latter years, and Jacobson considers them. However, it might also be helpful to factor in the maxim that absence of evidence is not evidence of absence.

Andrew Stewart
Reformed Theological College, Melbourne.

Constance M. Furey, Brian Matz, Steven L. McKenzie, Thomas Römer, Jens Schröter, Barry Dov Walfish and Eric Ziolkowski (eds.). *Encyclopedia of the Bible and Its Reception 18: Mass – Midnight.*
Berlin, Boston: De Gruyter, 2020. xxviii + 1228 cols. Hardbound. ISBN 978-3-11-031335-2. €259.00.

The comprehensive *Encyclopedia of the Bible and Its Reception* (2009ff) endeavours to treat not only the Bible comprehensively, but also its variegated reception in Judaism, Christianity, Islam, literature, visual arts, music and film. 'With this broad program of reception history, *EBR* moves into new terrain in recognition of the fact that biblical texts not only have their own particular backgrounds and settings but have also been received and interpreted, and have exerted influence or otherwise have had impact in countless religious, theological, and aesthetic settings' (Introduction, vol. 1, 2009).

Volume 18, which covers entries from 'Mass' to 'Midnight', contains several entries of interest to New Testament studies, specifically the entries on Matthew's Gospel; the disciple, Matthew; and the many entries related to Messiah. They offer up-to-date surveys by recognised international specialists in the field.

The extensive article on Matthew's Gospel gives a good indication of the nature and approach of this *Encyclopedia*. It begins with Lidija Novakovic's six columns on 'Matthew, Gospel of I. New Testament' (123–29) in which she treats issues of authorship; date and provenance; sources and genre; structure and theology, that is, Christology, fulfilment of Scripture, ecclesiology, ethics and eschatology; and, in closing, the socio-religious setting of the reconstructed Matthean community (its relationship with Judaism, with the Gentiles and other Christian groups). There is no reference to the debate about Gospel audiences in which the notion that the Gospels were addressed to specific communities and reflect their concerns was severely challenged—see R. I. Bauckham, ed., *The Gospels for all Christians: Rethinking the Gospel Audiences* (Edinburgh: T. &. T. Clark, 1998).

The following entry 'Matthew, Gospel of II. Christianity' consists of several sub-entries which trace aspects of the reception history: Brian Matz, 'A. Greek and Latin Patristics and Orthodox Churches' (129–31); Edwin Woodruff Ta't, 'B. Medieval and Reformation Times' (131–34); Ian Boxall, 'C. Modern Europe and America' (134–37) and Clyde R. Forsberg, 'D. New Christian Churches and Movements' (138). Like with other entries in previous volumes, the reception of biblical books or persons in Africa, Asia or Latin America is either not easily accessible (who, for example, would dare to write something representative on Matthew's Gospel in *Africa*? Yet some material is available; for example, the variegated notions of *Jesus in Africa*, based on Matt 2:13–15); or it is not worth mentioning (the situation is different for the following entries related to Messiah). This observation underlines that scholars from these continents will have to tackle this task themselves. See my reflections in the review article 'Recent Contributions to the Study of the Reception of the Bible and Their Implications for Biblical Studies in Africa', *Religion and Theology* 22 (2015), 329–83.

Ian Boxall sketches the receptions of Matthew's Gospel in literature and visual arts ('Matthew, Gospel of III. Literature', 138–40 and 'Matthew, Gospel of IV. Visual Arts', 140–44). Completely out of proportion in comparison to the other sub-entries under 'Matthew, Gospel' or other entries in the volume is Sven Rune Havsteen's erudite survey 'Matthew, Gospel of V. Music' (144–61) with its 18 columns. I would rather have had a detailed survey of current Matthean scholarship. Reinhold Zwick contributes 'Matthew, Gospel of VI. Film' (161–64), in which short reference is made to Mark Dornford-May's South African production *Son of Man* (2006), mainly Pasolini's *Il Vangelo Secondo Matteo* of 1964 and *Godspell* of 1973.

There are several related entries: Peter Gemeinhardt, 'Matthew, Gospel of Pseudo-' (164–65); Christoph Ochs, 'Matthew, Hebrew Versions of' (165–67); Peter Gemeinhardt, 'Matthew, Martyrdom of' (167–68) and the following entries for Matthew, the disciple of Jesus: Frank Dicken, 'Matthew (Disciple) I. New Testament' (168–69); Roland Deines, 'Matthew (Disciple) II. Christianity' (169–75; Matthew the evangelist, the Apostle, the missionary and the cult of the martyr; survey up to the Reformation Era); Christina Hoegen-Rohls, 'Matthew (Disciple) III. Literature' (175–77); Ian Boxall, 'Matthew (Disciple) IV. Visual Arts' (177–80) and Rhonda Burnette-Bletch, 'Matthew (Disciple) V. Film' (180–82).

The entry *Messiah* follows the same pattern: Mahri Leonard-Fleckmann, 'Messiah I. Hebrew Bible/Old Testament' (850–52) and Jens Schröter, 'Messiah II. New Testament' (the term 'Jesus Christ', usage in the Gospels). Schröter notes that 'The meaning of the designation "Messiah" or "Christ" changed significantly with its application to Jesus. "Christ" is not the anointed king, priest or prophet anymore, but Jesus, the Son of God, who was empowered by God's Spirit, acted with God's authority on earth as "Son of Man", was crucified resurrected, and exalted to heaven and will return at the last judgement' (856; the bibliography could have included M. V. Novenson's *Christ Among the Messiahs: Christ Language in Paul and Messiah Language in Ancient Judaism* (Oxford: OUP, 2015)).

The entry 'Messiah III. Judaism' is subdivided into the following entries: Matthew Neujahr, 'A. Second Temple and Hellenistic Judaism' (856–60; Messiahs in the Apocrypha and Pseudepigrapha, Messiahs in the Dead Sea Scrolls, Messianism in action in the Hellenistic Period); Günter Stemberger, 'B. Rabbinic Judaism' (860–863); Dov Schwartz, 'C. Medieval Judaism' (863–66, Messianic types, the Messianic personality, the Messiah and the Messianic era) and Gadi Sagiv, 'D. Modern Judaism' (866–69).

'Messiah IV. Christianity' is also subdivided: Martin Meiser, 'A. Patristics, Orthodox Churches, and Early Medieval Christianity' (869–71); Christoph Schönau, 'B. Medieval Christianity and Reformation Era' (871–73); René Dauser, 'C. Modern Europe and America' (873–76) and George D. Chryssides, 'D. New Christian Churches and Movements' (876–78; with the sobering conclusion that 'The many other messianic claimants throughout the centuries up to the present day have enabled mainstream Christians to find vindication of Jesus' prediction that many false teachers and messiahs would arise (Mark 13:22)', 878). For this lemma, there is a substantial survey of the understanding of Messiah or the Messiah in 'E. World Christianity' (Caleb O. Oladipo, 878–82): half a column on Africa; a few lines on Southeast Asia; the remainder of the entry offers generalisations about views in the 'Global South' or the 'Majority World', the bibliography does not contain a single book on the Messiah in non-Western traditions.

The other entries are: Todd Lawson, 'Messiah V. Islam' (882–83); Herman Tull, 'Messiah VI. Other Religions' (883–86);

Anthony Swindell, 'Messiah VII. Literature' (886–88); Richard R. Viladesau, 'Messiah VIII. Visual Arts' (888–97, 11 cols!); 'Messiah IX. Music' (subdivided into 'A. Jewish Music', 897–89 by Marsha Bryan Edelman and 'B. Christian Music', 899–901, by Sven Rune Havsteen) and 'Messiah X. Film' (901–904) by Marek Lis.

Related entries are Nils Holder Petersen, '*Messiah* (Oratorio)' (904–908) and 'Messianic Age I. Judaism', subdivided into the following entries: Matthew Neujahr, 'A. Second Temple and Hellenistic Judaism' (908–909); Dov Schwartz, 'B. Medieval Judaism' (909–13); Günter Stemberger, 'C. Rabbinic Judaism' (913–14) and Gadi Sagiv, 'D. Modern Judaism' (914–18); Michael Magree, 'Messianic Age II. Christianity A. Patristics and Orthodox Christianity' (918–19); Christoph Schönau, 'Messianic Age II. Christianity B. Medieval Times and Reformation Era' (920–21); René Dausner, 'Messianic Age II. Christianity C. Modern Europe and America' (921–23), George D. Chryssides, 'Messianic Age II. Christianity D. New Christian Churches and Movements' (923–25); Alex Mayfield, 'Messianic Age II. Christianity E. World Christianity' (925–26); Anthony Swindell, 'Messianic Age III. Literature' (926–28); Richard R. Viladesau, 'Messianic Age IV. Visual Arts' (928–29).

Similarly, detailed treatment is offered in the entries 'Messianic Banquet' (929–41), 'Messianic Judaism' (942–43); 'Messianic Secret' (943–45) and 'Messianism' (945–66). There are numerous other entries that will be of interest to students of the New Testament, including treatments of such varying topics as 'Massacre of the Innocents: New Testament' (Clement Greene, 21–22), 'Media Criticism' (Nicholas Elder, 289–91), and 'Mental Disorder II. New Testament' (Lena Nogossek, 679–81).

These entries demonstrate the approach, the opportunities and the limits of this inspiring *Encyclopedia*. *The Encyclopedia of the Bible and Its Reception* is projected to consist of 32 volumes.

Christoph Stenschke
Biblisch-Theologische Akademie Wiedenest
and Department of Biblical and Ancient Studies
University of South Africa

BOOK REVIEWS

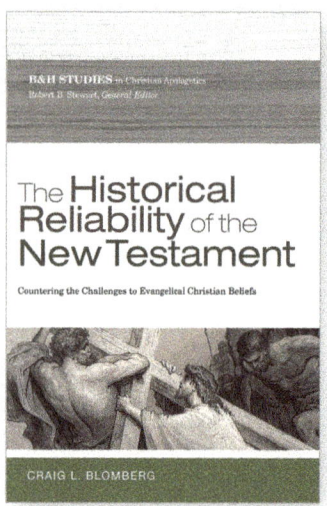

Craig L. Blomberg. *The Historical Reliability of the New Testament: Countering the Challenges to Evangelical Christian Beliefs.* Nashville: B&H Academic, 2016. Xxxi + 783 pp., paperback, ISBN 978-0-8054-6437-5. $40.00

For a number of reasons, one of the main concerns of evangelical biblical studies has been and continues to be the historical reliability of the New Testament. While evangelical readers of the Bible obviously are also concerned with the theological message of the Bible and appreciate the intricate relationships between history and theology, they rightly argue that the theological message and emphasis of the New Testament (God's revelation and intervention in human history in Jesus Christ and in the ensuing events) is closely linked to the historicity of the events.

> **The theological message is linked to the historicity of the events.**

Against this backdrop, the current volume, published in the *B&H Studies in Christian Apologetics* series, examines the historical reliability of the New Testament. In the introduction (xxi–xxxi), Blomberg provides a survey of research and explains how this volume differs from his previous contributions to this topic (*The Historical Reliability of the Gospels*; *Jesus and the Gospels: An Introduction and Survey*; *The Historical Reliability of John's Gospel: Issues and Commentary*; *Can We Still Believe the Bible? An Evangelical Engagement with Contemporary Questions*). He explains how he started out as a sceptic regarding the trustworthiness of the New Testament and, through some evangelical studies and his own study of the issues, came to espouse the position he has now defended over many years.

Part one is devoted to the Synoptic Gospels. It begins in *chapter one*, with an examination of the formation of the Synoptic Gospels (3–50; the setting of the Synoptics – authorship and audiences, dating; the Gospel genre – popular proposals, Greco-Roman biographies up close; the composition of the Gospels – source criticism, form criticism and oral tradition). Regarding the Gospels' genre, Blomberg notes: 'After careful inspection of all the proposed options, it turns out that Jewish and Greco-Roman biographies are indeed the closest parallels. Of course, we have to judge the Gospel writers by the standards of precision and excellence of their day and not anachronistically impose our modern ones upon them. Granted this caveat, they stand up to scrutiny remarkably well' (719).

Chapter two examines contradictions among the Synoptic Gospels (51–98). First, Blomberg describes issues arising from redaction-critical approaches and then he examines the infancy narratives, the initial ministry of Jesus, the peak of Jesus' popularity in Galilee, his later ministry and, in closing, his passion, death and resurrection. On this question, see also the detailed treatment by Michael R. Licona in *Why are there differences in the Gospels? What we can learn from ancient biography* (Oxford: Oxford University Press, 2017).

Chapter three gathers archaeological evidence, which corroborates the presentation of Jesus in the Synoptic Gospels (99–148) in the birth narratives, the presentation of John the

Baptist, Jesus' earliest ministry, great sermon, ministry in Galilee, withdrawal from Galilee, the Judean ministry of Jesus and the passion narrative.

Part two addresses the Gospel of John. *Chapter four* is devoted to the formation of the Gospel of John (151–188; authorship, date, context and sources, omissions and outline, genre and parallels, theological differences in christology, eschatology, faith and various dualisms). *Chapter five* brings together the evidence for the accuracy of John's Gospel (189–229; John the Baptist and Jesus, the different visits of Jesus to Jewish festivals, the bridge to the passion narrative – the resurrection of Lazarus, the anointing at Bethany, Palm Sunday – and the accuracy of the Johannine account of the death and resurrection of Jesus). Blomberg argues that a 'sequential walk through the Fourth Gospel again discloses, virtually in every chapter and major pericope, the kind of information that may be viewed as most probably historically accurate by a variety of standard criteria of authenticity' (720).

Part three covers issues of historical reliability in the Book of Acts and Paul. In chapter six, Blomberg first examines the historical credibility of Acts (233–295; setting and background, discussion of the disputed specific details in Acts; see the more detailed treatment along the same lines in the exhaustive four volume commentary by C. S. Keener). Blomberg concludes that Acts

> provides us with considerably more details that cohere with what we know from ancient history outside the New Testament. We are not aware of any form of fiction from antiquity that researched the setting, customs, places, and lay of the land with so much care and without any necessary errors, as if they were intending to compose fictitious narratives. Indeed, works of fiction usually tipped their hand by blatantly inaccurate information that most everyone would recognize. So much of what can be corroborated in Acts is fairly incidental to Luke's main points as well, so that it is difficult to charge Luke with inventing this material due to theological motivation. Whereas the Gospels were, first of all, biographies and, secondarily, historiography, with Acts the ranking is reversed, although, with the genre of "collected biography", we come close to what we find in Acts (720–721).

Chapter seven compares the presentation of Paul in Acts with the portrayal emerging from the letters of Paul, following the biography of Paul in Acts.

The remaining chapters of part three are outside the focus of the *Journal of Gospels and Acts Research* ("Forgeries Among the Epistles of Paul?", 347–411; "Is Paul the true founder of Christianity", 413–460). Other parts of the volume discuss the following topics: "The non-Pauline epistles – New Testament anomalies" (463–509); "The Book of Revelation – are historical matters even relevant?" (511–555); "The Nag Hammadi literature and New Testament apocrypha" (559–608) and "Textual transmission and the formation of the canon" (609–659).

A masterful, non-technical survey of the issues.

A final chapter of this comprehensive volume is devoted to the miracles in the New Testament world and today (663–715; the miracles are based in God's existence, a brief survey of the scientific and philosophical problems involved, modern miracles, on whether the accounts of miracles are myths or legends, criteria of authenticity, a discussion of the nature miracles and of the resurrection of Jesus). Blomberg concludes: 'Neither the miracle stories, in general, nor the resurrection accounts, in particular, have to invalidate all of the lines of argument that our other chapters have been pulling together' (715).

Blomberg's conclusion (717–725) briefly summarises the issues involved in the historical reliability of the New Testament and their implications for understanding the New Testament and the nature of Christian faith.

This volume provides a masterful, non-technical survey of the issues involved regarding the historical reliability of the New Testament by one of the doyens of North American evangelical New Testament scholarship. Blomberg's comprehensive and persuasive treatment of the contested domains affirms the historical reliability of the New Testament and provides a well-argued, persuasive defence of it. Evangelical readers will understand the complexity of the issues, and questions involved, and will enjoy Blomberg's erudite and clear answers. Other readers will find arguments that they will need to address and which they will have to deal with, if they wish to propagate a different assessment of the New Testament and its historical reliability. A persistent neglect of the case presented here will not do.

Christoph Stenschke
Biblisch-Theologische Akademie Wiedenest
and Department of Biblical and Ancient Studies
University of South Africa

Bruce Harold Henning. *Matthew's Non-Messianic Mapping of Messianic Texts: Evidences of a Broadly Eschatological Hermeneutic.*
Leiden and Boston: Brill, 2021. 276pp.
ISBN: 978-90-04-44416-4. €99.00/$119.00

Bruce Henning's study discusses the fulfillment of the Old Testament in the Gospel of Matthew and argues that the category of messianic fulfillment does not sufficiently describe Matthew's hermeneutic. In a book that seeks to contribute to our understanding of the use of the Old Testament in Matthew, Henning affirms Matthew's tendency to emphasise messianic fulfillment in Jesus. However, he makes the case that the phrase 'broadly eschatological' is more helpful for understanding all the ways Matthew alludes to the Old Testament (p.1). Henning validates this idea through his examination of four Old Testament metaphors found in Matthew's narrative—metaphors that could easily relate to Jesus as the Messiah but instead are used by Jesus to describe non-messianic individuals. Although Matthew could have exclusively fortified his Christology with metaphors such as the shepherding of a flock (Ezek. 34:23–24), the tending of Isaiah's vineyard (Isa. 5:1–7), the building of the temple (Ps. 118:22), or the heralding of the kingdom (Isa. 61:1–3), Matthew instead uses eschatological elements from these source texts to characterise the disciples.

Henning organises his four main chapters around the metaphors mentioned above. Each chapter includes a brief exegetical examination of the Old Testament source text(s), a discussion of Second Temple interpretations of the source text, and Matthew's non-messianic mapping of the source text(s) onto the disciples. Henning identifies his method as 'traditional', with a few elements of narrative and redaction criticism (p.16). In general, he utilises Christopher Hays' criteria for Old Testament allusions, but he also integrates into his exegesis cognitive linguistics or, more specifically, Cognitive Metaphor Theory. Henning frequently makes reference to 'Blending Theory' in order to show how Matthew reinterprets Old Testament messianic metaphors in fresh new ways (p.33).

In chapter 2, Henning discusses the first set of messianic texts that the Matthean Jesus applies to the disciples. Here the focus is upon the shepherding imagery from Ezekiel 34, Jeremiah 23, and Zechariah 10, especially in relation to the sending of the disciples to 'the lost sheep of Israel' (Matt. 9:36—10:6). Henning argues that the Matthean Jesus reworks a messianic shepherding metaphor so that it lands squarely upon non-messianic agents in the eschaton. Here it is the disciples that are given the task of tending the eschatological flock.

Chapter 3 explores the Matthean Jesus' use of the vineyard imagery from Isaiah 5:1–7 in the parable of the wicked tenants (Matt. 21:33–46). Specific attention is given to the role and identity of the replacement farmers at the end of the parable (Matt. 21:41). Henning provides fresh new insight into the parable by arguing that the disciples are these very farmers and that they fulfill various eschatological hopes rooted in

Isaiah's vineyard.

In chapter 4, Henning focuses upon Old Testament temple-construction texts and shows how temple building was often viewed as a messianic task. First, he reviews how the main texts for this imagery (Ps. 118:22; Isa. 28:16) were occasionally reconfigured in Second Temple Literature in order to stoke the flames of messianic expectation. In his next section, Henning again sheds new light on various sections of Matthew by demonstrating how the Matthean Jesus draws upon the same imagery to highlight the participation of the disciples in the construction of an eschatological temple (Matt. 7:24–27; 16:18; 21:41–43).

Chapter 5 explores the way the Matthean Jesus understood and applied heralding imagery from Isaiah 61:1–3 in Matthew 5:3–4 and 11:5. Yet again, Henning examines the possibility of a messianic interpretation for the herald of Isaiah 61:1–3 in texts roughly contemporary to Matthew (e.g., Targum Isaiah 61:1; 4Q521; Luke 4:16–30). In this instance, Henning admits that few, if any, early interpreters viewed the Isaianic herald as a messianic figure. However, the Matthean Jesus nonetheless alludes to this herald in Matthew 5 and 11 in order to emphasise the eschatological function of Spirit-empowered proclamation on the part of the disciples.

Throughout the volume, Henning delineates his research objectives and builds a convincing case for the application of four Old Testament metaphors to the eschatological activity of non-messianic agents. Though it is true that Matthew often centres upon Jesus as the fulfillment of messianic hope, Henning demonstrates that Matthew's Jesus does occasionally take messianic texts and apply them to the tasks of his disciples. Henning uses a variety of methods, but his focus is to offer a traditional reading of the Old Testament in the New alongside a less conventional tool: Cognitive Metaphor Theory. Interpreters interested in this rather unique combination will want to read his monograph, as will exegetes who wish to more precisely define Matthew's hermeneutic, especially as it relates to the characterisation of the disciples.

Chad Reeser
La escuela evangélica de teología
Barcelona, Spain

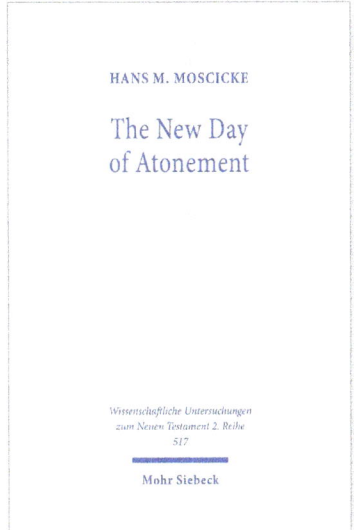

Hans M. Moscicke. *The New Day of Atonement: A Matthean Typology.* WUNT 2.517. Tübingen: Mohr Siebeck, 2020. 293 pp. ISBN 978-3-16-159393-2. €84.00. $118.00

In his volume *The New Day of Atonement: A Matthean Typology*, Hans M. Moscicke argues that Matthew appropriates Leviticus 16 and the Day of Atonement traditions into his passion narrative.

The study begins with an overview of scholarship concerning the passion narrative. Moscicke weaves together a fascinating summary of Matthean scholars who have explained the Passion Narrative with special emphases on Jesus' death, the forgiveness of sins, the new Exodus, the role of scapegoats, Isa. 53, and general views on atonement. Each of these approaches have their merits, but Moscicke argues that each leave at least one major question unanswered in their conclusions. Some of those questions are as follows: What is the role of Barabbas? How does Matt. 27:24–25 fit into the entirety of the narrative? How does Matthew's goat typology fit into the larger innocent-blood discourse? How does 'sin as debt' fit into the proposed schema? To those questions, Moscicke turns in the following chapters.

Chapter 2 analyses Lev. 16 and Yom Kippur traditions in the Second Temple period and early Christianity. Here, the reader will find the early church attestation to Jesus as the scapegoat. This analysis is coupled with explorations of Yom Kippur references in *The Book of Watchers*, 4Q180-181, *The Book of Giants*, *The Apocalypse of Abraham*, the book of Zechariah, *Jubilees*, and *11QMelchizedek*. Moscicke notes that the NT has relatively little to say about Yom Kippur except for a verse or two in the Pauline letters, the book of Hebrews, and a couple of passages in the book of Revelation. As Moscicke observes, the absence of Yom Kippur references in the NT potentially makes Matthew the most sustained treatment of scapegoat Christology.

Chapters 3–5 turn to Matthew's passion narrative. Moscicke splits the narrative into three episodes and devotes a chapter to each: the Barabbas episode (Matt. 27:15–26), the Roman-abuse scene (Matt. 27:27–31), and the death narrative (Matt. 27:50–54). Chapter 3 argues that Matthew crafts a typological correspondence between Jesus and Barabbas and the two goats of Yom Kippur. Chapter 4 argues that the Roman-abuse scene must be understood against the backdrop of the ancient practice of "elimination" or "curse-transmission" rituals. Once the background is established, Moscicke argues that the scarlet garment and crown of thorns become symbolic of the sins and curses put onto a scapegoat. Chapter 5 argues that Jesus' death (Matt. 27:50–54) is primarily about the forgiveness of sins. Moscicke argues that the death represents the role of both goats in the sacrificial system and the result is both the cosmic purge of sin and the possibility of God's new Passover and Exodus for his new covenant community. The volume concludes with a summary of the study and explanation of how a Yom Kippur typology rectifies problems with

> **Jesus' death is primarily about the forgiveness of sins.**

prior interpretations. Moscicke also includes an analysis of Matthew's theology of atonement considering the Yom Kippur typology.

Moscicke's volume comes on the heels of several stellar studies in Matthean scholarship which share similar emphases. Yet, he carves out his own space and does so in a fascinating and thorough fashion. Moscicke's biblical exposition is a nice corollary to the theological interpretations of the early church and their observance of Jesus as the scapegoat. While his conclusions are not necessarily novel, his implementation of method certainly is. He is also careful in how he interacts with his interlocutors. He is equal parts complimentary, and observant of the weakness in his review of scholarship. Although Moscicke necessarily limits his discussion to the passion narrative, it would be fascinating to consider other instances of forgiveness in Matthew. The debt language in the Lord's Prayer may be one case in which atonement is not in view. It is also difficult to see Pilate as a priest, given his historical description as ruthless and the implicit critique in the hand-washing ritual as the one who does not dispense justice. Notwithstanding these small observations, Moscicke has made a compelling case for a potentially explosive meta-narrative in Matthew's Gospel. The Yom Kippur motif provides a helpful framework and unifying thread for Matthew's views of sin, atonement, forgiveness, and Jesus' sacrificial death.

Charles Nathan Ridlehoover
Columbia Biblical Seminary, Columbia, SC

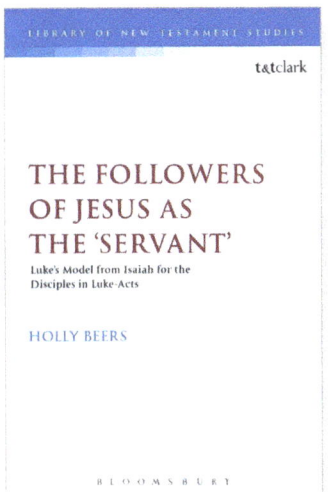

Holly Beers. *The Followers of Jesus as the 'Servant': Luke's Model from Isaiah for the Disciples in Luke-Acts.*
LNTS 535. London and New York: Bloomsbury T&T Clark, 2015. xvi + 213pp. ISBN 978-0-56765-652-0 (hardback). $125.00

Holly Beers' study of *The Followers of Jesus as the 'Servant'* is a significant project which bridges the divide which often separates biblical scholars into Old Testament and New Testament camps. On the one hand she sets out to define the function of the servant (or servants) of Yahweh in Isaiah; on the other she seeks to show how the Isaianic servant has been appropriated in Luke-Acts. This latter discussion has significant implications for discussions about the historical Jesus, as well as New Testament understandings of the atonement, Christology and ecclesiology. These implications are well summarised in the introductory chapter which sets the scene by summarising briefly the contributions of New Testament scholars Hooker, Litwak, Bock, Denova, Pao and Mallen. Her thesis is clearly stated at the outset and claims that 'Luke builds aspects of his portrayal *both of Jesus and the disciples* in Luke-Acts on the *human agent* of the Isaianic New Exodus in Isaiah 40–66, the servant' (p.1).

As this study of the servant motif in Luke-Acts seeks to understand how Luke appropriated the servant in Isaiah the question of intertextuality necessarily arises. Chapter 2 is an illuminating study of the philosophy and method of intertextuality. Beers examines the work of the French literary theorist Julia Kristeva and critiques a number of approaches ranging from those which prioritise the intention of the earlier author to those who radically de-prioritise it. Beers rejects positivist and phenomenalist epistemologies and argues for a critical realist approach which highlights the importance of story as a vehicle for communicating meaning. By combining critical realism with the insights of Speech Act Theory she creates a framework within which a well attuned reader can hear the many echoes of Isaiah in Luke-Acts, as well as making sense of the more commonly recognised citations and allusions. As she states later in the book: 'narrative echoes are powerful and produce resonance' (p.140). There remains, however, the danger that the reader may be so well-tuned to familiar themes that they hear the echoes they expect to hear. This is where the "critical" aspect of critical realism comes into play and the extent to which Beers has been critical of her hearing can only be assessed in the light of her exegetical conclusions.

Chapter 3 is an exegetical study of 'Isaiah and the Servant'. Although Beers acknowledges historical-critical studies of the various 'Isaiahs' she follows a literary approach and focuses on the message of the final form of Isaiah. Her aim is to identify the *function* of the servant in Isaiah 40–66, thus looking beyond the traditionally identified servant passages in Isaiah 40–55. The servant is Israel (though the question of whether this is Israel collectively, as a remnant or a representative is left open) and serves as the human agent of God's New Exodus (NE) whereby Yahweh returns to Israel, restores her fortunes, gathers the nations and establishes justice and *shalom*. This servant is called by Yahweh and Spirit empowered (42:1; 44:3); given the task of being Yahweh's witness (43:10, 12; 44:8); yet at the same time is described as blind and deaf (43:8; 48:8). Thus, no distinction between the faithful servant and unfaithful servant is recognised. Likewise, no distinction is made between 'the servant' in Isaiah 40–55 and 'the servants' in Isaiah 56–66 (p.44–45). 'The servants' take up the work of 'the servant' and continue as the protagonists of the NE. This reading of Isaiah 40–66 is foundational to Beers' understanding of Luke's appropriation of the servant theme.

Before moving forward, a few observations may be made. Beers does not make any allowance for the traditional understanding that at least some of the servant passages in Isaiah were prophetic in their reference to Jesus. This is 'the least plausible' understanding as it reads back from NT to OT (p.34). However, Luke may have regarded this hermeneutic as quite plausible. Moreover, the effect of this reading is to flatten out the references to the servant in Isaiah 40–55, and fails to do justice to the shifts in focus between (and even within) the servant passages. Might not the tension between the Spirit-filled servant of 42:1 and the blind servant of 42:18–19 be suggestive of a servant who will arise to do all that Israel had been called to do, and more? Moreover, it is hard to see how 42:7 justifies the claim that the servant of that passage lived 'a democratised existence' (p.37). It is hardly possible to discuss the *function* of the servant, without considering in a more nuanced way the various *identities* of the servant.

> **'The servants' take up the work of 'the servant'.**

The study of the servant theme moves from OT towards the NT by considering the appropriation of the Isaianic servant in Second Temple Judaism. That is the theme of chapter 4, which surveys the appropriation of the servant theme in the post-exilic prophets (Zechariah and Daniel); the translators of the LXX; the Dead Sea Scrolls; as well as deuterocanonical works, targums and non-Lucan NT passages. This survey seeks to locate Luke in a context in which Isaiah was read as a single literary unit, with an eschatological focus, and the servant was viewed as a composite figure. Yet, might it not be argued that the ministry of Jesus and the apostles has prompted Luke to challenge several of the common themes of Second Temple readings of the Isaianic servant?

The most important sections of this study are those chapters which survey the servant motif in Luke's Gospel (chapter 5) and Acts (chapter 6). Although the Isaianic servant is understood to be a composite figure, Luke alludes to him to describe Jesus as 'the ultimate fulfilment' of the servant (p.85), while acknowledging that the followers of Jesus follow the servant vocation 'in various ways' (p.86). The incidence of NE vocabulary and servant themes are surveyed in the main sections of Luke's Gospel (the Birth Narratives (1–2); the early ministry of Jesus (3–8); the disciples' training in servanthood as they journey with Jesus (9–19); the climax of Jesus' ministry as servant and his transfer of the servant task to his disciples (20–24). Along the way there are helpful sections offering a 'closer look' at significant passages.

In a similar way Acts is surveyed for NE vocabulary and servant themes: suffering and vindication; the empowerment of the Holy Spirit; God's choosing; witness; and mission to Israel and the nations. Beers argues that the presence of so many Isaianic themes, as well as their influence upon the structure and message of Acts, indicates how well Luke has understood Isaiah's message about Yahweh's NE. Although insisting that 'Jesus is the servant in an *ultimate* sense that does not carry over to his disciples' (p.138), the chapter argues that the circle of servants who carry out *aspects* of the servant's mission widens. Moreover, the servant vocation is open to all who respond in faith. Thus, the twelve (1:8); Stephen (6–7); Philip and the Ethiopian (8); Paul (9, 22, 26); Cornelius and other Gentiles (10); the Ephesian elders (20); and many others who are not named (11) take on aspects of the servant vocation.

Her view of the *openness* of the servant vocation allows Beers to offer fresh insight into a question which has puzzled Lucan scholars, Luke's apparent failure to attribute atoning significance to the death of Jesus. Beers asserts, on the basis of Luke 22:19b–20 and Acts 20:28 (pp. 87, 120, 149, 177), that Luke was aware of this idea, but downplayed it for two reasons. One is that vicarious atonement is a minor feature of the ministry of the Isaianic servant (p.115, 120); and the other is that only Jesus' death could have atoning significance (p.165). Thus, in order to highlight the continuity between Jesus the servant *par excellence*, and the *many other* servants who embody aspects of the servant vocation, the atoning significance of Jesus the suffering servant is downplayed.

In order to support her exegetical conclusions Beers marshalls a comprehensive array of linguistic and conceptual parallels. She catalogues the occurrence of 'Isaiah's favourite verbs' (εὐαγγελίζομαι, ἐκλέγομαι, διαμαρτύρομαι, παραδίδωμι) as well as recurring nouns from the servant passages (ἄφεσις, μάρτυς, ὁδός, σκότος) in Luke and Acts in order to back up her claim that 'narrative echoes … produce resonance'. Not every link will be convincing to every reader. For instance, readers may legitimately question whether 'being chosen' designates a participant in the specifically Isaianic servant mission (p.150); or the connection between Paul's preaching of the kingdom in Acts 28:23, 31 and the ministry of the servant like figure of Isaiah 61:1 (p.173). Nevertheless, this study provided much food for thought and models a fresh approach to the practice of reading Scripture intertextually.

Andrew Stewart
Reformed Theological College, Melbourne.

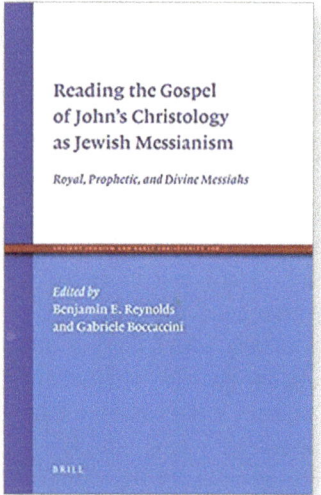

Benjamin E. Reynolds & Gabriele Boccaccini (eds). *Reading the Gospel of John's Christology as Jewish Messianism: Royal, Prophetic and Divine Messiahs, Mark, Luke and John.* Leiden: Brill, 2018. 489pp. ISBN 978-90-04-34975-9. €149.00/$179.00

This collection comes from the 2016 meeting of the Enoch seminar. The aim is to read John as a variant within Judaism, rather than something inherently external to it. The focus of this volume is upon how John may fit within Jewish messianic ideas. The background to the question of Jewish messianism in John is a struggle to reconcile John's high Christology with Jewish expectation. Previously, this has led to views that John is primarily a Hellenistic rather than Jewish text (so Bultmann, Dodd). Some still struggle with resolving the apparent contrast, describing John as Jewish yet non-Jewish, and this volume serves as a counterpoint to such views.

The volume begins with two essays that introduce some of the issues and relevant scholarship. Benjamin Reynolds highlights the disconnect between John's Gospel and scholarship on Jewish messianism. The scepticism around John's historical reliability is part of the problem, as is a tendency to read any differences as opposition to Jewish ideas rather than as a sub-group within Judaism. He closes with noting how reading John within Judaism might require rethinking some longstanding ideas in Johannine interpretation regarding its context. James McGrath follows with a survey of scholarship on messianism in John. He includes reflection on the diversity of Second Temple Judaism, with the implication that a differing view in John does not require separation from Judaism. He warns about reading in light of later trajectories, as the later separation between Christianity and Judaism was as much a matter of power structures and the ability to exclude as it was about theological difference.

The following section contains three essays which are linked by a concern for how John presents Jesus as Messiah. In the first, Adele Reinhartz focuses on Jesus' words, and especially on Jesus' connection with the Father (John 10:30). She argues that John collapses the distinction between God and Jesus, connecting Jesus' speech with the way that speech is the primary way God acts in the world. Thus, it is Jesus' words that portray him acting as God. Catrin Williams revisits her interest in John's use of Isaiah, considering connections between the Lord and the Servant in LXX Isaiah. She argues Isaiah presents Jesus as the visible embodiment of the arm of the Lord. 1 Enoch shows a similar combination of exaltation and judgement, albeit without the humiliation of the Son of Man seen in Isaiah or John. While both John and 1 Enoch use Isaiah, they do so in different ways, reflecting diverging messianic conceptions. Jocelyn McWhirter observes how John uses a different set of OT texts to what is commonly found in second temple texts about messianism. She builds a complex argument based upon shared vocabulary to link the texts used by John to those texts that are more evidently messianic. Her argument is that early Christian reflection began with Psalm 89 as a clearly messianic text, and used shared vocabulary to extend the number of messianic texts. While some of these connections that

McWhirter proposes are certainly plausible, at times they seem a stretch.

The remaining three sections deal with particular facets of messianic thought: royal, prophetic, and divine messiahs. In the section on royal messianism, Beth Stovell writes on the links between John and Davidic messianism. She uses conceptual blending theory, allowing varying subsets of messianic concepts associated with Davidic kingship to be present. She argues that John does exhibit some new blendings of messianic material but draws on precedents. Marida Nicolaci reads John as being centrally occupied with the question of the identity of the Messiah. She sees a continuity in Jewish messianism between a Davidic messiah and the high Christology of 1 Enoch. With John, she links kingship, sonship, and envoy Christology, with the Son sent as human but also demonstrating divine sovereignty. She concludes that the peculiarity of John in a Jewish context is not its high Christology but the attribution of it to Jesus crucified. Joel Willitts also tackles the idea of a Davidic messiah, but rather than identifying specifically Davidic features in the text, he argues that John sublimates David into Moses, and thus the Mosaic focus of John is part of presenting Jesus as a Davidic messiah. Willitts sees John following Chronicles and the presentation there of David as a new, better Moses.

The prophetic messiah section begins with Meredith Warren considering the connection between signs and the Messiah in John, though surprisingly without reference to the work of Salier. While the Messiah is rarely linked with signs in Second Temple Judaism, Warren suggests a connection with resurrection. A prophetic messiah tradition, building on the signs associated with Moses and Elijah, and the resurrection connection, provide a key link between the messiah and signs. Andrea Taschl-Erber writes on the links between living water, the prophet/messiah, and wisdom. She argues that John goes further than other second temple sources in linking wisdom to the Messiah, describing it as a creative intertextual reading of the Hebrew Bible. Thus, John reflects popular expectations but also transcends them. Paul Anderson considers the dialectical tensions between expectations of a kingly and prophetic messiah. He sees the eschatological prophet involving Son of Man, Elijah and Moses typologies. He argues the first edition of the Gospel presented Jesus as fulfilling the expectation of an eschatological prophet, making prophetic calls for justice and ethics.

In the final section on divine messianism, William Loader also explores the connections to wisdom traditions, although including a focus on *logos* tradition. He draws contrasts between the place of wisdom in 1 Enoch 42 and Ben Sira 24. Loader describes the way that the two-powers traditions already caused unease within Judaism, arguing that John adapted these traditions in a way that was unacceptable to most Jews of the time. Gabriele Boccaccini tackles the question of how and when Jesus began to be regarded as God, beginning by differentiating the human/divine division from the created/uncreated division, seeing the latter as more fundamental in Second Temple Judaism. While John may adapt Enochic ideas of a divine messiah, John goes further in placing Jesus on the other side of the created/uncreated divide.

> **The Son sent as human... demonstrating divine sovereignty.**

Ruben Zimmermann investigates whether the motif of bridegroom in John 2–4 reflects a messianic or divine title. While the use of the bridegroom motif for God is evident, Zimmermann identifies several messianic connections in Second Temple Judaism literature. Thus, he concludes that 'bridegroom' in John is not clearly either messianic or divine, and that there may be overlap between the two. Charles Gieschen draws out implications of the name that Jesus possesses for his identity. In second temple texts, God's primary messenger might share his name, while the name is also linked to power and creation. Linking *logos* to the divine name, Gieschen argues that John focuses on believing in Jesus' Name, thus his true identity as YHWH in flesh, rather than *logos* ever referring to Jesus' teaching. The final chapter from Crispin Fletcher-Louis investigates the high Christology of John 5 which is nevertheless set in a Jewish context. He explores the Danielic backgrounds, not only Dan. 7 but also the indication of a double resurrection in Dan. 12. This is considered alongside Enoch, arguing that both the Parables of Enoch and John 5 use the Son of Man tradition as a response to pagan ruler cults, with John 5 indicating that Jesus is to be worshipped alongside God.

> The Son of Man tradition as a response to pagan ruler cults.

There is an overall continuity to the essays in this volume, as each starts from a Jewish context. There are a range of texts used, and methodological approaches, but the goal of reading within or at least alongside Jewish tradition in a way that is sympathetic to similarities provides a coherent focus. All the authors argue that what John does is to push things a little further, although for some the principal step is not about how the Messiah is understood but applying such ideas to a specific figure.

This book provides a helpful methodological corrective. Where there might be a tendency to assume that John, as the other Gospels, reflects a distinctively Christian concept of the Messiah, that can lead to an overemphasis on the differences. Instead, it is appropriate to start from an assumption that a text fits within its context, and only to assert divergence where features of the text can be shown to be incompatible with that context. The recognition of the diversity of Judaism is also useful, encouraging NT scholars to go beyond the Hebrew Bible in defining what Judaism and its ideas in the first century may have contained.

While most of the essays in the book include attention to canonical texts, the wider range of sources helps broaden the range of ideas that may be associated with messianism. It also facilitates the understanding that differing concepts do not necessarily exclude a text from falling within Judaism. Thus, while John is not identical to any second temple documents in its messianism, those differences alone do not place it outside that context.

At the same time this appeal to diversity is potentially problematic. The fuzzy boundaries of Judaism allow for the assertion that a text such as John fits within it, as there are no criteria for differentiating between a variation in Jewish tradition and a departure from it. In this context, motifs of conflict and exclusion within John are perhaps underplayed, muting the way that John presents his ideas as unacceptable to many within the Judaism of his day—not merely as distasteful but as grounds for exclusion or violence. Thus, even without appeal to later trajectories, we may have grounds to question just how well John fits within Judaism.

Overall, this is a helpful reading of John's messianism in light of a range of second temple texts. It would be profitable reading for Johannine scholars who seek to understand John within the diversity of his Jewish context. It also points towards potentially significant implications for broader questions of interpretation. If we accept the premise that John is to be read as a primarily Jewish document rather than one opposed to Judaism, it may require rethinking around the setting of the Gospel, an issue which has relevance for the breadth of Johannine scholarship.

Christopher Seglenieks
Bible College of South Australia

BOOK REVIEWS

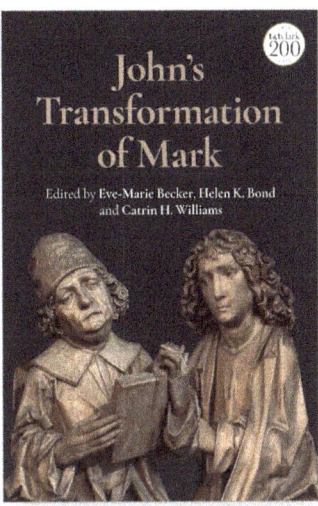

Eve-Marie Becker, Helen K. Bond, and Catrin H. Williams (eds). *John's Transformation of Mark.* London: Bloomsbury, 2021. 344pp. ISBN: 978-0-567-69189-7. £24.99.

John's Transformation of Mark consists mainly of a collection of essays presented at a conference held in Athens in 2018. Edited by three prominent female New Testament scholars, this compilation of essays explores the perennial New Testament question concerning the relationship between the gospels of John and Mark. Across the seventeen essays, various methodologies are employed, several themes and motifs are explored, and after careful analysis and consideration, each of the contributors concludes that John had in some way or another transformed Mark. Thus, this edited volume contributes the growing consensus that John knew and used Mark.

Following an introduction by the editors, the essays in this volume commence with a history of research written by Harold Attridge. In this concise survey, Attridge offers a selective yet representative overview of the debate concerning the relationship between John and Mark. He offers a balanced presentation of proposals from scholars who either argue for John's dependence on Mark, or for John's independence from Mark. He concludes by observing that many scholars have now come to recognise that there is a notable relationship between John and Mark.

The next three essays utilise different methodological paradigms for considering the relationship between John and Mark, and they demonstrate how these approaches help make sense of the relationship between the two gospels. Firstly, Jean Zumstein employs intertextuality, or more specifically hypertextuality, and suggests a free literary and theological transformation of Mark's gospel by John. Secondly, Chris Keith uses social memory theory, or more specifically critical inheritance, and proposes that John both accepts and rejects aspects of Mark's gospel. Thirdly, Catrin Williams utilises rewritten bible, and argues that like Jewish authors with the Jewish Scripture, John rewrites Mark's gospel.

The following three essays explore various aspects of Mark's gospel that John is seen as having developed. Firstly, George Parsenios argues that John recognised and further developed Mark's use of concepts from Greek philosophy and Greek drama for his presentation of Jesus. Secondly, Mark Goodacre provocatively proposes that John should be regarded as a fourth Synoptic gospel. That is, John borrows Mark's phraseology, his structure, and his concept of the hidden Messiah with the resurrection as the interpretive key and develops this in his own presentation of Jesus. Thirdly, Eve-Marie Becker suggests that John recognises Mark's historiographical approach and like Luke, uses this genre and develops it further in his own gospel.

The final ten essays are presented in roughly a sequential order and compare material that appears to be present in both John and Mark. Christina Hoegen-Rohls compares the opening material in both gospels, Steve Hunt and Troels Engberg-Pedersen explore the passages concerning John the Baptist, Gilbert Van Belle looks at the pericopae relating to the paralysed man, Jörg Frey covers eschatological material, Oda Wischmeyer focuses on ethical material, Susanne Luther deals with speeches, Kasper Bro Larsen assesses temptation material, Michael Labahn considers the material relating to the plot to kill Jesus, and Helen Bond concludes this section with an analysis of the passages concerning the death of Jesus.

Each of these essays comes to the conclusion that John reworked material from Mark's gospel albeit for a whole host of different but complementary reasons. However, the understanding of the nature of the dependence of John upon Mark is varied among the contributors. For example, Steve Hunt assumes that John was directly dependent on Mark. In a similar vein, Troels Engberg-Pedersen, Gilbert Van Belle, and Oda Wischmeyer suggest that John had read Mark. By contrast, Susanne Luther is more tentative, proposing that John may have had direct knowledge of Mark or knowledge of Mark from the reception of the Markan gospel in other early Christian gospels. While Michael Labahn argues that John was dependent on a re-oralised Mark.

The contributions in this edited volume are written by internationally recognised experts in John, Mark, or both gospels. The essays employ different methodologies and explore various comparable passages and themes within the two gospels. Notably, each essay concludes that in some way or another John has transformed material from Mark. This plurality of broadly complementary approaches adds significant weight to the growing scholarly consensus that John knew and used Mark. As such, it heralds a new stage in the understanding of gospel interrelationships.

Elizabeth Corsar
St Padarn's Institute, Cardiff

BOOK REVIEWS

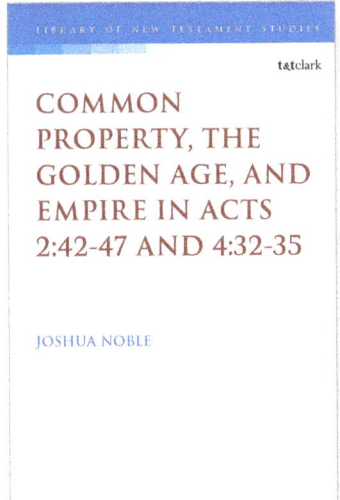

Joshua Noble. *Common Property, the Golden Age, and Empire in Acts 2:42–47 and 4:32–35*. LNTS. London: T&T Clark, 2020. 208pp. ISBN: 9780567695819. $170

Noble's *Common Property, the Golden Age, and Empire in Acts 2:42–47 and 4:32–35* explores how 'the golden age myth' can colour our understanding of the summary statements describing the early believers in Acts 2:42–47 and 4:32–35. The 'golden age myth' is a literary topos that categorises different ages of human civilization with different metals (gold, silver, bronze, etc.), with the greatest age of human civilization being labelled golden, and being characterised variously by peace, concord, common property, and direct access to the gods. Noble's central argument is that Luke's description of the communal sharing of the early Jesus community in the summary statements draws upon this golden age motif, with the implication that Luke is making a supra-imperial claim by using this motif.

This book has five chapters, with the first acting as a summary of the previous literature on communal sharing in the summary statements. Noble categorises previous attempts to understand the Hellenistic context of this communal sharing into four main streams: friendship traditions, ideal state descriptions, primitivistic accounts, and golden age accounts. He shows that the golden age context is 'relatively unexplored' (9).

The next two chapters address the golden age myth in Greek and Latin sources (chapter two) and in Jewish and Christian sources (chapter three). Noble notes that in the early Greek literature, the golden age myth included depictions of concord, peace, direct access to the gods, and spontaneous food. While with the Latin literature, Noble identifies Virgil as a significant innovator in the golden age myth, introducing the ideas of the return of the golden age (linking it with the rise of Augustus), and communal property. From here, Noble notes in chapter three the appearance of the imagery of the golden age in Philo and Josephus, and most significantly, the extensive use of the golden age myth in the Sibylline Oracles.

In chapter four, Noble establishes two contextual links between the use of the golden age myth in the broader Jewish literature and the summary statements. First, he argues that Luke creates an eschatological setting for summary statements with the addition of 'in the last days' (Acts 2:17) in Peter's Pentecost sermon, which he links to the eschatological setting of the golden age myth in the Jewish literature. Second, Noble argues that Luke-Acts takes a supra-imperial (not pro- or anti-) stance towards Rome, again linking it with the use of the golden age myth to critique Rome in the Jewish literature. It should be noted that this anti-imperial link is built predominantly upon the use of the golden age myth in the Sibylline Oracles 8, which Noble dates to the late second century.

In the final chapter, Noble interprets the summary statements themselves, arguing that they are distinct literary units which allude to the golden age myth. There are two pivotal arguments in this chapter. First, he emphasises the distinctness of the summary statements compared to the rest of Luke-Acts, the NT and indeed the Bible, on the basis of vocabulary, context and content. Second, he establishes numerous parallels between the golden age myth and the summary statements, including in the descriptions of favour, unity, harmony, and common property. This position then leads Noble to associate this use of the golden age myth with the coming of the eschatological Spirit and as a supra-imperial claim in Luke-Acts.

> The golden age myth…as a supra-imperial claim.

The strengths of this book are its clear prose and its straightforward outline and argument. As a reader largely unaware of the golden age myth, Noble's writing was clear and accessible. However, the book could be strengthened in a few areas, and in particular, chapters four and five. As Luke's eschatology is a major topic in current studies in Luke-Acts, Noble's treatment of Luke's eschatology is brief (85–91). A further area of research could explore how Noble's study could be complemented with the contemporaneous study on Luke's eschatology in Kylie Crabb's *Luke/Acts and the End of History* (2019). Likewise, Noble's argument for the distinctiveness of summary statements (119–122) needed to be nuanced by engaging with the insights of literary critics on the summary statements, who emphasise the commonality of these statements and the surrounding narratives, e.g. S. J. Noorda's "Scene and Summary: A Proposal for Reading Acts 4,36–5,16" (1982). Overall, Noble presents an interesting and engaging thesis, creating an interpretive context that has largely been unexplored by Lukan scholars, and which hopefully will lead to fruitful discussions concerning the communal sharing of the earliest believers in Jesus for years to come.

John D. Griffiths
Alphacrucis College

BOOK REVIEWS

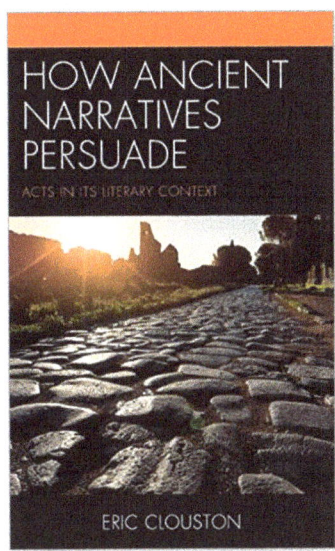

Eric Clouston. *How Ancient Narratives Persuade: Acts in its Literary Context.*
London: Rowman & Littlefield, 2020. 267pp.
ISBN: 978-1-9787-0660-6. £73.00/$95.00

In this book Clouston sets out on the ambitious task of not only analysing techniques of persuasion in Acts, but of setting out a method for assessing persuasion in narratives. He begins with the context of narrative approaches, which have set the groundwork for this sort of study, as well as rhetorical criticism. Such work has taken ancient texts on rhetoric as their starting point, which presents a problem for assessing Acts in that their focus is upon speeches rather than narrative.

Having set the scene, a substantial chapter sets out Clouston's method. After a literary analysis identifying the narrator and implied audience, one of two key parts of the method is identifying the various ways in which a character might be accredited or discredited within a story. These are features that influence the audience's attitude to the text—trusting or distrusting characters within the narrative. These can prepare the audience to respond positively (or negatively) to the words and deeds of a character.

The second key part is identifying the techniques of persuasion, which are features that encourage the audience to attitudes or actions beyond the text. These range from overt instruction from the narrator or characters in the story through to plot and the arrangement of events. Clouston expects many of these devices to be present in any given text, working together towards overall patterns of persuasion. He admits there may be other, perhaps more subtle techniques of persuasion in addition to those he lists. Yet these, Clouston suggests, require more information than modern scholars possess, leading to speculative interpretation. Appendices are provided listing both the accrediting devices and the persuasive techniques that form part of the method.

Rather than simply declaring a method and applying it to Acts, Clouston then proceeds to use four non-biblical texts as tests for the method. This serves both to demonstrate the general applicability of the method, as well as producing comparative data. These four texts are Philo's *Embassy to Gaius*, Josephus' *Jewish War*, *Joseph and Aseneth*, and the *Letter of Aristeas*. These are narratives from a comparable date, a Jewish context, and with some evident persuasive function. In each case the persuasive techniques are identified, with conclusions drawn about both the types of persuasion used but also what the persuasive features might reflect about the audience and the function of the text.

Clouston then returns to Acts, devoting several chapters to his analysis. First, a literary analysis deals with questions of narrator and audience, along with cataloguing previous views on the purpose of the narrative. Acts is considered alongside Luke as connected works, albeit allowing that Acts may differ in genre, intended audience, or purpose from Luke. Clouston cautiously identifies a broad audience who may not all share the worldview of the text, and a purpose connected to the prominence

> **A character might be accredited or discredited.**

of the proclamation of the resurrection and accompanying call to repent and believe.

Following the literary analysis, he works through the persuasive features in Acts as a whole. This includes a visual depiction of the distribution of persuasive features in the narrative. Unlike many narratives, including Luke which he uses as a comparison, Acts does not cluster accrediting devices in the opening chapters but towards the middle, notably chapters 10 and 15. This suggests the author deliberately seeks to shape a positive attitude to the characters in these sections, and thus the persuasion that features there. One of these is the subject of more detailed study—the Cornelius episode in Acts 10:1–11:18. Clouston selects this story in part for the concentration of persuasive devices here, in order to demonstrate the applicability of his method at a more detailed level. He identifies Acts as having a greater focus on accrediting Paul than accrediting either Jesus or Peter. Meanwhile in the Cornelius episode, there is a significant shift from presenting Peter as a leader to be respected, to being the object of empathy, encouraging the audience to engage with his journey—coming to include the Gentiles.

Following the analysis of Acts, Clouston makes a brief comparison of the persuasive features found in the various texts addressed. Overall, the persuasive features of Acts are not novel but are found in the comparable texts. There are some noticeable variations, both between Acts and the other texts, but also amongst those other texts as well.

A chapter on the purpose of Acts is the final part of the argument. Clouston revisits the range of suggested purposes for Acts that have been proposed in scholarship. He compares these with the purposes that the persuasive features of Acts appear to suggest. He argues that the central purpose of Acts is legitimation of the Christian movement, albeit with particular attention to legitimating Paul and the mission to the Gentiles. The persuasion addresses both insiders as well as interested (but not hostile) outsiders, seeking to persuade them to the views of the text. He makes the interesting conclusion regarding the dating of Acts, that the persuasive intent makes most sense if published at the point the narrative ends, rather than after the death of Paul.

Clouston presents a clear and plausible method. What is demonstrated in this book gives a solid basis from which to talk about the persuasive intent of a narrative that goes beyond simple assertions. It gives helpful insights into the purpose of the text by highlighting not merely the topics covered in the text but also the persuasive thrust. At times, the work's origin as a doctoral thesis is evident, for the format is systematic in a way that can tend towards repetitive. However, such repetition may serve as a persuasive technique for what is a novel method.

Clouston is open in acknowledging that there is scope for developing and refining the method. There is a need for a wider range of texts to be analysed with this method to refine the method and the conclusions, whether that be the Gospels, the LXX or other contemporary texts. One of those potential refinements relates to some persuasive techniques explicitly excluded from the method. In rejecting more implicit persuasive techniques, the use of the Old Testament, beyond explicit claims to fulfilment, is excluded. A wider study of persuasion in Jewish literature may provide sufficient basis to include discussion of the persuasive effect of the implicit use of Scripture in narratives, those connections identified in approaches such as figural exegesis. While Clouston is sceptical that such readings can go beyond speculation, a wider study of their persuasive use would enable taking into account what would seem to be a significant persuasive tool that is excluded by this method.

This book could form a useful companion

to Stuart Liggins *Many Convincing Proofs* (De Gruyter, 2016) as they take a different approach to their study of persuasion in Acts. Both are contextual in focus, but Liggins focuses on the topics used to persuade, where Clouston draws attention to the literary features that are used to persuade, such as the characterisation and plot.

This is an essential resource for those interested in the function or setting of Acts. More widely those interested in narrative persuasion will find it useful, and it may provide a launching point not only for other NT work, but also for those working in OT or Second Temple texts. It is not overly technical, and anyone with a passing familiarity with narrative approaches should find it accessible.

Christopher Seglenieks
Bible College of South Australia